Stay Me,

Oh Comfort Me

Also by M. F. K. Fisher

M.F.K. Fisher

 Stay Me,
Oh Comfort Me

Journals and Stories,
1933–1941

Pantheon Books
New York and San Francisco

Portions of "Bern Journal, 1938" were originally published in *Antaeus* by
The Ecco Press in 1988. The "Epilogue" was originally published as "Spirits of
the Valley" in *Geo* Magazine in 1984.

Grateful acknowledgment is made to Peter Owen Publishers, London,
for permission to reprint an excerpt from *Opium* by Jean Cocteau, translated
by Margaret Crosland.

Library of Congress Cataloging-in-Publication Data

Fisher, M. F. K. (Mary Frances Kennedy), 1908–1992
Stay me, oh comfort me: journals and stories,
1933–1941/M. F. K. Fisher.
p. cm.
ISBN 0-679-75825-9
1. Fisher, M. F. K. (Mary Frances Kennedy), 1908–1992 — Biography.
2. Authors, American — 20th Century — Biography.   3. Food writers —
United States — Biography.   I. Title.
PS3511.I7428Z468   1993
641'.092 — dc20   93-768
[B]

Book design by Cheryl Cipriani
Manufactured in the United States of America

First Paperback Edition

9 8 7 6 5 4 3 2 1

Contents

Introduction

Norah Kennedy Barr

In these journals, letters, and short stories, Mary Frances Kennedy Fisher tells her story of the death of her marriage to Alfred Fisher and the beginning and tragic end of her "fifteen minutes of marriage" to Dillwyn Parrish. Mary Frances put this manuscript together before her death in June 1992, because she wished her life to be read as it really happened to her and as she felt it at the time, not as interpreted later by a biographer or even by her older self.

After their marriage in September 1929, Mary Frances and Al Fisher spent two idyllic years in Dijon. While Al worked on his doctorate at the university and on an epic poem, "The Ghost of the Underblows," the world of the senses opened up to Mary Frances. Al already knew that he was a poet; Mary Frances was alive with creative energy but undecided about the direction it would take. Her strong family feelings brought her back to the Ranch in Whittier, California, for a vacation at the end of the second year of her marriage, and then our mother Edith persuaded her to take me, her youngest sister, back to Dijon with her.

Journals are fascinating in part because of what they do not say. Mary Frances was hurt at the easy way in which Al had agreed to a separation of three months, but she faced this only seven years later in an unsent letter to their close friend, Lawrence Powell. She may even have unconsciously welcomed the presence of a fourteen-year-old sister in their third year of marriage as a shield against her feelings of betrayal.

After Al earned his doctorate, we three spent the winter months in Strasbourg, then went to Provence, where we were joined by Lawrence Powell. He had spent the previous year studying for his doctorate at Dijon, and he returned there for a second year after Al, Mary Frances, and I boarded an Italian freighter in Marseilles for the long trip home to California.

The Kennedy family to whom the young Fishers returned consisted of our mother Edith, our father Rex, our sister Anne (Sis), caught in an unhappy marriage to Ted Kelly, and our thirteen-year-old brother David. During the years covered by these journals, Edith began having bouts of pain that culminated in a severe heart attack in 1939.

Nothing in France had prepared Mary Frances and Al for the Great Depression. They had been insulated from its devastation by three years as poor students on a fixed stipend. Our father Rex, as editor and publisher of the town paper, knew its full extent, although it touched our family only indirectly. As a community leader, Rex tried to muster some sort of work and food for the hundreds who had lost their homes and who were wandering the roads, subsisting on free oranges from the surrounding groves. By 1932, when we returned from France, the great experiments of the New Deal had just begun. The overpowering uncertainty and feeling that the entire country was close to revolution was strong, as Mary Frances's journals reflect.

Al immediately began to look for a university teaching job, but two long years went by before he was offered one as an English instructor at Occidental College in Los Angeles. Those two years were spent at the Kennedy family Ranch in Whittier or at the summer cottage in Laguna Beach.

The Laguna cottage was built before World War I by my father and willing friends. It stood under six enormous eucalyptus trees, next to a deep arroyo and a short block from the ocean. Once the Coast Highway had been built through Laguna in the 1920s, our block filled in with other cottages, but ocean and trees were always within sound and smell. Each summer in our childhood we made the hour-long expedition from Whittier with a two-burner stove, discarded quilts, and bent pots and pans for three glorious months of freedom. Mary Frances loved Laguna, as did we all. It was not, however, an ideal place for Mary Frances and Al to begin their new life in the United States.

Al faced the death of his father in August 1934. This, and perhaps life in Laguna, had a disastrous effect on his creative life as a poet. To me, he was always remote, kind, beautiful—a man I was confident would eventually be acknowledged as a new Keats or Andrew Marvell.

Friends were important to both Mary Frances and Al during their two years in Laguna, and some mentioned in these pages remained close to Mary Frances for the next sixty years of her life. Most important of these was Lawrence Powell, who found a place near Laguna Beach in 1934 for himself and his bride Fay. After an apprenticeship at Jake Zeitlin's famous bookstore, Larry became an authoritative writer on Southwest literature, a critic, and a novelist, as well as chief librarian at the University of California, Los

Angeles. The journals also talk of Mary Frances's warm friendship with Gloria Stuart Sheekman, a beautiful and generous movie actress, who has become both an artist and fine-book designer.

The central event of these two years in Laguna was her meeting with Dillwyn Parrish and Dillwyn's very young and beautiful wife Gigi. Dillwyn, who was fourteen years older than Mary Frances, had met Gigi while working as a tutor to relatives who were wealthy expatriates, raising their large family in Europe. Earlier, at Harvard, Dillwyn (Timmy) had joined the Volunteer Ambulance Corps and had been sent to France. There he was under repeated gas attacks—a possible cause of the circulatory illness that later cost him his leg and finally his life. Tim's deft and insouciant handling of depressed times, his worldliness, deep sensitivity, and compassion, sparked his correspondence with Mary Frances during 1935, when the Fishers were at Occidental College. I am confident that it was Timmy who helped Mary Frances begin to focus on her gift for writing.

Timmy invited Mary Frances to accompany him and his mother on a voyage to France and Switzerland during the summer of 1934. Gigi had decided to concentrate on a career that held much promise as a movie actress, and she was deflected from this only by meeting her future husband, John Weld. As Timmy's marriage ended, he returned to Europe with his sister Anne and bought a crumbling house, Le Pâquis, in a vineyard above Vevey. Al and Mary Frances joined him there in a wildly ingenuous idea that somehow they could succeed in communal living. Al escaped this situation a year later by accepting a position at Smith College, and at the end of 1937 Mary Frances made the trip back to Whittier to announce her intention to divorce Al and marry Dillwyn.

One year of life (1937–38) together was allowed Mary Frances and Timmy before he lost his leg. In the summer of 1938, not only Mary Frances's brother David and I but also Timmy's sister Anne and a good friend came to Le Pâquis. We were together on a weekend jaunt to Bern when an embolism struck Timmy and, in its progress up his leg, destroyed it, so that soon after a first operation, a second one was needed to amputate. He was never without pain again.

After Bern and Adelboden, Mary Frances did not write again in her journals until she and Timmy bought their house, Bareacres, in 1940. This remote, barren, but beautiful ranch near Hemet, California, was to be her home and base of operations for many productive years.

The year between the Parrishes' return and their purchase of Bareacres was spent undergoing two more operations in Wilmington, Delaware, and making a frantic trip back to France to procure the drug Analgeticum, which was essential to relieve Tim's pain.

Timmy's sister Anne proposed a trip to the Mayo Clinic in 1940, which is described in the Bareacres journal. There Timmy and Mary Frances learned that there was no hope of recovery or even of relief from the progression of Buerger's disease.

Timmy, during the painful years before he shot himself in the summer of 1941, worked every day at painting. His paintings are a treasure that Mary Frances guarded until her death, but she was generous in giving them to friends who wished to have them.

Mary Frances, of course, had to live on, day by day, after the loss of her love. Although she always considered herself a "ghost" after Timmy's death, she was very much a person who continued to love and be loved during her long productive life.

Stay Me,

Oh Comfort Me

1
Laguna Journal,
1933–36

In the last three days, the currents have changed as many times. I feel them shifting all around me. It makes the thickness of a blue rug and the hard beauty of zinnias in a bowl seem more than ever things to feel and see.

Tonight Father and Al and the children [David, thirteen, Norah, fifteen] are playing poker. They started out with Father facetious and Al quiet and the children bickering, while Mother laughed with pleasure at Dave's dullest sayings. By now they are leveled out, all quietly chattering and amiable and good to listen to. It is good to see Father's face lighter. When he is low, he seems to be thick and rather gross; his table manners are unpleasant; he speaks little and then in a rudely taciturn way. He has been so for two days. Today both the kids asked me, Noni in the car and Dave while we were oiling tools in the barn, about the family finances. Dave said, What's this about our getting poorer?

I forget what Noni said. She is a little sour about it—feels, I think, that Sis and I had an unfair chance at boarding school and clothes and so on. Really, she is not rancorous, but occasionally she is a little sour.

When Al and I went away and drove through all the little villages with our faces like insects' behind dark glasses and my arms burned scarlet, everything that had piled up in two days seemed not to exist. I don't think we thought. It was hot, so we took off almost all our clothes. Our tongues were dry, and we stopped and ate a watermelon so propitiously that we were bathed in a sensual rapture by its color, its icy crisp flesh, its delicate faded taste. Or we stopped for beer, which I have never enjoyed, though Al says he has tasted one brew that is as good as the good beer of Strasbourg. It all has a fake taste to me. Perhaps it is because it is served mostly in hideous roadside eating places.

We ate, slept, bathed, loved each other. I thought of starting a vague diary, an attempt to tell of the fourth year of our life together in this fourth year since the Crash. Fifth, I mean. It was our fourth anniversary, September 5. Yes, it seemed quite clear— in San Jacinto. Now I feel bewildered, set upon by my unruly wants. And there are all the complications of my love for the family, my interest in our friends. The main thing, though, the only thing, really, in the whole disturbed scheme, is Al's and my private life. That I will fight for. It is important and should live through more than a mere world revolution.

12.ix.33

We went to Laguna with the children and that night, Saturday, took a basket of food and piles of old coats to the cove north of Emerald Bay, where there is a deserted camp. Cliffward from a beached log, we made a little pit, and Dave threw down jagged stones for Al to line it with. Later, one stone exploded three times, showing its scar very white in the coals and blackness. Noni and I picked up wood, which lay untidily against the rocks under the point of land near our log and our fire. When we had deep coals, we broiled steak and put it into buttered round buns. I liked mine better in my fingers, hot and dripping and tasting delicately of wood and smoke as only broiled beef can. Just before the steaks were done, there was that still moment of no color, when all the things and the sky and all the hills seem to exist in some other way than the one we suppose. Then we saw Venus, and then two others —stars they were, though—and I thought that I would watch to see if Venus made a path where she neared the water. But later, when I looked, she had gone. We were very warm after the good meat and in our many old clothes. Dave and Noni had dug little hollows up the sloping sand of the cliff bottom and lay with their feet to the fire, not talking. Al and I sat under a rug, our backs to them and the fire. Occasionally he kissed the top of my head gently. It was very dark and cold. Then we all drew together and began to talk and sing, and in a minute were telling a long silly story. Finally we went home.

Yesterday was the first day of school, and both the children, Noni especially, were very tired and depressed about Latin. Al helped them, and they were cheered. We played poker and I broke even. I usually do that or even get a little ahead, but I make astonishing blunders. Four times now I have blandly passed on a straight flush. It makes us all laugh. Today Mother is pickling figs, and the house is filled with a tangy smell from the spices and the vinegar and brown sugar. Occasionally I think it would be very pleasant to be an old hausfrau of means in the last century, and have a great cellar and pantries filled with things in crocks and jars and kegs, and a reputation through the countryside for my special pickles and mincemeats. Or it would be as good, or better, to have a spice trade in the late eighteenth century, with a little redolent office and ships buying from the far countries. Just for the names —and the smells.

And that reminds me that for this Christmas I am going to make a lot of that fruitcake Sis and the kids like, from Mother's old book, and give nubbins of it to people. It will be nice to give, and nicer to receive than anything I could buy.

Larry is back. We saw him first at Ritchie's. He was very nervous, and then when Ritchie and Gordon came, he began to show off with vigor and bombast. He had an accent, a slurring of inner r's, rather Scotch. Going home, Al condemned him until I told him that when we first knew each other, he himself at times used an English accent or an Eastern one. I think that months in England and relatives and a *petite amie* with the typical English repugnance for our flat sounds had made Larry self-conscious. And three days later, when we saw him Sunday night at Bieler's, it was almost gone, and he was calmer. At Ritchie's, with us all there watching him and looking for changes after his long absence, he was on the spot. And he knew it. Sexually he is even more sure of himself than before, after a year of good hunting. He has a new trick of looking long into women's (my) eyes, with his own very deep and blue. For the first time, I found myself wanting to touch him. I would have been glad to lie with my arms around him or my hands in his. I was not moved sexually at all but was glad to have him back, to see him by me. Here when I use *I,* I mean Al and me, because I have never been able to think of Larry without feeling that I was Al, too. Perhaps I am mistaken.

Larry and Al and I were going today to Laguna for a few days, but L. phoned that he couldn't leave until Thursday, as he is looking into a job. When Al told Mother, he said instead that Larry was seeing about his book. He didn't want Mother to think, Well, Larry's getting a job and Al isn't.

Today I wrote to Grandmother Holbrook's friend Wilhelmina Loos about her date ranch down in the Imperial Valley. It is warm there and isolated and perhaps cheap, and Al and I thought we might go there or to Mecca, three miles from her place. I'm afraid Murray Brush* will decide that he can afford us, and then we'll have to go there. And if we go there, we'll do all the dirty jobs for the whole faculty. But it would be interesting, too, and would only last nine months.

I really wouldn't care much. I'd feel awfully silly playing hymns for all the little boys in morning chapel. But we'd get at least our room and food, and now that is quite a lot. Maybe we'd be paid a little, too. That would be good, because our money is going fast enough. I think we might be able to do our own work, too, in spite of our "duties." I'd like to get some work with French —tutoring or something—or I'll forget what I know.

13. ix. 33

Al, talking with Rex and Denny† (Joanne's husband, here for a night), is telling of J.B.'s communistic turnings. Denny says communism is growing. Al tells of the increasing number of intellectuals who swing to the Left. Rex sits with his face redder, his eyes half-interested, half-scornful. Al and Denny say that if their families hungered, they would grow rabid. What do you mean, rabid? asks Rex. Denny says, Smash, steal, kill! What good would that do? from Rex. We'd join with others and overthrow the government! And who'd control, the hoodlums? No, Al says, the other men like

---

* Headmaster of Thatcher Preparatory School in the Ojai Valley near Santa Barbara.
† Harvey Denham, married to Joanne Holbrook, M.F.K.F.'s first cousin.

Denny, like B. Well, Rex says, there are several hundred men on starvation wages or alms here in Whittier. Now why don't they band together and storm a grocery store? Why, they are afraid! And it is amazing what people will take, what they will endure. They are afraid. Mother puts down her book and tells of Ethel's brother-in-law who works for the county at what the county, formerly for fifteen days a month at about $3.50, now pays for nine days at less than $3. He is supposed to live on that and raise the new generation. And so on. A little talk of the strikes in Iowa and so on. Then talk of Rex's manorial system, with the children on the farms, all a self-supporting community. We would even knit our clothes, says Al, and Denny, knowing I knit, says, Rather hard on Dote! Yes, Mother says, we'd have to be nudists, but that wouldn't shock anybody in this family!

Now they're talking of Russia, and Denny says to Rex what I often say and think, that he shouldn't read only the memoirs of the ex-grand-dukes. Rex's reading on Russia is guided by a business partner, who never having visited the country nor known a Russian gives lectures to service clubs about the evils of the five-year plans and communism in general. In the middle of the talk, Denny leaves to wash his hands and *faire pipi* before taking the tram back to Los Angeles.

A letter from M. Brush says that he can't let us know about being at the school until the day it opens. I doubt if he can have us there. If there are no emergencies, our money will last at least six more months or maybe longer. Then what? We'll have to live off my family, as Al's, after thirty-five years of serving the Lord, is almost destitute. I have an allowance of $300 a year from Mom, which I expect her to be unable to continue much longer, and about $20 a year in dividends. Al has nothing and an insurance premium of about $60 a year to meet. If his Aunt Helen would die, we *might* get $5,000, of which we owe $1,000. Last night I was thinking that there are only two ways to live with any promise of bread through the next few years: (1) tie in with some power— France, Japan, Russia, États Unis—as secret agent or as official correspondent or as propagandist, perhaps, and live in the centers —always, of course, a target, but good while you last, a good life; (2) go far into the land, there to dig for water and plant and spin, there to live the life of a slave but with, certainly, times for looking at things and for love. But being a professor, being a good novelist —I doubt them, for the next years.

Tonight Father and Denny talked at each other for an hour or so, sometimes one at a time, sometimes together and trying to drown out each other. From the talk I gather that they both think the N.R.A. [National Recovery Act] doomed, Denny a Democrat and Rex Republican. D. says it is too complex. Rex, scornful of a handful of economists controlling a nation's industries, thinks immediate war the only alternative to chaos and revolution, and one that Roosevelt will choose rather than see his plan a too-obvious failure. He says the national press is primed now to such an extent that war with Japan (or, second choice, Latin America) will be accepted as natural and inevitable by the people whenever it is declared. Men long unemployed will welcome enlistment and drafting and will be sent over after the first shock has been taken by the C.C.C. [Civilian Conservation Corps] forces, now beginning to be toughened and strengthened for warfare. Rex gives it—this state of present peace!—a year or eight more months. Then war, to save our face. And so on. Talk talk talk.

Why, Rex says, are we killing a hundred thousand hogs to raise the price of pork while ten million people are hungry? And why are we plowing under every fifth row of cotton when so many children are naked?

Today Mother and I drove to Los Angeles for various reasons and stopped on the way home at Lucca's pastry shop café, bulging with NRA and affluence—the latter due to the fact that they give people too many little cakes for dessert and then invite them to take them away free—in a box that they provide for five cents. Accordingly, many hundreds flock to pay seventy-five cents for a dinner in order to take away those free cakes. Mother bought two dozen of them and just now has come to turn on the radio for the ten o'clock news, with two in her hand. Those cakes certainly aren't much good, she says as she licks a little piece of chocolate from her finger. They have no taste, just a mouth of fuzz. While she waits for the news, a woman with a clipped voice tells against a background of Chinese music about the Hotel Blahblah in colorful San Francisco. A man says something about Standard Oil. Then the news.

Today at lunch I remembered, as I watched an imitation Russian waiter (we ate at the Russian Eagle in Hollywood)—can't write while the radio talks— When I saw the waiter bend his knees slightly as he poured beer from a bottle into a glass and slowly straighten as the glass filled, I remembered seeing Al do that last night with ginger ale and then seemed to see dim hundreds of bent knees grow straight as wine, and porto-cassis, and Dubonnet filled glasses. I must watch. I think I remember all those knees.

One of the reasons I am glad to go to Laguna tomorrow with Larry is that then it will be easy to eat simply, of milk and lettuce and yeast and vegetables. Tonight my side caught as I crouched on the fender to warm myself. That was because for about ten days I have eaten what was served, both here and in restaurants, from politeness and laziness and a certain pleasure in the knowledge that sooner or later I would be sorry. Now I am sorry. If I don't go to Laguna but stay here and continue to eat potatoes and rice pudding and cakes, I shall be even sorrier. Because rather than make an effort, and not even a great effort, I shall continue to eat what Mother orders for her cuisine. I eat it knowing it will hurt me, but God knows I hate to see Dave and Noni eating it.

Just now I went into the desk for more ink and when I came back here and sat down, I thought, Did Al come in and touch me on the arm and shoulder? I am quite sure he did not, as he sits calmly by the fire some thirty feet from the desk. I do not ask him, for I am quite sure. But still I can feel where he touched me. I can still feel on my arm and shoulder the loving touch of his—hands or what, I don't remember. But I thought without thinking, I *felt* him on my body.

I do not read any of what I write in this book, once it is written. Much of it I certainly would not say again, if I remembered it, nor if I thought much would I *ever* say some of it. But I think that for myself later, perhaps even for others much later, but certainly for myself now, it is a good thing to put down some of what seems to me now a disturbed life. Tonight Denny said, What about forty, fifty years from now? And Rex said, Oh, we'll be riding along. Whether we will or not, now I am alive, and I see that there is movement, a new troubled aching everywhere.

Tonight I ate a passion fruit, a rather new fruit here, from Australia, I think. It is small and dark and hard, very uncompromising. It needs a knife, a sharp one, to cut the shell. And inside is a viscid yellowish mess, all filled with olive-green hollowish seeds growing neatly from three sides of the shell and filling it as if it were a little bowl. To be sucked out or eaten with a spoon. The mouth is pleasant long after. It is a delightful fruit. The man we bought them from puts boxes under the vines one day and picks them up the next day filled. They do the work, he said, and grinned rather sheepishly with his wide thick mouth and his blue pig eyes. A big sign over the road stand said his name was Slim Craddock.

22.ix.33

It has been some time—a week or so. I find that I am lazy—
lazier, that is, than I had planned to be. And I am often in a frame
of mind that might be too monotonous. When I write letters now,
they all veer away from chitchat to stewings and sputterings about
"conditions." I don't know what good it does to talk—but always
it comes round to that. Of course, I think about things. The day
A. interviewed a pompous man with more conceit than tact, I was
quite disgusted. It sickened me to think that a man as fine and
intelligent as A. should be forced to have *anything* to do with such
a person. And there he was asking him for work as a ditchdigger!
A man with A.'s mind! God, I was sick. And there's still a chance
that he may get the job. I am afraid when the phone rings. There
is so shallow a well, for all we take from it, and what Al uses
heaving dirt all day will be just so much lost. It's not right, in his
case, to talk of "interesting experience" and all that. He's done it
before, and worked in the oil fields, and hauled potatoes in sacks.
Now is his time for writing. And he must exhaust himself to feed
us. I wish I could do something. I've thought of everything, but
there are a hundred people for every job. My only chance, I think,
is radio work—maybe. But that means going to town again—and
so on. I can carve rather nice little toys—but they can be bought
at the five-and-ten for less than I could make them.

We've seen Larry several times—at Gloria's one night, two
days he spent with us at Laguna, last night at his place. Next week
we go to a dinner given in his honor by the arriviste president of
the college that was so embarrassed, at the time, by L.'s presence.
Now he has a doctorate—now he is somebody! A pox on them.

All our plans to go away, get away from the twenty-four-hour
attention, always loving and generous and thoughtful, have gone
by the boards. The only sensible and decent thing we can do is to

go to Laguna for the winter. In many ways we are glad—the water, the quiet, the room for Al and me to work in, and the piano, and the bathtub, and on and on. But I did want to go *away*. I do these people no good—open a few car doors for Mother, run errands, be present for talk and this and that. But they get along as well, sometimes better, without me. And when I'm here, I worry and scheme and stir up and smooth down, and when I'm away—away too far to telephone or summon—I am all in one piece. That is what I want, to be whole. It's Al and our life that count for me. These people, my family—they all have to go their own way, with no help. I am no use to them. I've chosen my way. I want to go. But now things are hard to buck. For years we went as we should, and now we are tangled up in the intimate living of between six and ten people. For some people, others, that is all right. But I suffer when I hear Dave sniffle. I think of crying, and what I can do, and go from that to Mother's apathy (between earaches) and from that to doctors and then back to M.'s discipline and swing to Noni. I think of her laziness or worry about her clumsy, pained walk or her embarrassing bursts of tears. I suffer. I sound very silly and like a tender lily wringing its sensitive emotions like a wet handkerchief. But it is true. And when I am away I don't hear that sniffle from Dave. He may do it. But I can do nothing about it, and there is no reason for being here to listen and fume and fuss and use up energy I want to save or spend on A.

Today A. saw a ragged little boy sitting on the curb, his feet in the gutter. In his lap he held a dead cat, very stiff. He was picking the fleas from it.

24. ix. 33

Laguna—at night on a tuffet by the fire. Edwin Fisher [Al's younger brother] is playing—mostly Bach. He looks very funny, so tall and awkward and not yet of a piece, with his hands going as fast and delicately as mice. He plays well and, when not well, with a constant love of playing. It is good to hear him. When he said last night that he really wished to be a concert pianist, I said, Well, it's not too late. But I wonder if it is. He has no money, no prospect of anything better than the salary of a classics professor!

I remember writing that Larry's eyes were blue. They are the gray that is greenish or tawny—not blue. However, I felt that they were very blue.

I think it will be good to live here at Laguna again. This time there will be no baby coming,* no trip east for Mother to call us up to the Ranch as happened last year. Of course, there are other things to interrupt, but in the meantime—my housewifely instincts are out in full armor, and I look at each old piece of furniture and long to make it new. I shift everything in a room, as some people strip the clothes from a desirable body, without moving more than the eyeballs. But this house is familiar, every crack in its floor and stain on its ugly walls, and I can do little but imagine how charming it might be. The best thing would be to raze it and build again.

Last night we took Edwin to dinner, from the aunties' in Pasadena, where he had driven them the day before from Palo Alto. It was Sunday, so we inserted a few equivocal remarks about dinner with friends, invitation, and so on. Both Edwin and Al are good at that kind of lying—long training in a Christian minister's family. Before we got away, we heard at great and round-the-mulberry-bush length about the aunties' trip to Sitka—about the

---

* Shaun, Anne and Ted Kelly's son, was born in San Francisco in 1932.

salmon fishing, and the glaciers, and on. We looked at many post-cards. The aunties are remarkable chiefly for their enthusiasm. They will be seventy soon. Their spirits are about as old as their minds—seven or eight. It is very tiring to be with them, for aside from the fact that I must avoid religion, drink, etc., as conversation and be careful of my goddamns, my attention must be theirs constantly and without wavering. They dart and rush from one subject to another, and when one is breathless from inane chatter about nothing, the other dashes in, her eyes snapping with enjoyment. It is with guilt and embarrassment that you realize a second's lapse of attention. You feel that your eyes have glazed, that your mouth has sagged open like a dolt's, and you snap up in your seat and listen visibly and nod and beam. I was very glad when we left. We went to a Japanese place for sukiyaki, which E. did not really like, and sake, which he did.

It seems that things are bad with the Fishers—he lumping up in the lymphatic glands with what is said *not* to be cancer, she insomniac. Al will probably go up there when Edwin goes back, at the end of this week. I am very sorry. I think that one of the foulest things about the way a human life is arranged now is the last part of it. For the human rats, there is really little difference between old age and the rest of it, but for fine people who have spent many years of labor and struggle, the living decay of their bodies is even more horrible than the slowing down of their brains. They should be able to die decently—no bad odors, no ignominy. It might be fairer to start out at puberty in a state of general decrepitude, and for several decades grow stronger and more beautiful than any youth ever could be, and die as clean as young corn in the fields.

31.*ix.33*

The last night of the month. In October I am going to eat more as I should, less as *la cuisine de ma mère me dicte. C'est difficile, mais nous allons à la plage dans une semaine. Au moins, espèrons-le.*

Al est parti à 7 h. ce matin pour Palo Alto. Son père est malade —mourant peut-être. On ne le dit pas, mais—

Hier soir, sa derrière nuit, nous avons peu dormi, et ce matin, debout à 6 h. moins le quart—et maintenant je dors yeux ouverts. Je n'aime pas ce lit froid, morne. J'ai mis des petites fleurs pourpres sur la table près du miroir. Je les vois. Mais je suis trop seule, trop seule. Encore une semaine. Ce matin je lui ai dit, Reste donc à Palo Alto—tu vas aider tes parents, les réjouir un peu. Reste donc—deux, trois semaines. Mais j'ai menti quand j'ai dit que j'en serais heureuse, de le savoir loin de moi.

Je vois que le français m'échappe. Et je l'aime tant.

Dix fois par jour je vois une chose, ou je le sens, ou le touche, ou le goûte, et j'en pense pour ce cornet. Mais ça passe si vite, les choses venues. Et maintenant ma vie n'est pas à moi. Je suis compagnon de dame.

*Encore dix jours—une semaine même—et nous vivrons à deux —à un. J'ai sommeil.**

---

* . . . my mother's cooking dictates. It is hard, but we are going to the beach [Laguna] in one week. At least, we hope so.

Al left at 7:00 this morning for Palo Alto. His father is ill—perhaps dying. No one says so, but—

Yesterday evening, his last night, we did not sleep much, and this morning, up at 5:45—and now I am sleeping with my eyes open. I do not like this cold, mournful bed. I put little scarlet flowers on the table near the mirror. I see them. But I am too alone, too alone. Still one week. This morning I said to him, Stay in Palo Alto—you're going to help your parents, cheer them up a little. Stay—two or three weeks. But I lied when I said that I would be happy, knowing he is far from me.

I see that French is escaping me. And I love it so.

When I think of Al's father and then of his mother and then Rex and Edith, I wonder that after so many thousand years of training we continue to be surprised when our friends die. We are well hardened to the fact that more will be born.

In 1930 I read *Opium,* by Jean Cocteau, and its pain and some of its ideas impressed me. Tonight I reread some of it, and I find that I am still impressed, certainly in a different way because of the time between then and now, but still glad to read it. One thing I remember well: *"Il y a chez l'homme une sorte de fixatif, c'est-à-dire de sentiment absurde et plus forte que la raison, qui lui laisse entendre que ces enfants qui jouent sont une race de nains, au lieu d'être des 'ôte-toi de là que je m'y mette.'*

"Vivre est une chute horizontale.

"Sans ce fixatif une vie parfaitement et continuellement consciente de sa vitesse deviendrait intolérable. Il permet au condamné à mort de dormir.

"Ce fixatif me manque. C'est, je suppose, une glande malade. La médicine prende cette infirmité pour un excès de conscience, pour un avantage intellectuel.

"Tout me prouve chez les autres le fonctionement de ce fixatif ridicule, aussi indispensable que l'habitude qui nois dissimule,

---

Ten times a day I see something, or smell it, or touch it, or taste it, and I think about it for this journal. But things sensed pass so quickly. And now my life is not truly my own. I am a lady's companion.

Still ten days—perhaps a week—and we will live two together—like one. I am sleepy.

*chaque jour l'épouvante d'avoir à se lever, à se raser, à s'habiller, à manger. Ne serait-ce que l'*album de photographies, *un des instincts les plus cocasses de faire d'une dégringolade une suite de monuments solennels. L'opium m'apportait ce fixatif. Sans l'opium, les projets: mariages, voyages, me paraissent aussi fous qui si quelqu'un qui tombe par la fenêtre souhaitait se lier avec les occupants des chambres devant lesquelles il passe."**

3. x. 33

I have just finished a good novel, written this year by Josephine Herbst. It is strong and robust. I met a man last summer, and when by some chance one of us mentioned J. H. and I said that she had published *Pity Is Not Enough* and had many good notices,

---

* "There is in man a sort of fixative, that is to say, a sort of absurd feeling stronger than reason which allows him to think that the children who play are a race of dwarves instead of being a bunch of 'get out there and leave room for me.'

"Living is a horizontal fall.

"Without this fixative any life perfectly and continually conscious of its speed would become intolerable. It enables the condemned man to sleep.

"I lack this fixative. It is, I suppose, a diseased gland. Medicine takes this infirmity for an excess of conscience, for an intellectual advantage.

"Everything convinces me of the functioning, in others, of this absurd fixative, as indispensable as habit, which conceals from us each day the horror of having to get up, shave, dress, and eat. Even if it were only the photograph album, one of the most comical ways of turning a helter-skelter into a succession of solemn monuments.

"Opium gave me this fixative. Without opium, plans, marriages, and journeys appear to me just as foolish as if someone falling out of a window were to hope to make friends with the occupants of the room before which he passes."

(An excerpt from Cocteau's Opium, *translated by Margaret Crosland [London: Peter Owen Publishers])*

he was delighted. He had known her when she was a husky, silent woman who cooked for many talkative and intellectual menfolk. He was glad of her book, because he used to look at her as she went about her work so stolidly and think that she could say more than all the rest of them, if she wanted to. Now she has written this good novel, and it and her first one have made her an important woman.

I haven't heard yet from Al. Mother had notes from C. Y. F. and Edwin today, but of course nothing was said about H. H. F.'s health. I'd be very happy if Al telephoned tonight that he had died. I am afraid of a long and harrowing end for him.

Today was very hot. It reminded me a little of the days off Guatemala last year, when my bones felt gone from the flesh, leaving a limp yawning emptiness. But today I felt sleepy, and all afternoon fought against drowsing by changing my position often and violently as I lay on the chaise longue.

Yesterday Douglas Kennedy* was here on his way to Stanford from Buenos Aires. He is a pleasant young chap and is amusing because of his scatterbrains, but more than a day of him is too much.

It is night, and Mother on the couch has dropped into a little nap. She breathes in short, abrupt puffs. Suddenly one of them changes to an awareness, and I know that she has dreamed that she is asleep. For a minute I cannot hear her. Her breaths start again to make audible puffings, and then she clears her throat and moves briskly and picks up her book again. I do not look at her, but if her eye met mine she would smile with embarrassment and perhaps say, Well, I almost dropped off!

Upstairs I can hear Dave taking a shower. He is growing used to football practice again. For two weeks or so after it started, he

* M.F.K.F.'s first cousin from Buenos Aires, Argentina.

was so tired that he was far from civil—and he still expresses disapproval or grouchiness by a discarding of all politeness. He is a fine boy and a charming one, but when he is sullen there are few humans more unattractive.

The other day I bought new oxygen-grass and cleaned out Father's fishbowl and put in new fish. Since then I have felt much more interest in the bowl, which has been there on the music cabinet for several years without more than casual looks from anyone but Father. He sits watching it from the chair by the radio, or from his chair in the living room sees through the dining room into the side porch and through one side of the bowl, with the fish glinting slowly among the green weeds. That is what I like, too, to look up from my book and see the two fish moving counter to their reflections, slow and easy and very lovely in the many-colored water.

A letter from Dillwyn P. to A. says that there is a slight chance of selling the scenario they wrote. I hope it comes off—for many reasons.

All the time I eat and talk and live here I am full of the consciousness of A. He is all through me, like a virus, and I doubt if I will ever get over him.

28. xii. 33

I think that many people want to write, but of them few have the will to. I write more than half the things I do or say or think. I can see the words on the sheet of paper and see the pen writing them. And in my head a voice, a kind of silent reading voice, reads them not from but to the paper. Often what is read is good. There is a quick sureness about some phrases. At times they come too patly, with a smart-aleck tone. But I *don't* write. I write a few letters, which grow less interesting as I age. But that is all. It is because I am lazy, and that is true of most of the people who think in prose. Laziness and a vague fear.

I sit here, sleepy on top and thinking of the long steaming shower I shall take in a few minutes, but my mind is buzzing with many things to say. Christmas is over, a good one with us all in gay humor, weather cold for a fire in the morning by the tree and warm and sunny for walking after the dinner, which was not too big. The next day we all felt gay, too. Gordon Newell* gets $26 a week under the P.W.A. [Public Works Administration] for carving two panels of the Spirit of America. They are to go in a new school. H. W. R.† gets the same for hand-setting copies of the Declaration of Independence. Same destination. I have suggested that Al's penchant for writing lusty ballads might be turned into a flow of patriotic hymns for eighth-grade glee clubs. A fine chance for equivocal punning. Larry goes to work in Zeitlin's bookstore next week. He and Gordon sup with us tomorrow night, Rex and Mother being on their way to Carmel and New Year's with the Kelly ménage. Saturday Al and D. and N. and I go to Prado, where A. and I went just when I started this book. It is a gathering of bowed-down Mexicans and a few hard Italians who sell their pottery. The Mexicans work hard, using the soil they live on. They live in great poverty. They seem sweet and dull. The pottery, too, is very simple, with a few lewdly painted jars for the imitation balconies of suburban "Mediterranean" houses. Once in a while there is a little joke—a pig bank turned quietly into a monstrous elephant by some clayey fingers or a squatting dog bank with a crude human head.

---

* Gordon Newell, sculptor, lifelong friend of M.F.K.F. and Larry Powell.
† Harry Ward Ritchie, book designer and fine printer, another lifelong friend.

There is too much noise in this life. At Laguna it is better. But still there is too much. I listen with disgust and with my ears sickened to the radio now, telling news.

30. xii. 33

When I put pine branches in the rooms, we said, How they will smell nice when we take them down. But now, standing by the fire warming my knees, I pulled a little branch from behind a candlestick on the mantle and squatted down to hold it against the flame. The needles spat and burned up. When it grew too hot, I dropped it, but the room is scented almost disagreeably. Perhaps we were remembering a myth about the perfume of burning pine. This is rather *écoeurant* [stifling].

It is raining now. It seems as if I know about the grass reaching up and how green the leaves feel when newly washed. One sensation I've long desired—a California hill, dry after summer, being rained upon.

New Year's Eve, 1933

The radio mumbles a "cross-country dancing party," with bad bands and throngs saying, Whoopee, and Oh, boy, into the microphone. A minute ago we switched to another station just in time to hear a farmer announce by telephone that he could not leave his place, cut off by flood. It has been raining steadily for about thirty hours now, but we hadn't thought of flood. It is a likely thing, however. So many hills are stripped bare by fire. The rain scoots down their black sides.

It is 11:30. In a few minutes I'll make a hot punch and Noni and Dave and A. and I will drink. Mom and Rex are in Carmel with Sis, stormbound. I feel slightly moved, rather sentimental, though not much about the New Year, I think. For me, the years begin September 5. As for resolutions, I have always wondered at my impatience with them. I used to think something was wrong with me that I could not resolve to do certain things on a certain date. Now I do not mind.

The radio grows louder and more maudlin. Here the fire burns bright. A. and I have just taken showers, and our hair is damp around the edges. Noni in a burning-colored dress looks cool. She is reading, and I see that her face is flushed. She and Dave were excited by the snatch of flood news. He sits by the radio. I think he is rather sleepy. He has black paint on his fingers from a drawing he made and burned, of a tree blowing and a little shepherd sitting under it in the falling leaves.

Now I will make the eggnog. I can't find a recipe. I'll heat milk, beat the eggs and sugar, add them, and stir in port and a little brandy. It may turn out—a kind of thin zabaglione, I suppose. I hope we'll sleep untormented into 1934.

11.i.34

My pen is broken, and I have not written because of that, putting it off each day with a feeling of disappointment and relief. This old pen of A.'s makes a startling difference. If I wrote long, I should be cramped.

I smell the shellac from a plaster mask Hal Bieler made of A., which he gave us for Christmas. I can't put it on the wall. There is something unpleasant about a known face breaking abruptly from a flat surface. With a grotesque or even a thing like Beethoven's mask it is different, but I couldn't stand this green, dull look of A.

It is a good mask. I am glad to have it, too, but I think I'll put it away.

Tonight we have supper with Ann and Bud Leland at the Hinchmans'. Mr. H. is to be cook. He is a stubborn, shabby man, always a bit dirty but very unperturbed and comfortable. Ann says he looks like a tipsy plumber. He is cheerful in a brusque way and at times speaks a surprising jargon of very "advanced" art. His wife is quiet, with a withdrawn, fine, melancholy face, like an Italian painting.

12. i. 34

The supper chez Hinchman was one of the worst meals I've ever eaten, but the people were good. There was a great tub of spaghetti cooked with cheap oil and hamburger meat and no imagination, a salad so badly mixed that the salt and the oil and the garlic came in gobs, and, most god-awful, saucers of pink gelatin. I was almost too depressed to be revived, but the people were quite interesting. One, an old sailor who held himself in because of the "ladies present," had the hearty, knee-whacking mannerisms of a professional "salty sea dog," but was genuine for all of that. When we took him home and he wanted us to slow down in front of his house, he said, Slack away there, slack away!

Just now when I went to the bathroom I thought of how good it was to live intimately and freely with someone so that the sounds of washing teeth and urinating and so on were not something annoying, to be hushed and ignored. I like privacy and am quite modest, too, but without any talking or exhibitionism, we never make a fuss over functions of the toilet. I haven't said quite what I mean.

I must make some tooth powder. It is something we started

this winter. We like it and save quite a sum of money. We use about three parts each of powdered magnesia and baking soda, and one of table salt, with one drop per teaspoonful of essence of peppermint and wintergreen. Mix well and bottle. Our teeth look all right. So far.

Larry may come down tomorrow or Monday for a few days. He sold an article to *Touring Topics* for $50. I'll give him the little panel I made of the Lawrence phoenix emblem. I don't think it's very good, though the coat of hot oil and wax improved it some. I wish I could have made something really beautiful and give it to A.

Letters from France today, in answer to my Christmas notes. Miss Lyse wrote a long incoherent letter on Christmas Eve, sitting alone in her little attic room. She spent some of the $3 we sent her on some flowers, some English holly. She said her friends lamented that the birds, this hard winter, had eaten the berries from it, but she told them it was right. The birds were made to eat berries, even English holly berries. So she tied red ribbons on the twigs. It is hard not to become very sentimental about Miss Lyse. She is highly pathetic—the kind of little old lady who would delight the hearts of imitators of K. Mansfield—but she's a fine little old lady, too.

13. i. 34

With my pen back from hospital, I should write often!

Today the family came and went in a jolly mood. I think they like to come. We eat, and have a highball before lunch, and afterward Mother and I sit by the fire and chat while the others take a little walk. Then they go, and Al and I do the dishes and feel warm and hospitable and glad they're gone. We're usually restless and not able to work any. Tonight, par exemple, we'll probably go to a show even though we don't want to.

I am reading *The Way of All Flesh*. It is a fine book. I'd like to have, someday, a style one nth as simple and direct.

Last night we had supper with Bronson Barber and stayed late. The air was heavy with counterromances and alcohol-inspired plottings. I hate gin and can't drink it without several days of malaise, so I was very sober. But most of the others were tipsy. It was rather tiresome, and I was saddened by some of the emotions I felt around me. People thought I was or should be piqued at Al because he talked for a long time in the kitchen with two women while I sat by the living room fire—but we came away feeling that we were the only ones there who really knew what they were doing. All the others were uneasily living, suspecting and fearing and not knowing what everything was about. There is too much suspicion and fear between men and women.

On the mantle are some Chinese lilies from the Ranch. The warm room makes their perfume breathe out quickly. I suppose they will die sooner because of that, but it is nice now. Dave polished the little man I carved on a block of oak—not very well carved on not very good wood, but he liked it. I was going to give it to him but was afraid to because I had nothing for Noni. So this week I'll make a little thing for her, before Friday if I can. We're going up then while Rex is in Santa Barbara.

Al came in very wet from a walk to the village in a cold and milky fog. Now he is dozing on the couch. I wonder at the things that work constantly in his brain. I know that when he sits looking at his pipe or talking so nicely to any person, his head is working hard on some mad paragraph. And when he suddenly needs a little nap, I am for some reason as proud of him as if he had climbed a high mountain, because I imagine what has tired him.

Last night he was the best person at Bronson's party, because he talked with two queer girls who sat unnoticed except for him, while other people laughed and whispered meanness about them and pitied him. He was nicer than I. One of the two women I disliked very much, a boringly affected little thing about thirty-five with a flat yellow face and the blue hair and puffed lids of a Eurasian. She and the other women were closeted for a long time in the kitchen with Al. Finally she came near me by the fire and with many silly and attemptedly "deep" remarks tried to comfort me for being neglected. I parried all her thrusts in the same affected, semisubtle style but more cleverly. And finally she grew quite excited by me, and forgot Al, and would have leapt at any advances. I could have had her under the sheets. But I hated her. I am too curious, I think, and quite detached. If she had been attractive to me, I'd have led her on farther to see how she'd act. But this woman was odious to me. I was prejudiced before I knew her personally, first irritated indirectly because she and her friend were causing talk about Al and me, then definitely annoyed by her lavish commiseration of my "neglect," finally revolted by her oozy interest in me.

There is something very coarse about the attitude people have about married couples—like mother-in-law jokes in the funny papers. If Al and I had sat holding hands all evening, it would have been stupid and stupefying. But because he learned what he could from other people and so did I, there was almost universal conviction that he was philandering, that I was neglected, that I was secretly raging, that he longed to be unfaithful. And when we finally left, I saw glances between the two kitchen women, saying, She's dragging him home by the ear! And all this came without the slightest hint from either of us but simply out of the minds of all those people who saw us as they were themselves and from habit and repetition interpreted us as a conventional "married" joke in the Sunday comic supplement.

Eucalyptus leaves half-float in the dim fog, and more than ever before I can imagine myself living in the sea.

27.i.34

I meant not to answer it [a letter from Sis], but I did. I love her very much indeed. The thought of her boredom, so young and intelligent and fine to look at, is almost intolerable to me. But now she is not being intelligent. Of course, that is very easy for me to say.

I feel an increasing triviality about what I put in this journal. I'd like, for instance, to tell something that has happened, perhaps a whole incident. But I think, In fifteen minutes I must put on the cabbage, or go to bed with A., or do something else. It is very disgusting to me. I really want to write, and I can write—but I'm not driven by a fire intense enough to make me say to hell with A.'s supper. I make beds and clean and wash and manicure my nails because I *want* to be clean for him and make him comfortable. If I really were an artist, his comfort and even his opinion of me would be secondary things. And so would my own. I'd work and, if I did not starve first, perhaps do something very fine. As it is now, all this sincere but ineffective piddling with chisels and journals is to keep me limber. I won't be all stiff and dulled when my time comes. If it does.

Al is fumbling through a book of German songs. Sometimes he plays softly and sweetly, although he is very uncertain, but tonight he hits each note hard. It hurts my head a little. The piano is rather off-key, too.

I notice many similarities between Balter and Gide, at least in their sentiments about the family.

I can't continue. The noise A. makes is really hideous.

19. ii. 34

Tonight there is a gentle rain, with sound all around us from the eaves and, outside that, the noise of water in the waves. They are rolling in fast and heavily, with much foam all along the shores and some lifted into the air.

Today I told the head of the little tutoring school that I could not continue my two hours daily of watching the children and teaching music and reading. For several days I talked back and forth to myself. I was uneasy at the thought of not finishing what I had started. I was afraid I'd lose some self-respect. And I thought I was a fool to turn down $10 a month for work I really could do. But in the end I did tell Miss Johnson. I think she was relieved, because now she has a chance to get a real teacher, one who has studied child psychology and pedagogy and schoolroom ethics. I am relieved, too. Little children are lovely. I like their fresh smooth bodies and their slender necks and many of their speeches. But in a classroom I hate their smells and their dirty noses and their bitten fingernails and their flat blank innocent eyes and the way they pout their red mouths. I hate their guts, in other words. But I still feel uneasy about the $10. I have a feeling that I can make it up, though. I'll make five or so on the stool I'm doing for Mother to give to Betty Benson, and I have made two little boxes I may perhaps be able to sell. They are very well done and ought to sell. I'll have photographs made of them and the bench, and send them to Hammold and anyone else I can think of who might have some jobs. We'll see.

I like the rain. I remember one time lying most of a day in bed in the Ranch guest house, listening while rain fell all around me. I could hear it on four sides of the little house, and it made a shell over me.

The sweet alyssum is growing wild now on the vacant lots. I have three bowls of it in the house. The first day the dusty, cloying smell was everywhere, but now there is none. And the eucalyptus trees are more than ever in flower. Last night we drove under the trees in front of the house and looked up at them. The sky was high and dull, and the flowers glimmering like stars in fog above us. In the daytime bees are busy at them, and all together make a continuous hum.

Sunday I heard Toscanini conduct Beethoven's Ninth with the New York Philharmonic and the Schola Cantorum. There were 270 voices singing. At the end of the last movement I was swept up by them, and tears welled out the corners of my eyes, but I was not weeping. It is celestial music, and there is a movement in it like the swift unearthly lines in some of Blake's drawings. Or Dante.

I can hear a frog, quietly enjoying the rain, like me.

In three days we start to drive to San Francisco with Dillwyn and Gigi Parrish. We are excited. We like them. And it will be fine to be in S. F. together.

T. had an abortion performed Saturday. I am glad it was all done decently by H. B.—no scuttling, no drunken doctor. She stayed in the clinic. Last time she went home and worked and then was sickly for months. She deliberately misuses her body, in a kind of complicated masochism and as a silent reproach. Many women are that way. They will iron longer than they need to so that the backache they acquire, even though they never tell anyone they have it, can be used as a little incentive for the recrimination they never utter: While you sit reading, I work, my back breaking. It is very complicated. Long after, they think with pleasure of their years of silent sufferings, especially if they are dying of cancer or heart trouble. Then sometimes they tell of their slow martyrdom and bask in their families' abject abasement. It is a kind of revenge, but how many know for what?

King Albert of Belgium fell down a mountainside and died, and last week, after a short revolution in Paris against the corruption uncovered in l'affaire Stavisky, Austrian socialists fought for four days. For a time that looked like the spark Europe waits for, but now things have quieted. On the surface.

We finished *Les Faux-Monnayeurs* last night, one of the most artfully arranged books I have ever read. It is very mature—a contrast to Wilde's precocious sophomoric style. The last sentence was bad for me—the first semblance of a leer. The rest of the book I found very pure and real.

The other day I wrote one page of a letter to Gloria S., and when I decided not to send it after all, I put it in this book to copy. But tonight when I read it over, it sounded so damned noble and frank and disgusting that I threw it in the fire. That is, I threw it around the gas grate we burn for lack of wood, and it hit the edge of the hearth and rolled under the piano. But I am thinking of how words change on the page. It is very disturbing. How do we know what we write? There were the letters I put down, my mind aggravated by G.'s suspicions and small grievances and my heart somewhat hurt at the numbing of a pleasant friendship. But my God, how hollow and how nobly frank they read tonight—not what I said at all. Words shift and reform themselves in the mind, folding onto themselves and begetting new connotations like colored glass in a kaleidoscope or cells in a plant. What did Mr. W. S. really say when he said, To be . . . Whether to take arms against a sea of troubles?

The rain is quiet now. A heavy drop falls here or there from the eaves, and the waves are slower and stiller.

In S. F. I want to ride on the ferry at night and listen to the music in the Chinese Theater and take baths in the hotel. I also want to buy Gigi a corsage from a corner flower stand near the Palace and take Al to hear the bird whistle at Gump's. That is one of the funniest sounds I have ever heard, so breathless and embarrassed and ending with a few bars of "Over There." Now I begin to think of many more things I want to do. But those are the main ones.

Later

I just realized that the uncomfortable need to write in this and the constant realization that what I write has no significance are almost what I feel about carving. I have to do it. All the time I despise the work I do, but I go on simply to be ready. I don't know what I need be ready for, but there is evidently something. How strange if I lived all my life doing things almost without wanting to, always feeling that they were just a substitute for what I was really meant to do and never finding what that was.

1. iii. 34

We didn't go to S. F. Gigi got a job on a Barrymore picture— and the weather was bad, anyway.

Now Al is giving his weekly lecture. In an hour I'll get him, and we'll go to see a picture called *Thunder over Mexico*. Tomorrow he will earn $3.50 by sweeping and cleaning a house that has been empty so long that the windows are broken.

We came back down after a night at the Ranch, I very discouraged. The Kellys were there, biting and jibing at each other. Shaun [their baby] was there, with tension between Sis and the maid over open safety pins and so on. Noni was in bed with a bad cold. Dave was impudent and thoughtful by turns. Father was low as a snake because he'd had a cold and rheumatism in his chest for ten days and, in spite of many pills and light treatments, was no better. Mother was in the hospital with a cold, demanding constant attention, alternately wheezing out coughs straight from her toes and snoring violently. And so on. I thought, Hell, what a family—all at cross-purposes, muddling along! I fled with my tail between my legs, leaving Sis fuming and griping at how they imposed on her and how indispensable she was. I used to feel that way, but now I know it's not true. They'll get along just as well or better without me, and I'll spare myself a scarred heart if I can only remember that. A scarred heart and many a gray hair. It's hard, though, to be impersonal. But I'm beginning to realize that it's as important for me to inoculate myself against my family as it is for hay-fever victims to stay away from goldenrod and mimosa.

I dread tomorrow because I *have* to sharpen tools. I can put it off no longer. I have an idea to read a few books on photography, borrow Father's good camera, and learn all I can by myself—so that I can present a project to some foundation: a thesis, illustrated, on Scandinavian folk carvings in wood. Of course, learning the languages would be another thing, but I could handle that. God, if I could only swing it, I *know* I could make a good piece of work. Of course, I have no American college degree and only a minor French one and have never gone to an art school. But I think the idea might do, especially if I could publish one illustrated article first in an architectural journal or some such thing. Of course, photography is a field in itself—but I have a fairly good eye for light and shade and pattern and ought to be able to learn how to develop and print. Well—I've had so many big ideas—but *I want to pull out.* It is necessary for Al and me. We're sinking now, slowly.

11. iii. 34

Late Saturday night. I have just pushed Al away from here to dance down in the village. He wanted to go and felt he should not. He has been waiting on me all week, bringing grapefruit juice and listening to me blow a cold away. Tonight he was twitching to be off. I urged and coaxed and commanded him to go, and I really didn't want him to at all. I hate being here alone tonight, I am lonesome for him—and *I* told him to go, for heaven's sake. I don't want to go to bed and I don't want to stay up and every car that passes I hope may be his returning, and I urged him to go and stay a long time and go on to parties if he could. I don't know what I'll do. It would be awful if I seemed sad or grouchy when he came back, yet I am so sad that I could easily be that and grouchy at once. I am probably sad because I still have a cold in my throat, enough to give me a dull senseless monotonous cough, and I am three days late with the curse and have abortion-$75-curettage-abortion in a corner of my mind. And my nails need manicuring and my hair shampooing so that I am not well groomed, and that always disturbs me slightly. And today Sis and Ted drove the children down and for a few hours I was in the thick of an atmosphere of veiled bickering, affection, strain. I am so sorry for Sis because she loves me, and Ted does not and doesn't want her to, and she is torn and is as yet incapable of any balance between two such diverse loves. She is bewildered and pained and sulky. The children are puzzled by two couples before their eyes, Sis and Ted and A. and me. They wonder at us and no doubt try to make us the proof of many theories.

Gloria came down, as usual laden with exotic jars and bottles, South African gooseberry jam, and Stilton cheese in port wine, and Russian cake. She stayed four days. Although no one even hinted at her long silence, the first three days never quite reached the open-eyed friendliness of last summer. But the fourth day had the old easiness.

Gordon was here two days and sharpened all my tools really sharp.

The day G. and G. left, Fay and Larry came with the baby. Everything happened to make it a bad visit, but if nothing had happened, I still would have wished them nevermore with me. I knew the minute I saw their car at the curb that I should not see them, for our common happiness. I reached the saturation point during their visit here, and now if I heard them coming, I think I would run up into the hills. The second morning they were here, I woke up and told Al that I couldn't see them. I was staying in bed with a cold, and I thought it would be easy, but all day they were with me. I was desperate. I don't know just why it is. I am very fond of Larry and occasionally I almost love him, and although I am not fond of Fay and never have been, I do not actively dislike her. At times I feel very friendly toward her. I wish A. would come back.

Tonight I put the designs on the legs of the bench for Betty Benson. I hope Mother will like the design. I am almost through with the third and last box. I hope I can sell them. I wish I had something made for Mother's birthday, but it is the twenty-seventh, and here it is the eleventh, and we may go to S. F. with the Parrishes next week. I might be able to. Begin anyway, show it to her.

A. bought me some Transvaal daisies, different shades of

coral. I look up at them on the piano from my tuffet; half-wilted and drooping, they are like fireworks, stars shooting out from long green stems. Very delicate. I love them and the tulips he gave me in Dijon that came every morning fresh from Holland, some of them black. The brodiaea are out now on the hills and every vacant lot. Gloria called them water-nuts when she was little, because of the little bulb at the bottom. She ate that. I will eat one this week. I have seen some lupine and a few poppies. I remember when Father bought the orange orchard in Puente, poppies were solid gold between the trees. We didn't pick them, but in three or four years they had disappeared, as everywhere. I think the cultivating buried the seeds too deep.

I sit quite stolidly, but I feel that at each window are faces peering. And when leather creaks on a chair seat, I jump inside, or when a eucalyptus bud hops down the roof, I wish Al would come. I think I'll go to bed. But I'm not at all sleepy.

6. iv. 34

What I mean to do and want to do is write something every day. Many small interesting things come to us, like letters and people for lunch and perhaps an idea. But I am lazy and I put off, and also I am often tired by late night. Now, for instance, it is about 11:00. Al, who cleaned a vacant house today for Tom Harper and for $3, has just hobbled to bed. I want to go soon, before he is asleep. I am rather tired. I didn't get up until 9:30. The morning was dark gray. By noon I had done a lot of dishes, taken a bath and breakfast, made the beds and done the usual bedroom straightening, and cleaned most of the house quite thoroughly. Then I got lunch and, after we'd eaten it, washed the dishes. I went to the beach for an hour and read *Ulysses,* into which, past my first wild gallop, I've settled at a steady pace of about fifteen pages at a time. I'm at the spree between the lying-in home and the brothel now. While I read it, I turned myself neatly to brown on both sides in the sun, which had come out beaming. Various reports of the resultant horrors of the suntan craze had almost decided me against any brown, but the sun is so warm and the sand so soft and lying flat out in the heat so delightful. And I am so nice looking when I'm brown. So now I have a judiciously done three-day coat of tender pink.

Between 2:30 and 6:00 I carved, made a chocolate cake that stuck to the pan but looks all right frosted, went shopping, and got a very good dinner. Of course, Al cooked the steak, and we bought a piece of coconut cake at the Kooky Krock—but I assembled it all and timed things to be done at 6:15. And that is something. We had yams and bananas and artichokes and steak and cake and coffee—rather heavy but very good. And before dinner we found some bourbon of R.'s we had thought all drunk and made a little old-fashioned with it and with some bitters that Larry found in his garage and gave us. Then we went to a movie—and from its end until I began this, I carved. I finished a leg of the Benson bench. It is all right.

9. iv. 34

Yesterday, another sunny day, Mom and the kids to lunch, with Father on a stag party, and, of course, I had a steady flow of talk from Edith. Every Sunday is the same. Off she bundles the family, to start to talk to me with eyes ashine. Sometimes I give her nods, or even tell her something new, or perhaps I just say, Ah and Yes and Oh, no. Almost always now she discusses the Kellys. God, how tired I am of them. I love Sis. I love Mother. I am not jealous.

But oh, God above, how sick I am of hearing about the Kellys. I don't like Ted; I think a divorce is the only good end and that soon. I am sad that Sis is unhappy—but why in God's name so much talk? Over and over the same ground, over and over he said and I said and I think and I just told him and what do you don't you I really I'm just.

Anne was here for a night. She and I talked until early morning in the stuffy room. She asked me what I thought and what I'd do and so on, and at first I kept clear. But in the end I told her. I told her I'd go to S. F. with the baby, borrow money if necessary, and live alone for a time and try to find work. She said little, but next morning told me she'd decided to do that. She was bitter at the family's discussions of her most intimate problems, and without saying that the best way to stop that would be to keep quiet herself, I suggested that she say nothing of this venture until it was well started one way or another. She agreed. It would be easy, since Mother already knew she was hunting for an apartment and would not think to ask for how many people. But Sunday I found that Anne hadn't been able to resist, telling just enough—that she was looking for an apartment for S. and herself—to throw Mom into a wild state. Any suggestion of actions not fully predisclosed to her puts her into a frenzy. Anne says that when she has nothing else to fret about, she'll begin on Al and me—how do we live, what is to become of us, why doesn't Al find work—and it all boils down to a fuming anger at her own ignorance of our "plans." It is inconceivable to Mother that we might have none. She feels that we are living independently, secretly almost, and her impotence makes her rage.

Last night we went to a cocktail party in Timmy and Gigi's canyon house. It seemed dull and messy without them. Everyone was drunk. After my second or third glass of the gin punch, I felt very careless, but with the next one I became sober and saw everything with a too-clear eye. The women looked ghastly, their faces gray, their lipstick half gone and discolored. The men looked very silly. The host has the pop-eyed foolish face of a gutter terrier in permanent erection.

We left at 10:00 and hurried down the coast to Larry's house, for we'd told them we might come. But the windows were dark. We felt badly—it's annoying to wait or half-wait for people. And this morning when I found they'd had a bottle of wine for us, I felt worse.

We had a picnic at Emerald Bay with them. Bart barked a lot, and the baby gnawed at a soggy sand-coated zwieback, and I had the curse, but it was all right. I'm at one of my off times with L., when everything he says is either dull or annoying, and all his actions bore me or disgust me. Sometimes I like him so much. He and Fay seem quite happy. I think they ought to get some kind of radio—it would help Larry a bit.

12. iv. 34

A day in bed, long awaited. It is most weak and selfish of me to continue to eat chocolate and cake and things I know so well will lay me low. Al is miserable when I am not well. And I can avoid being so.

To a stupid party chez Harper this week, and yesterday to the Ranch.

I go to night school almost every night, on the Emergency Educational Program. Al makes $7 weekly for two two-hour lectures—we are living on that and my allowance and an occasional dollar he makes cleaning houses for Tom Harper.

Today a letter from Stelter at Occidental asking if we'd consider a part-time job for next semester. We answered yes and suggested that the bigger the salary, the more we'd have to eat. By that time our money will be kaput. I'd like to live on the hill between Broadway and the library in Los Angeles. Last night at dinner with Painter the Old Sea Dog, he told of an immaculate room he gets there for $2.50 a week. What I'd like to do would be to rent two or three rooms unfurnished and borrow enough stuff to live with. The family would squirm at our living in such a quarter.

16. iv. 34

I know that three years from now I'll look back with a certain longing at this time of careless living. Even now I feel it—a nostalgia for the present! But I'll be glad of change, any change. I want life, want to feel, to realize it with all of my being. And it's only now, bit by bit, little by little, that I am becoming conscious. Gradually I see myself shaping up, forming. For years I've been fetal, in the egg shape. I've known it all along. Now I begin to hear, to smell and feel, still through the shell, but I do hear and feel and search. Always before, I've known that I might. I've been uneasy and half-conscious of life outside of me. Other people suffered and were joyous. I was, too, but in an unfilled way. I was living as the reflection in a mirror lives. Now it begins to be me.

Well, no doubt I've written incoherencies. There are times when I feel very acutely my own tiny forming. This is one of them. Often after I've had the curse I seem more acute. That is more than a physical purge, certainly. It has its value. If it weren't so futile, I could easily rage and rebel at its demands. It is so damnably inevitable. Affairs most important, an absolute need for beauty or action or nerve—and no matter, it comes. I am dull. I suffer. I am helpless. I feel a pariah. It is hell. What a god-awful waste of time.

A month or so each year of actual pain, a year or so each decade. God, how mean, how very mean and ignominious a treatment! But, yes, it has its value. If I could live simply and healthfully enough to reduce it to its bare demand of a day or two of annoyance, I'd be months ahead. I could get more done.

That is the joke, of course. Get what done?

Last night we started *Moby Dick.* I think we'll like it.

Today I began to write a quasi-serious article about Laguna: to be or not to be an "artist colony." I want very much to sell it. I'll try to finish it before Thursday. Then when we come back from two or three days at the Ranch (to have the roadster doctored), I'll peer at it again. I do want it to be good enough to sell. I'd like to make a few drawings for it. It would be wonderful to make a little money to give Al, so he wouldn't worry. I'd give him a little present first. Maybe we would take a little trip—to Catalina for a night, perhaps, or Caliente. Well—counting my chickens.

The children were here for the weekend. When Mother came down for lunch on Sunday, she was twittering with excitement and kept saying, Come, Dote, I want to talk to you—I want you to do something for me—Come, I have something to ask you. I thought, Oh, Lord, she's going East and wants us to take care of the kids or something. She dragged me into the bedroom and closed the door. I kept thinking, Oh, hell, what now. Dotey, she said, and her eyes were very bright, I want you to trade me your old black dinner dress for this. And she had a lovely dress, long and slim, with full sleeves and a funny round collar and jabot of sequins. I was very happy. I tried it on to show to Father. He sat by the fire and said, Now *I tell you,* those lines are—now those lines—turn around, let's see the back—well, *I tell you,* those lines are *good.* I found I was a bit fat, especially my buttocks. I've been eating too many avocados.

Tonight I went to Hinchman's class on modern art and got in

a half hour of typing at each end of it. I want to improve my typing: maybe I could get a job if we were in a city next year.

Last night Fay and Larry came for supper. For a time Larry will be moons away from me. Marriage is making him see many new things about women, and he hates them and feels victimized, so he'll hate me as a woman who has been close to him. He'll suspect me. Perhaps *she* has tricked me, he'll think. It is interesting to watch him change and turn and grow new corners and new colors. Soon he'll begin to rebel. Already he is ready to imagine every kind of wifely imposition. If Fay asks him to lift a heavy pail, Henpecked! he thinks to himself.

When I wonder what Dürer's mother looked upon, I am filled with amazement and with fear, too. I am helpless. She looked into another world, beyond us, and she looked, at the same time, back and in upon her own past and the lives of all her loves and hates and the lives of every person she served in her own life. She looks and looks. There is a kind of expectant immobility, her soul like a pointing dog waiting to leap away from her.

17.iv.34

Finished an article on Laguna that Al likes. Also did a fairly good sketch of bust and shoulders of a woman, a life class. The clothes are a bother.

26.iv.34

Beautiful days at Laguna after a short week in Whittier. I went into the water this afternoon. The beach is hot and good. I do little work, other than dishes. Night classes continue in spite of several more contradictory letters to the contrary from various boards and committees.

16. *v.* 34

It is late, with A. long in bed. Tonight people for supper caused me to drink coffee, so I'm not sleepy. I usually write in this late at night. When A.'s up, I don't want to.

Tomorrow night, after A.'s class, we'll go to Whittier for the weekend.

Today I finished a charcoal drawing for a bookplate for Dave's birthday. I am not much pleased by it. I must do one for Noni before tomorrow night.

5. *vi.* 34

I sit in a low chair by a good fire. I wear soft black velvet pajamas with green on the neck and sleeves, and my nails are stained green from painting this house. It is the Parrishes' beach house, and we are cleaning it and earning $30. Today we painted hard until late afternoon. Then a rainstorm blew in on it all and floated the paint right off the railings. It was very depressing, but it was fine to be so near the ocean and be rained upon. Now the waves are rather sullen and make a steady peevish noise that sounds all around us instead of just on their side.

Gloria came down with her usual load of strange victuals and a bottle of fine cognac. So I have drunk a little of it here tonight by the warm fire.

Since I last wrote in this book, a great many things have happened. But I think that they really are not very important. Or else they are so complex as to be beyond my writing. If I followed the several separate plots of my own life or anyone's, with all their developments and with all the people who never touch out of their own tales, I'd write all day and perhaps all night. And soon I'd never see any people, and the stories would kill themselves.

I seem to have made a grand big blob of a blot.

My toenails are very long, because I forget to bring scissors from our house every time I go there. It makes me remember reading about a man who was almost overcome by a fearful disgust at the thought of all the whiskers growing in the world on millions of chins, growing and growing and being shaved off and growing more ferociously.

Al's father is dying of Hodgkin's disease. According to some medicos, this is a tubercular infection of the lymph glands. Others call it cancer, glandular cancer. Honky and Bieler call it thus. They say it is cruel and foolish to try to dispel the lumps by rays—the treatment H. H. F.* is following. They say it tortures the victim and leaves his family in debt. H. H. F. writes that for three weeks after a roentgen-ray treatment he lies in bed in great pain (kidneys, spleen, and so on). And I know the Fishers have borrowed money.

This week Father and Mother and the children start for Victoria. I think their trip will grow very wonderful long after it is over, but really while it happens it will be scratched up with many bad moments. They are, all four of them, very selfish people in different ways. The children are most so, of course, because they have never yet realized the existence of any other real people in this world. And Mother, in spite of her pose, justified often, of a self-forgetful and self-sacrificial mother of four fine children, is a most demanding and pettish woman. And Father, half as his "just due"

* Herbert Fisher, Al's father.

and half in self-protection, simply takes, or does, or says—if he wants to belch, he belches, by God.

So they'll all hate each other and sulk and perhaps cry a little bit and feel very much abused or misunderstood. But it will end, in a few years, rosily.

I try not to think of finishing the painting and cleaning the cupboards and washing the windows and waxing the floors and seeing the curtains are back from the laundry by June 14. I hate things like this. And having the sink mended and calling the electrician. Hell, I say.

The ocean still rushes and snaps all around me, and the fire and the cognac cool. My feet look quite far in front of me on the rug, and very thin and elegant in black pumps, because now I am almost always soft-shod in espadrilles. If I wear shoes for a long time, it is reversed, with occasional espadrilles making me feel quite naive and sophisticatedly rustic, like a drawing of the Duchess of Dalrymple Sunning Her Dogs on the Plage.

Jobs look vague. Occidental dwindles, and what looked mildly encouraging at Stanford now seems hopeless. A tentative chance to ship as scab steward and -ess to New York, thanks to strikes, can't be decided for some few weeks. A letter to a friend of Aunt Bess about a job in a Detroit prep school is probably a wasted stamp. And so on. Our money will last a month more, anyway. Then it means debt. I wish Aunt Helen would die. But we still love each other, so I am content.

27. vi. 34

Several months ago I began to write in this book because I thought that what was happening to us was interesting. Or rather,

I thought that the effects of today upon two young people in love would be of value on paper. But it's not the Depression that is happening to us. It is almost unrelated inner things that I cannot or shall not write about. I am sincere when I say that this book is not for anybody. It is perhaps for myself—to read in ten or twenty years and wonder about. But when I think of writing about the real things, I am outraged at the thought of their ever risking others' eyes. They are bitter and tragic and damning and very beautiful, too, and hopeless with the hopelessness of all human passion, and they must stay locked in our own silent hearts.

Al is in Palo Alto, after a week of trying to find work in San Francisco. He tried newspapers and boats, mostly—all with no luck. A bad strike is on among the longshoremen. He was in danger. But what really disheartened him was the first night in town, when he fled at 1:30 from a crawling bed. He suffers so about little bugs. (I remember how I had to wash the lettuce, in France, seven or eight times, with a trip to the faucet in the hall each time. And there'd always be bugs left, when we ate it.) So he was miserable and probably imagined itches all the time he was in S. F. And his pocket was picked. So finally he gave up and went to Palo Alto.

He has written several letters from there, with never a word about his father. Perhaps he's better, but probably worse. A. meant to come back yesterday but instead will come tomorrow, because Herbert [Al's older brother] arrived from China this afternoon. He is invalided home with Chinese dysentery, supposedly—but I sense a scrape. We'll see.

The way we feel now, we'll borrow enough money from Father to go north and will settle in a shack somewhere on the Peninsula. We'd go now, if I hadn't agreed to care for the children until their school starts. We both feel that we must get away from

Laguna. Al's work has come to a standstill, and I don't think he'll be able to start again here.

A good letter from Dave today, in Victoria. He writes tersely but well, of fishing trips and shopping tours and the funny English hotel with its murmuring tea-sippers who so delighted Mother's pussy heart. He wrote, "fished at the mouth of a creek, just where the swift green current met with the blue of the lake." When Sis read that, she looked very disgusted and said, "Well, little Davie's going arty on us! Can't you just see him getting an A in composition for that?" All of which is partly true, but it explains a lot about the scarcity of good letters in our days. People are shamed out of saying anything more polished than "Dear Mamma, We're having a swell trip. Wish you were here. Rained this morning. Love to all." I remember how I guarded against stepping out of that formula all the time I was at school. As I grew older I became a little freer, but I have never written a line to Mother without watching my words to save her embarrassment. For it does embarrass people to read good letters, except in books. I don't mean by that that mine were good—but they would have been much better if I had written more as I wanted to.

14. vii. 34

I am working hard. Dave and Noni are here, and although they are very helpful, there is much to do. I carve as much as I can, though I seem to go at snail speed. I am still paring away at the mahogany bench legs—which are *not* for B. Benson, I suppose, since her engagement is indefinitely postponed. I can probably sell them, or keep them.

The night A. came home from the North, Ben Stelter arrived,

very sheepish, with a job for A. at Occidental—part-time instructor of English at $750 a year. So now we're trying to find a house, and I'm scouting for a job. I want to work anyway, but for money, too, this time. We'll need it. If we possibly can, I want to pay a little of Mr. Bright's $1,000.

I sold the Laguna article to *Westways* and may sell three or four drawings. Don't know yet how much I'm making. I hope it's a fat check. I'll take the kids and the Kellys and Rex and Noni on little parties, and the rest will make me feel easier about buying what we'll need for a house. Yesterday I went to town with Noni and bought two beds (box springs with legs, and hair mattresses) for $42.00. They were repossessed.

The longshoremen's strike in S. F. is very ugly now, with a general strike declared and the town in siege state. It's a hideous mess. This Labor-Capitalism business will be our death in the end. I think it may be necessary, before the country is in revolution, to avert such a seeming catastrophe by declaring war on another nation. But that will just put off for another twenty years an inevitable thing.

J'ai une élève—une jeune fille de dix-huit ans, de Kalamazoo. Elle hait le français, et elle ne le parle jamais. Chaque leçon est une supplice pour tous les deux—elle s'ennuie horriblement et moi je souffre de son manque total d'intérêt. Oh, well—fifty cents an hour.

---

* I have a student—a young eighteen-year-old girl, from Kalamazoo. She hates French, and she never speaks it. Every lesson is a punishment for both of us. She is horribly bored and I suffer from her total lack of interest.

25. vii. 34

The air jerks and flutters with news of the murder of Dollfuss. After the Nazi "blood purge" of June 30, people sit uneasily. Trouble fills all our brains.

This week I made many quarts of chili sauce and Baltimore relish, for some reason. The reason, I suppose, is my weakness for old odorous recipes. They were given to Mother by a fine cook, one who kept slaves in old Illinois and had a Preserves Pantry. I feel like a cloud of vinegar fumes. My hair, my hands—

I keep thinking about this assassination. The San Francisco strike has almost sputtered out—longshoremen and train drivers still on strike, but the siege over. It seems almost entirely futile. It did throw a little scare into la bourgeoisie, as Comrade Harry Carlisle dates himself by calling it.

Once a young woman walked every afternoon along a stretch of beach. She was tall, with a slender tanned body, and her bathing suit was very short and tight and of a soft gay green yarn.

Every afternoon as she crossed the warm sand to the steps up the cliff, she passed close by a rug, on which sat two people. She was conscious that they both noticed her and waited for her. Especially she knew that the man watched her. She walked very straight and stuck out her two small round breasts a little.

It surprised her that the man and woman were together. He was a tall rather soft man, a few years away from being very handsome. He wore bathing trunks and was busy tanning his skin. The woman rubbed oil on him, and even with her strong hands rubbing him, he watched the young girl pass by. His eyes were spoiled and laughing, the slightly moist brown eyes of an attractive middle-aged man.

That was what surprised the girl, his blatant charm and the woman he was with. There were so many lone lovely women to be with him, but he was always with the plain, gray, strong woman who never spoke but sat watching over him and rubbing his skin when he wanted it rubbed.

The girl thought they were probably the same age. But the man was still boyish and his eyes roved, and the woman was a stocky middle-aged person, blunt looking and never dressed in anything but a white apronlike dress and a coarse misshapen sweater of dull gray.

Every day the girl grew more conscious of the man. She knew he waited for her to pass. She could feel him watching the rise and fall of her little round buttocks, and she was glad that her legs were straight and firm. She stuck her breasts out proudly and wondered about his staying always with an old stubby woman.

One day she walked past them. The man half-lay against the woman's shoulder, and she was humped strongly like a rock to support him. His hand dropped lax beyond a raised knee.

He watched the girl. The woman seemed not to. The girl was very conscious. Just before she got to the steps, she turned and for the first time looked at the two people. Her head was up, very triumphant, because she knew she would catch the man finally with his bright roving look and hold him.

He smiled confidently into her eyes. Then the woman leaned slowly around, and with her white clean teeth she caught hold of the soft sidepiece of the man's hand, the piece from the base of the little finger to the wrist, and she bit it. Probably she did not bite very hard, but it was a stern, an authoritative bite. And it told the girl suddenly of a deep real passion she had not known yet nor even thought about.

The woman looked at the girl. Her eyes were clear and impersonal and swung from the young face out to the ocean. The girl turned and walked quickly away, and for a long time felt very young and humiliated.

On the beach—my first picnic in a long time.

Much is being made of the coincidence of the Dollfuss murder with that of the archduke in Sarajevo, which happened exactly twenty years ago, almost to the hour.

The saddest thing, I think, is that such a devout little man was denied the last sacrament or even any religious comfort at all. That would be agony for him.

I thought I had much to say, but I have not. I might put down here something about the house. Perhaps later.

While my French pupil scratches her small soft head over an easy examination, I sit very uncomfortably on a wooden chair. It makes me wonder why something bad doesn't happen to the flesh on the human bottom that is so often pinched and ground between bones and seat. It might so logically mildew or turn to leather warts.

One of the things I wanted to put in this book, one of the interesting things, was the trip we made to San Pedro during the strike. Or did I? I never look back in this book—too dull and plain disgusting.

We had a rendezvous with Del Mouran, whose friend, chief steward on a big boat, might get us a job because of the strike. We made wild plans of shipping round the world as steward and stewardess. It turned out to be nothing, all the way. But what was exciting was the atmosphere on Terminal Island. We were very neat and white-collar looking, deliberately: we had debated going in old clothes, in rags, and so on. The streets of working-people's shacks were very quiet. When we crossed the loading tracks and swung onto the wide street that runs along by the docks, we were suddenly in the midst of a strike. Men stood very quietly along the near side of the road, moving slowly up and down with their hands in their pockets and never forming groups. They talked a little but mostly just drifted sullenly along the road. On the other side, the dock side, hundreds of special police, in plain clothes, bustled officiously in cars and in and out of the huge buildings. They were big ugly men mostly, all armed very ostentatiously and all wearing large billies, which they swung from their wrists. They seemed to be delighted by making sudden fierce gestures with them, rapping truck tires and then guffawing and saying, That's what I'd do to 'em. They always had their eyes turned sideways across the road, but they never really looked at the strikers.

The air was hot and gray and horrible with hatred. I was moved. I had never seen men carrying clubs before, and it seemed very awful. The ones with the clubs were so viciously pleased, practicing delightful head-smashers, and the ones without clubs were so ominously and silently hateful.

All my sympathy, my human sympathy, was for the strikers. Of course, if they had ceased their sullen pacing and attacked, I'd have been one of the filthy bitches of the bourgeoisie soon smashed. I may be smashed anyway, before I die another way, by the mad workers. It won't be my fault or theirs.

Hindenburg died, Hitler declared himself supreme ruler for life, the Austrian civil war is curbed for the moment, and stock markets shudder slightly while we all wait to see what will happen.

This week I went to town and for the first time in several years tried on many beautiful dresses and finally bought one. I was crazy to do it—I can't bear to think of all the bills we'll have to pay somehow, the next three months—things like garden hose and window screens and clothesline and dishpans. But I bought it and I'm glad I did. It is a long thin dress with a short jacket, made of a soft silk patterned rather gaudily in clear bright colors. Sis says I look like the cover of a seed catalog in it, and I do. I like it.

Our house shapes itself in our minds. In three weeks we'll go to the Ranch and from there go every day to Eagle Rock. This next week we'll go up to look for a carpenter and a plumber. There are many puttery things to do, like moving shelves and putting on faucets. When we get through, we'll have a jolly little place. We are going to spend about $150 on it, instead of paying rent.

As it is now, the house is made into small stuffy rooms, except for a fine big enclosed porch. We'll knock out the partition and make one big room, with French doors across the front. We'll move the johnny from the back porch to the bathroom and have a little dining room on the porch. The big porch I'll use as a workroom at one end, and at the other our beds will be dressed like couches in the daytime. Al's study will be our main expense, and we plan to use old lumber for it and do all we can ourselves.

The location of the house is wonderful. It is on the saddle between two very high hills. On one side we see down past and over the campus and all its tall trees to the far hills. And on the other we look into the face of the mountains, blue and close. At our feet on that side is a playground. We see only green grass and trees, but shoutings from children come up to us.

Sunday we leave early to go to a cocktail party chez Gloria Stuart and her new husband Sheekman. He is nice—hypersensitive with a too-fine face and sad large brown eyes. Gloria is completely gaga —introduces him as her "honey baby." He is very good to her. His attentions seem thousandfold after Gordon's* slapdash manners. They want us to stay all night, but we want to start on the house Monday morning. But perhaps we'll have drunk too much. I think not, though. I'm gradually working out my own system of intoxication—a pleasant long glow with no bad waking up.

I hope the Parrishes are there.

Leaving Laguna is strange. I am sad and very much relieved. It is exciting to change. It is funny to go from one awful old shack to a worse one, but the new place will be ours, and all the things in it. That will build over us like the sky an inviolable armor. Here we felt helpless, like hermit crabs without shells to back into. But chez nous it will be good.

I have been and still am making a skirt and dress of the blue cotton Herbert Fisher sent from China. It was very stiff and hard blue, so I sent the whole forty yards to a laundry, with instructions to treat it roughly. It came back in a great squishy roll, soft as old linen and of a clear high blue. I can see that it will fade unevenly to gray colors. I am glad. The scarlet and the moon-colored silks still lie in a box. I am stumped by their narrow width—too hard to make a dress—and a pity to use anything so lovely for such quick passing. I'll think of something.

Just then, as I looked out the window, all the light changed very suddenly; the fog had given way to sun. It made me wonder a little, with the slight feeling of awe and skulduggery afoot that you

---

* Gloria Stuart was first married to Gordon Newell.

have when the one window at which you look in a dark building suddenly squares with light—or when a leaf, the one you are watching, trembles on a still tree. It is a coincidence that stirs and soothes us by its promise of strange things meant only for *us,* for a certain person. Our ego puffs itself. Astronomy is successful with a like system.

I was just paid $20. With it I shall pay a seamstress $9.50 for making over one of Mother's dresses and a coat for me, and this afternoon I shall startle my girl by taking her to tea when she thinks she is to have a verb lesson. Then I shall buy Al a good pair of shoes. And with what is left I'll pay a little on our milk or ice bill.

I had a good time with the $35 I got from *Westways.* I bought four dollar books—*Crime and Punishment* for Al, a mystery omnibus for Dave, Shaw's *Intelligent Woman's Guide to Socialism and Capitalism* for Noni, and *The Well of Loneliness* for myself. I paid Mother $10 of the large sum I owe her for beds and stoves and so on. Then this week I took her and Rex and Al to Hollywood. We went first to Don the Beachcomber's for a cocktail. Then we went to Sardi's, where we had a good table, good waiter, good dinner, good wine and coffee, and a very amiable time. Then we went back to Don's where Rex bought fine cognac for us. We tried to call the Parrishes, but when we couldn't get them, drove slowly home in the warm dark night, all very comfortable and pleasant.

The rest of my money I used for food. This summer has been very agreeable. Dave and Noni have been nice all the time, with never any fussing and always ready to help. They have been well and seem very happy—for people their age.

Muscat grapes begin to be raisins already. That is the only good result of a dry year. Papers and radio news say, The worst drought in America's life. Occasionally ghastly newsreels are shown of cattle falling over on dry naked plains or bellowing with cracked voices in stockyards, with their hipbones almost through their hides. And people sitting listlessly at their bare blazing door-steps, while their fields show sharp rows of twelve-inch corn, which turns to dust in the fat hands of the cameraman's assistant. Not many such pictures are shown. They disturb people. And people must not be disturbed.

In the Middle West farmers are beginning to say that the drought is God's punishment for Roosevelt's plan of plowing under every fifth row and killing surplus hogs—all to raise prices last year. Now there is too little instead of too much, and good pious farmers mutter of God's wrath. It may be Roosevelt's doom song. It is ominous, Rex says, when religion mixes with politics.

21.viii.34

At the Ranch. We came up Sunday, piled to the gills with an incredible amount of what seemed junk at the time. I still do not understand the human faculty for collecting social increment. We took eight or nine large boxes of books, papers, letters from the house, and yet it didn't look much emptier. And then all our clothes, and linen, and blankets and knives and forks. The relent-less piling frightens me. We've fought it ever since we married.

Sunday evening we went to a cocktail party given by the Sheekmans. It was very restrained—many too-cultured voices and silver-fox capes, with everyone there for business. Except us and Dillwyn. I can see that he may be of value to Gloria—but why us? Everything seemed very shoddy and pretentious and terribly and dreadfully dull. A strange difference from G.'s parties of a year or so ago, so noisy and alcoholic and littered with interesting tramps. This was alcoholic enough—but badly "refined" by large incomes and Hollywood architecture. We left early.

Monday morning we spent looking at French doors donated

to our house by two of Father's friends. In the afternoon we took old Trueblood the Quaker carpenter to Eagle Rock and spent two hours or so going over the house. It emerged a very amusing little place, as we had expected. Then the proprietor appeared. He hummed and muttered for almost an hour to tell us what we guessed at his first sentence—the property had to be sold, and the house was to be wrecked immediately!

I was really much disappointed. So was Al. We hurried home silently and had a drink of whiskey. After dinner we went to a fight with Rex. We sat in ringside seats, and for a few minutes I was a bit overwhelmed by the thudding and gasping of two bodies so close to me and the occasional whiff of sweat. But soon I forgot. The fights were mediocre, except for two lightweight Negroes. I liked looking through and across the white ring to the steep wall of people watching. At the beginning of the late rounds, the air was full of bright drops where the boys struck, because they'd been doused to make them springier.

This morning we started out to look for another house. We drove toward Eagle Rock, going up and down streets that looked as if they might have shacks on them. It was tiring. But we have a fine six-room house on a wooded slope of hill, almost invisible to other houses and in need only of a little plumbing and a lot of paint. We are delighted. It is roomy and full of light and air from many windows. The living room and bedroom are large, and Al will have a workroom and I a screened porch for my carving table. The bathroom is bad—small and dark—but more than we had in France, ever.

19.ix.34

Now I am in our house. We have lived in it ten days and nights, and we are very happy in it. It is a good peaceful little house. We grew tired before we finished painting, even with much help from the Parrishes. And after the Sunday we moved—on a truck from the *News* office, with Harrison's help—we were quite numb and incoherent. For several nights we slept like stones in our new beds. Now we are wide awake again.

There are many windows still to be scraped and washed and other little things to do. But the country lies flat with heat, and here in the house I move languidly and do only the basic things like dishwashing and the making of beds.

Al is well set into the routine that seems so necessary to him. He has classes in the morning, and in the afternoon he works in the library after he has eaten his bread and cheese and fruit and drunk a little bottle of milk. At night we eat a simple but rather large dinner slowly by candlelight. The dining room is white and cool, with the silly yellow organdy curtains with big white polka dots on them moving across the sill silently in the air. Then Al goes to his study and I read or write or bathe. Then we read—now *Crime and Punishment*—and go to bed.

Two days ago Anne had her stomach split, an ovary removed, her uterus shifted about, and several ligaments tied tighter. All that was caused probably by careless haste after Shaun's birth. The repair of such damage is very important. It may rescue a woman from frigidity and ill health and neurasthenia. Anne needs rescuing. She insisted on a spinal anesthetic and watched the operation with interest that dwindled to faintness by the end of the forty minutes. She felt very miserable for two days, but today was better. She had been stimulated by an intravenous injection of glucose, and her voice was very dreamy and lilting. I took her some rock sugar on three little strings, wrapped primly. She was reminded of other times—not special ones, but just times—as I was when I first spotted the dusty jar of crystals in our corner drugstore. They are scarce now.

Our house is very nice. It is a Sunday afternoon after a soft rainy night. The air is cool and clean and thinly lighted. Ashes crack metallically on the hearth of our square, ugly, yellow rock fireplace, which was so hideous until we put bookcases on each side of it. Tonight we are going to supper with the Powells, because we'll have to sooner or later and might as well get it over with. It's horrible to feel that way about people who may be our best friends. I like Gigi and Dillwyn very much indeed and think they like us especially well until I see them being just as nice to dozens of other people. They are right to be so withdrawn in their intimacies—we are the same—but still it is sometimes disturbing. But the Powells bore me completely—and I think it is mutual.

When I was putting some papers away, I looked at several diaries I have kept during the last ten or fifteen years. I am struck by their dull sameness. It is far from interesting and utterly unimportant to record that on June 11, 1927, I felt very bored and wondered what I was meant for and wished I could work or do or create. That went on and on. I think that it is better to write of food or people or sleep, after all. I've always disapproved of "Line-a-day books" that say, Rain today—twelve quarts of milk, three dozen eggs—J.'s earache. But now I think they're better than pages and years of incoherent dissatisfaction. Perhaps from a genius such mutterings would be valuable—significant, anyway. But God, how dull from me.

Yesterday I read about sixty freshman English papers. Al assigned an autobiographical sketch. Most of the girls became very introspective. Their papers sounded as if they were saying, "See how frank, how self-understanding, how subtle I am! And how complex, how unusual! How misunderstood—but what a sense of humor!" I retched to recognize myself. And the glib ones, too: there I was, the facile, occasionally clever and very self-conscious student who came to college with straight A's in high school English. How plodding and forced was my would-be sparkling irony. And how very wide-eyed was my wonder at my own depth.

But I really couldn't help it, nor can they. They do stand above the average high school writer. Their teachers, numbed by years of misused English and grateful for even a faint glimmer of enthusiasm for the language, flatter them and accept their most idiotic papers as a kind of manna. They become very self-satisfied and glib. And then the hell of it is that when they get to college, there is rarely anyone to help them. If some older, keener person had only shown me how crude, how cheap my papers were, how makeshift my work, I'd have been forever in his debt. I know I was recognized, just as I recognize these children. But nobody bothered. Perhaps they thought it labor lost.

I believe that I began to write today with the firm belief that only incident matters in a diary, that people and objects are much more interesting than my own badly expressed beliefs and dissatisfactions. Belief on the brain. So I have covered several pages with belief.

Last night Gigi and I went to see Mrs. Leslie Carter in *The Circle*. Ten years ago Mother and Father saw her and Drew in it, and since then I have thought of it as a very lively comedy that made them laugh for many days. But last night it sagged horribly. Not one line was funny. The cast was ill at ease. The only good parts in it were very poignant and almost melodramatic. Mrs. Carter was an oddly misshapen monster with enough of her old fire to shift the audience from a dismayed gasp at her first entrance to a politely enthusiastic series of final curtains. Her buttocks were pulled up into the small of her back by bad corseting, and her heavy shoulders and breasts made her old-woman arms and legs look like brittle sticks. She was very bad until the last act. Then she revived and was almost grand. The curtain came down on a fine, sparkling old actress—and suddenly her third or fourth curtain showed a little witch, collapsed and death-tired, clutching at a chair in the middle of the empty stage.

24. ix. 34

Above the tub in our small white bathroom is a square window that once opened into the yard. Right there a room was added to the house. Now it is Al's study, and when I go into the bathroom quietly and try not to make too much noise on the johnny (the obsolete kind with a resounding well of water into which a tinkle hurls itself like Niagara), I peer on tiptoe over the tub into the lighted room. Al taps on the typewriter or writes minute tracks on little scraps of paper. He smokes a pipe with a kind of absent-minded sensuality, or holds a cigarette gingerly in his fingers. His hands have the arrested movement, the unreality, of great carving. He frowns slightly.

Last night at the Powells'—an evening that started rather dully with us feeling rather de trop, and ended smoothly and amicably at nine o'clock after a bad dinner and going out into a cold hard night that you could feel go in and out your nose—last night Fay gave me a strange red and black garment. It looks Tibetan, of thick crisp wool like a good blanket. The neck, V-shaped, and the pudgy sleeves with uneven mouths halfway between wrist and elbow are edged with black silk tape. A black stripe, about four inches wide, runs from the right front to the bottom, and on the back it is on the left. The robe has four openings, the neck, the sleeves, the bottom: there are no buttons. It falls straight down, in thick clumsy lines, from my shoulders past my knees. There is a fading smell of camphor about it. I wear it tonight, in this rather cold room, and I feel that I shall wear it for a long time. I like Fay for giving it to me. The color is not an ordinary red but a high clear pungent color, like a perfect young tomato or an English horn.

In this robe and fur slippers, I could work well in a very cold room, except for my hands. I really love this robe.

25.ix.34
Faculty Women's Club Meeting

I go at 2:30 in spite of my resolve to be an hour late. Even so early, I am the last to arrive. The house, new and waxed and with the carefully planned discomfort of synthetic "genuine pieces" and catalog Orientals, bulges snugly with women. It is horrendously refined.

My hostess, new president of the club, is a singer, wife of the music department manager. She is tall and very vital, with crisp gray hair that grows at right angles to her scalp rather than parallel to it. Her dark eyes flash professionally, and her tall stout body seems always ready to breast an aria.

Women rise up at me, curiosity hard on the heels of their warm cordial words. I make smiles and hide behind the part of Our New Member Young Dr. Fisher's Wife She Is Really a Member of Our Family. Yes, '27, or was it '29? I find myself kissing Mother's old music teacher, who gives piano lessons out here and watches her diet because of neuritis in her hands. Finally I sit down.

The large careful room is ringed with women. They are not distinguished. A few have kind faces. Some are dressed with clumsy consciousness of La Mode as exposed by advertisements in the *Times.* One or two are very strange looking. The secretary, sitting with a black notebook of minutes, her hands trembling a little, has a round pale face that looks quite normal from the front. But when she is in three-quarter profile, I see that her eyes are set in her head sideways, like a rabbit's. Another woman with small meek shoulders wears round glasses with lenses ground to so many different strengths that her eyes appear to be at the far ends of two long gleaming tubes. Her clothes are a caricature of the frowsy faculty wife. Where are such hats made, where sat upon? Her shoes are improbable.

The meeting is called to order by my hostess, and for an hour and almost another, there is much parliamentarian formality, much Madam Presidenting and seconding of idiotic motions. The president holds her little black book below her bosom with that gesture peculiar to divas. I feel that she really is peering discreetly at it to remember the second line of "Tes Yeux, Tes Jolis Yeux."

The secretary takes trembling notes, after reading last year's leavings. She speaks English softly and well and occasionally lifts her strange eyes obliquely. The treasurer, a compact, efficient woman who reminds me of a business school director I once knew, reads a report of money lent to girl students, of a large bank account, and of eighty cents for postage stamps.

There is talk of how to make more money, all woven through with All those in favor signify—and I move that the motion be—and so on.

I look around the room, behind my mask of the New Member. A hairpin keeps slipping down, and I wonder if I have on too much lipstick. I smooth at my upper lip with one finger. The president's wife suddenly looks out at me from behind a far sofa.

Her large flat blue eyes flicker with comprehension. I feel better. She bends her chic head down and knits at a blue skirt. She is the only one who is occupied.

A lean bright-eyed young woman plays rather well on the cello. Then the wife of the dean of men tells of last year spent in China. At times she is quite interesting. Her pronunciation is good, without affectation, but her English is involved and most of her sentences get away from her. She is dressed rather well except for very vulgar kid gloves with colored appliqués on them, but her figure is inexcusably ugly. She is evidently unconscious of it, for her clothes, bought with some care and pleasure, accentuate by their cut her loose belly, her swayback and sagging breasts, and the rolls of fat above her hips. She is distasteful to look at. Her face, too, is one of those pudgy, heavy white faces with dark eyes and rather thick peevish mouths—the face of a passionate woman with a sallow disposition.

As she talks, a man's voice mumbles in the hall, and I know it is four o'clock and teatime. It is the biology professor who comes first and tiptoes straight to the dining room. It is college legend that frightened coeds at sorority banquets can and do put themselves and him at ease by talking voluptuously of food. He is most sparkling about the heavier dishes like German fried potatoes and pancakes with sour cream. Then his little round eyes peer most jovially over the tops of his spectacles, and the coeds feel very worldly and able to make conversation.

Now he heads a straggle of men. The president looks anxiously at the wife of the dean of men, who continues talking for several more minutes, her mouth secretly peevish. Finally she invites people to look at a satchel of her little boy's Chinese clothes and some little dolls, and the women flock politely toward the dining room. The biology professor stands by a large tray of little sandwiches. He has put down his teacup to have two hands for eating.

The noise is frightful after the cultured elocution of the hostess and the gurgling murmur that welled swiftly up from all the women like one big bubble after any of her mild waggishness. Now the men's deeper mumble holds it only one notch below monkey-house pitch. The tea makes a fine decent smell in the air. I finally get a cup and drink it. People pluck at me, and I listen beamingly to many almost soundless shoutings.

Finally I go. I am exhausted. My face is stiff and my head rings. As I go out the front door, I remember taking ether and how the voices go in and out, *boom* sway away *close* boom away. And I see the controlled nervous face of the president's wife, flushed and smooth and like one hideously wrenched underneath, as a tall stringy woman crashes down two steps to the floor. She is the wife of the head of Religion. People rush politely to pick her up. The president's wife goes on knitting, and the sudden red in her face fades slowly until she is very pale.

10.i.36

I sit close to the basket of coal fire, alone in our sweet neat dear little house. A. has gone to see his mother, somewhat alarmingly depressed, last night at least, with a cold and the realization of a year now past since her husband died. On my knees, crooked over the pillow on the walnut love seat, is an elaborate pattern made of *War and Peace,* Toby the kitten, and this unwieldy copybook.

It is maybe a year since I last wrote here. I haven't looked. My mind steams with words. I am on the point of beginning a novel, and may God help us. I have good material—the founding of the Quaker town of Whittier. I have no experience, except for the book I wrote last winter. It is a strange and satisfying thing to finish a book. I'll finish this, and it should be good. I suppose all writers think that.

This vacation—Christmas—Noni, home from Wells, and I took an afternoon's ride into the country between home and Prado and back, a slow circuit over empty back roads. I remember saying, as we drove into the old finished town of Orange, that if I should sell a book it would be queer, because then I'd be called the "writer" of the family, and really I have no more talent than any of the others. Noni laughed in agreement. Then today, as I hoed ferociously in the side yard, preparing a bed like a big grave for seeds when this rain comes, I thought, That's right but not right, because I shall have *written*. They'll not. Comparisons are not possible.

I know, after correcting several thousand themes from every kind of class, Junior League to freshman, that there are countless, yes, countless people who *could* write. They could write much better than I. But they don't. I do. I don't know why. I seem to have no special interest, *no* interest really, in selling things and seeing them printed. I believe there are too many books, too many people writing, above all too many women writing. But I write, without really wanting to. I write probably ten hours a day, mostly in my mind. Now I am writing while I garden, mulling over and over, almost like the daydreams that flow with somnolific music, the actions in this damned, this goddamned novel about Whittier.

On the radio a Handel program trips and bounces smoothly. The fire putters flatly, like butterflies.

Tonight at the dinner table A. and I talked prosaically—my God, is there such a word?—of having a child next fall by our own work or by the courts. Is he sterile? Am I? Are we fools to get a child? Will we breed a fiend or adopt an idiot? Would it be better to grow old alone, unbothered, dry, inverted? Or shall we oil our joints with the troublous juices of children all about us? I see the heart tearings, the million small anguishments of a parent. But I grow to believe them better than the sapless life of old lone beings. Our years in England, in Russia, in Italy, and dear France I see swing irrevocably into dimness, and in their places are the illnesses, the lies, the cruelties of new humans—we in their power and forever relegated to second rank. But I choose it so. Six years alone with A. have given me a fortitude that I know will withstand any torture. Children, much as they will cost us, cannot but bring joy, too. At a puppy or a kitten we laugh and exchange quick sweet glances. How much more at a child, our own by flesh or law? And I feel this might be better for it, too—to feel free from us from the beginning.

My garden gradually smooths itself down into an ordered chaos. I pull leaves off iris plants now and wait for rain, although I know the soil is bulging with wild barley seeds that will grow madly at the first moist encouragement.

I look forward to a summer here, although I feel that next June will find us going somewhere again. Our courtyard is most pleasant, and if we were going to be here all summer, I should feel justified in buying a few big canvas chairs and a lantern or two. As it is—I shall once more plant it with yellow flowers and hope to be able to care for them.

For seven months now I've written to Timmy instead, really, of writing in a journal. I think that by this time he has started on his travels, and my correspondence with him has ended, at least for a time. It has been good, in many ways. He is, both unconsciously and by intent, a master at drawing people out of their commonplace shells into the full glare of introversion, self-appreciation, and neuroticism. That is very valuable, and for that and many other reasons I value my friendship with him, and my true love and affection.

I feel foreboding and a weight of ominous sorrow about C. Y. F., as always when someone I love is even partly ill. I remember how I went to see Mother a few hours after she went to the hospital with influenza. She lay, gray and enormous, under the light covering on the bed. Her chest rose and fell quickly under the uncouth wrappings of a pneumonia jacket. I tried to talk to her, but she answered perfunctorily, as if breathing and even living were much more important at that moment. I left, and as soon as I had got out the front door and down into the high bushes that lined the walk to the parking space, I was contorted, inside and out, with bitter sobs of suffering and anxiety. I felt that Edith was surely near death. My little mother, so young, so old with suffering, so annoying, so endearing, was near death. And I was helpless. What could I do? I suffered, trying not to cry aloud, there in front of the implacably noncommittal building that hid her preoccupied breathing.

The next day when I went to see her, full of dread and resigned to that awful moment, she was gay and quick, her skin its usual creamy brown and her brown eyes bright. I felt strangely cheated, even in my elation.

I notice that same feeling now that A.'s Aunt Mary draws hesitantly near what she calls Home. Her death will be double for Aunt Evvie, bound to her by the mysterious veins of an identical twin. We call each day to see if Mary has died. We are prepared for it. But if, after all this, she recovers, we shall feel that shameful disappointment known to all men whose dear friends have almost but not quite died. I think it is because we really hate life. When a man dies, we feel that at least he—we, vicariously?—has escaped. Then if he comes back, we are irritated. So nearly to have put off all the trivia! And how painful, how wearisome, again to resume them! We suffer for him, and for him take up once more the grim burden of brushing teeth, excreting waste, buying gasoline. Why the hell didn't he get out of it when he had the chance?

I have a fine new dress, purple in daylight and a silver-grayish purple at night, with a low décolletage and a full-skirted soft-flowing coat. I think it should have been made of some stiff material to be as dashing as its picture. But in this soft crepe it has a certain dignity, rather too mature for my taste. (The first sign of maturity, to resent that?) I shall wear it tomorrow night to a fraternity dance, with silver combs in my hair and silver slippers, a judiciously heavy makeup, and an air of preferring to be with the fraternity rather than anywhere else.

A. is home, with a sack of chocolate peppermints and the news that his mother, in bed and looking like a girl with all her wrinkles smoothed out, is better and much happier.

I hear, between recordings of a Mozart quartet, that rain is predicted for tomorrow. Well, I had planned to finish peeling the iris leaves in the lower meadow. But it is better. I should clean the house. Rex and Edith come for supper next day, and she, like most rather lazy housekeepers, is very conscious of other women's dust. Then Monday I drive to the Ranch for a rabbit to jug* for Wednesday and, I hope, on to town to get a decent pair of shoes for A. Tuesday we should go to Occidental for a lecture. Wednesday Guy Nunn and his girl come to supper. Friday we go to the theater with a couple whose male half A. has met at the Huntington. Saturday there's another dance. Sunday—and so on. But this is a good life, I think. I have a fairly good body, an active if insignificant mind, a charming house to live in, and most important, all-important, my dear love by my side and all about me.

---

* Rex Kennedy raised rabbits (as well as pigeons and chickens).

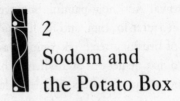

2
Sodom and
the Potato Box

Sodom looked once more into the dark depths of the half-covered potato box. It was hard to see in there. Down in the canyon behind the sloping eucalyptus wood, Sodom squatted among the dark, wet leaves, his head bent half-fearfully over the old box. It was a serious task he had set himself, this burying of his soul, and he wished that he had never heard the troublesome word. He'd have to go through with it, though, or else be tormented for the rest of his life by a feeling of self-apology. Once before he had been nagged by that itching emotion, when he had delayed for weeks the simple and easily told end of a story for his father, and he knew too well the unpleasant fatigue of such weak procrastination.

He frowned and peered resolutely through the crack in the top of the box. It was growing dark, and the cool earth of the little canyon sent up damp odors from among the tree roots. He must hurry.

A moldy mass of sodden papers, pages of print and pictures torn from journals, and with them three pale silken strands of ribbon, stained and faded, showed in the blue light. He shook the box gently and felt the bottle bump against the side and then roll into view—an old green bottle, its unmistakable color glowing dimly, glassily, through a mist of innumerable scratches. Beside it lay the skull of a rabbit, tiny and finite and sharply white in the deep shadow, but connected with the darkness by a string of beads that curved through the eye holes and away into the black corners. Sodom rattled the box once more and squinted anxiously into the crack in the top as if he were rather afraid that something else would slide into view. He heard the bottle thump heavily into the lowest corner, and the beads rattle quickly after, but nothing more. A look of quiet satisfaction crept over his face. All was ready, then, and he was about to dispose in the most gentlemanly way of his encumbering soul. He sat for a minute in the dim little canyon, his hands resting lightly on the box and his eyes half-closed.

It was queer that he had found out so easily about his soul and had known so clearly what to do with it. He remembered that day very well. He was in the window of his father's study, sitting on a pile of books behind the long red curtain. Outside slow drops of autumn rain slipped down the pane of glass, and he could see the eucalyptus trees twist and bend through the tiny wet paths. He was almost asleep.

Suddenly he heard his father, with a voice that jerked him awake as if his dreams had been cut short by a shriek, a groan, anything but this dull soft sound, say an interesting thing. "You are a creature without a soul, Lydia." Sodom heard his mother walk toward the door, and he peered quickly around the fuzzy edge of the curtain to see what she would answer to this puzzling observation that seemed to hurt his father's throat. Lydia stood with one hand on the dark wood of the open door, as if she were thinking. With a quick movement she threw back her head and laughed silently, then closed the door sharply behind her.

Sodom pulled back his shoulders so there would be no chance of his being seen and sat waiting for his father to leave the room.

His mind was jumping with excitement. He realized keenly that the ever-present sound of his father's pen had stopped, leaving a kind of buzzing shadow of itself in the dead silence of the room. Not even a breath came from the still figure of the man seated at the cluttered table, and Sodom himself had forgotten that his own breath came and his heart still beat. What was the thing his mother lacked, the thing his father spoke about as if it were a curse, a magic spell? Here was something more to know, something so important that the mention of it could make his mother move from her accustomed pattern of gestures and toss her head with a laugh almost audible. As the little boy realized that he had finally seen his mother smile, he felt a shock, a thrust of horror that made him dizzy. What was her soul? He wondered eagerly if he had one, being a man instead of a woman like Lydia, and then hoped passionately that he had not.

He felt as if he must know, but how to do it? There was only his father to tell him, and Sodom knew that something had made the subject unpleasant to him. He turned the situation over and over in his teeming brain, feeling that if he could not find out about this new thing he would die.

Then the luncheon bell rang, and Sodom kept himself from leaping to his feet until his father had walked slowly out of the room. The dining room was silent except for the restrained chewing of the three people at the table. The man and woman sat stiffly in their places and ate in a politely businesslike way. Sodom, between them on his lonely side of the table, looked from under his eyelids at them. How could he ask them a question that they themselves had planted violently in his mind a half-hour before, when now they looked as if nothing had ever happened to disturb their usual deliberate behavior? He felt as if he were going to explode—or be very sick.

The meal dragged on. Finally he saw in a kind of agony that his mother had wiped her lips and then put the napkin beside her plate of nutshells and desolate-looking grape skins. He must say something before she pushed back her chair.

"Father," he heard his voice squeak in a high, defiant tone, "what do you call the soul?"

The room seemed suddenly full to the brim with startled and rather disapproving attention. Sodom felt that his mother had stopped breathing, but from the corner of his eye he could see that her fingers still played casually with the edge of her folded napkin. His father looked at him seriously, as if he were some interesting but slightly distasteful animal. The boy thought for a minute that he was not going to be answered. Then the gray man's lips opened slowly, and from them fell slow words.

"The soul, Sodom, is a collection of emotions that is deified by weak men into an intangible idol upon which he turns his own punishments from God," he said with a sly look into the blank eyes of his son. Then he glanced quickly up at his wife, who sat across from him stiff with attention.

"The soul," he continued in a quiet voice that chilled Sodom with remembrance of the one he had heard that morning in the study, "is the result of emotion. It can be hidden, but it is immortal because it grows from love, sentimentality. Hate has no soul. Sodom, if you ever have a soul, hide it. It is precious junk . . ."

For several seconds the man and the woman looked at each other, as if they were discussing things long ago dismissed from their common conversation. Then Lydia lowered her white eyelids, and as at a signal her husband stood up and walked deliberately from the oppressive silence of the room.

Sodom knew for the first time that his mother hated his father. That is why she had no soul.

He went quickly on to the next problem, having solved that one so neatly. His father advised him to hide his own soul, if he had one, and since he was quite without hatred, he realized that there must be one belonging to him. He was puzzled. He looked quickly at his mother to see if she would remind him of anything and found that she was staring at him as if she saw him for the first time. When she saw that he looked at her, too, she started and then smiled into his bewildered young eyes with the ghost, more tender, of her morning's quick laugh. In a flash she went away from the table, as if she'd had enough of such nonsense.

Sodom left the room in a fog of thought. He felt sure that he had a soul. What was it his father had said—"a collection of emotions . . . hide them . . . precious junk"? Yes, precious junk. That was it.

The boy was filled with relief, his bewilderment dissolved by the words of his father, which still sounded in his ears with a kind of rhythm. He walked rapidly to his room and pulled his old wooden box, once made for potatoes, from under the bed. That had been almost three weeks ago, and now he was ready at last to hide his soul. Here it was, in the box beneath his hands, its various parts rolling and rattling to his slightest touch. He wondered idly if it would mind being so thoroughly dismissed from the warm, secret life of his room, where it had lived so long with him. And he hoped he had chosen the right parts from the collection of precious things that he had been making all these years. It had been rather hard to know what was really his soul and what just things, but he had finally decided on the oldest and most valued of his clutter of junk.

It was almost dark. He rose stiffly to his feet and picked up a little garden trowel that he had brought with him. He worked fiercely in the thick dusk, digging with rapid thrusts into the wet mold of the canyon's side. Roots of the trees that whispered distantly above him twisted through the earth and out into the calm air of the ditchlike little gully and made it easy for him to hollow between their bendings a tiny cave. He worked furiously for several minutes, and then, panting and sweaty with effort and an almost unbearable excitement, he thrust his short arm into the black hole. Yes, it seemed big enough. He picked up the box, holding it on a level so that the green bottle would not roll about, and tried it. He laughed. The hole was really too big, too high.

He suddenly had the idea to turn the box on its side; then the dirt would not fall down through the crack in the top. He did this gleefully, then shoved with all his might against the end of the box until he could feel it pushing bluntly against the spongy earth at the back of the cave. His arms ached with tiredness, and he wished that he had dug the cave lower down instead of on a level with his face. However, it was done now, and a fairly good job he had made of it, he decided.

The visible end of the box was a faint yellowish blur in the canyon side, about a handbreadth in from the face of the ditch. He pushed a few fists of sticky loam against it, pulled a vine down over it from the bank, and then stepped back to view the resting place of his most precious junk, his soul. It was hidden now even from him. He and the dusk and the wet earth had worked well together.

He walked home, stumbling a little in the cool dark and feeling rather lonesome. He began to hum a song he had thought of several days before, and slapped the trowel against his trouser leg to make still another sound in the hushed evening air.

—Laguna Beach, California, 1936

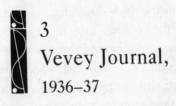

3
Vevey Journal,
1936–37

31.x.36
Vevey

A week ago last night we were together for the first time. Al and I came at noon, inwardly very nervous: would T. be here, would he still like us, would he want us to live with him when he saw us? Outwardly we were quite calm, remembering the gargantuan omelet we had tried to eat the night before in Bâle and the pocketsful of monies we had juggled on the wagon-restaurant from Holland, drinking coffee in Lausanne, looking for Le Pâquis as we raced along the lakeshore toward Vevey. And then T. was not here.

But Otto Trettman met us, tinier than ever, shaking and flushed, with tears of nervousness and perhaps emotion rolling slowly in the corners of his sharp fierce eyes. As always, he took care of everything and came with us to the pension where we are now. (It is the usual excellent Swiss establishment, clean, chaste, filled with ancient dames and damsels and a few grumpy men in toupees, all of whom totter slightly as they walk through the ugly dining room to their tables ranged with tonic bottles and tin boxes of laxative biscuits. Oppressive—we feel like rowdies if our voices rise above a low hiss.)

Here were chrysanthemums, gold ones growing and ragged lavender ones in a bowl, and sherry, and brandy, and cigarettes. "At Mr. Parrish's orders," Otto explained, but we thanked him, too. We drank together, two tears rolled for every one before from his eyes, we toasted each other and T., and he left.

When T. came on the 6:10 train, we had a little advantage over him because we had bathed and settled our bodies if not our souls, but all three of us were jittering for many more reasons than could be written. Otto disappeared discreetly toward the baggage while we kissed and touched each other and tried to see months in a few seconds. T. looked well, strong, handsome. Al was almost knocked down to see the change in him, from the broken man so old and wounded who had cried as they had gone to the station eighteen months ago in Hollywood, to this young man with the calm eyes. And not only physically, Al saw, had he changed. I was glad that Al felt that, too.

We nibbled politely at dinner and talked too fast, interrupting almost every sentence and laughing at nothing. Later we went to a café, two cafés, and drank rather a lot of vin de Vevey but not too much.

The next day, a Saturday, we took a car through Chardonne to Chexbres and ate soup and salad and cheese in the café of the Lion d'Or. Then we started slowly down the road toward Le Pâquis. It was a clear cool day, with the thin sunlight of October on all the yellowing leaves of the vineyards. Windows were open; we could hear women singing and stirring things in bowls. Cats and children sat on the doorsteps. A black dog barked from a balcony.

Al saw Le Pâquis first. The rusted iron door was off its hinges, but we lifted it back and walked in again to feel really there. Leaves still hang on the trees, and the grass is short and green, with still some purple clover and an occasional snapdragon or harebell in it. The little source trickles peacefully, as if forever, clear and very cold, and the brooklet is very busy and tiny, like Otto.

We went into the house. I was surprised at its size and good condition. There is the skeleton of a fine little stair in granite. The two rooms are airy. There is a funny little toilet, a privy, with one seat for people and another, much lower, for children.

The whole place was unbelievable. Since the first day I saw it, last March (the last day it was, too), I've been warning myself that nowhere would there be anything as lovely as it was that day in the first of spring, with the burgeons reddening and swelling and violets thick in the grass. And I was right. It is even more beautiful. The lake far below, the mountains, the curve of the land, and the strong fine smell of the air are more than seem fair for one spot on the world. But there they are, all. I saw them again, felt the trees growing and the earth beneath me, walked through the sturdy cottage, drank from the source and ate mint beside the brooklet. It exists, and so do we.

We were very happy.

The next days are important because we did so much and with such amazing ease—thanks, of course, to Otto. We drew many plans, one night in the Buffet de la Gare, over beer, then supper, then coffee, and finally a bottle of champagne, and the next morning met with Otto and an architect. He was a tall, taciturn man, competent looking, who reported the house in good condition and put our plans into his portfolio.

That was the day we started early, with Nicolas conducting, first to Le Pâquis and then across the road to meet our neighbor the head vigneron of the *faverges,* the vineyards of Fribourg. We went to his cellar, the old site of a convent, with a fine vaulted ceiling. The wine was in fermentation, and the air full of heady decay. We closed the great door to keep the temperature right and

in the light from one bulb drank several bottles of *faverges* 1934—
the architect, Otto, Nicolas the chauffeur, T., Al and I, and the
vigneron. He is a strong, heavy man near sixty, shrewd and probably violent in anger, inquisitive but impersonal—a good peasant,
and a good neighbor or a bad one following our own behavior. I
think all will be good.

We visited the *pressoir*, descended to the cellars for more
wine, talked interminably of crops and rival vineyards. Finally we
left, with the germ in T.'s and Al's heads to make Al winemaster
of Le Pâquis. (By now the idea has matured, and Al plans to study
the art and perhaps practice it—and perhaps, with his training and
intellect and some acquired experience, contribute to the Swiss
industry. Why not?)

On to Otto's for a drink of wine and an introduction to
his wife, a round, soft-voiced woman from Czechoslovakia. The
daughter Anna was there, too, round and soft and pretty, speaking
better French than her parents, pale and spoiled. And a white
cat, Zizi, who has already caused fourteen kittens, Anna told me,
although he has not that many months.

Lunch with Otto and the architect, who is not much socially
—very shy, I think. Then to Lausanne in Nicolas's car, and visits
to various garages for a car. Finally we bought one—a *voiture de
luxe* in appearance (old de Soto with special sport-cabriolet body)
and very inexpensive: $500. Nicolas gave it a fiendish test ride and
enviously reported that it was a *belle occasion*. I hope so. It's very
handsome and comfortable, anyway.

We were exhausted, but the day was far from finished. At
8:30 that night Otto appeared and led us to his house. There we
spent a strange evening. At first we tried to put some limits on our
drinking and our hours, but we soon saw that any such plans
were useless and commended our souls to our hard-drinking Irish
ancestors. The result was interesting and pleasant, although not to

any of our tastes its procural. We started with coffee and liqueurs
—one liqueur first, kirsch, until we started discussing distillation
and Otto had to introduce us as well to his *pruneau,* cassis, and
some other white liquid. Then we got down to business and, as T.
said later, had a wine dinner without the dinner—white wine of
the country, an excellent Côtes de Beaune rouge, much champagne
(for which Otto couldn't resist letting on he paid only 3.40 francs
a bottle), and finally (I never thought I'd see myself drinking this!)
Türchenblut. We ate very good sandwiches of ham and pâté and
smoked a great deal.

By the time we reached the Turk's Blood, Otto was weaving
and shrinking by the minute, and when we left, perhaps just in
time before he disappeared completely, he was curled up like a
little child or a goblin, frowning fiercely and very gaily, waving his
tiny chapped hands and trying to imitate an American millionaire
with many strange sounds.

At the beginning of the evening, his wife tried to squash him,
afraid perhaps that we would laugh at him if he lost his dignity.
But soon she realized that he was safe with us and went docilely
whenever he said, "Another bottle, Anna." She chattered softly to
me of her child's delicate stomach, of preserving pears, of the cost
of servants in Switzerland. I listened and nodded and smiled, trying
at the same time not to miss too much of Otto's increasingly vague
mumblings of the menace of Freemasonry in Suisse and of his
secret society of rationalists, most of the members hotelmen who
can control the visiting tourists—out with bad Jews, encouragement of good Jews, and so on. And of the franc, down again in six
months, and of the pound, down, too, with the dollar alone a good
investment. I wonder.

Coming home we laughed a lot but walked quite straight. The
next morning I felt well, except in stuffy rooms.

And then we have looked at apartments, and rented one, and

bought an electric stove and lights and percolators and so on. And we've signed many contracts—everything takes a contract, even a stove. And furniture, secondhand—a beautiful round tip-top table, three or four chairs, two fat little armchairs with slipcovers, a desk, a kitchen table, a bureau.

And on and on. Now we wait for our furniture, which is on its way and should arrive Monday. I hope very much that it does. It will be good for all of us to live more quietly, more regularly, than is possible in a pension where one's main impulse is to stay away. Staying away means cafés and cafés mean drinking, and even such fine nectarial water as the white wine can be hard on unaccustomed systems. We ate well, but not natural.

Last night T., tired from a week of bustling and emotional strain, grew very fidgety in the theater where we were listening to a poor play. We got him out just in time; he collapsed on the stairs —not a vertigo faint but what Hal would probably call a nerve-bile crisis. He was unconscious for perhaps fifty seconds, very stiff for thirty with a gray face and his eyes rolled up. He made a few snoring sounds. Then he relaxed, and we bent his head over his knees. Immediately he flushed and broke into a cold sweat. He became conscious and mumbled like a child for us to go back to the play. We sat for a few minutes more and then walked quickly home and to bed. (I was collected at the time, but in the night lost my nerve and existed through a kind of half-waking nightmare until morning. Today he looks tired but all right.)

It is snowing now in the Savoys. Each morning more white has filled the ravines and the meadows. The air is colder today but clear. Women hurry toward the churches with pots of white chrysanthemums for All Saints' Day.

This morning the architect came with four projects, all bad as far as we were concerned. He, so far at least, has missed completely our desire to build a house "of the country," not new and garish and "chalet" like the Villa Rose-Baloy that went up near Le Pâquis this summer. His plans are for suburban villas, and it is, of course, incomprehensible to him that we *want* the old house left as a kind of germ, or nucleus, for the new. "It's not worth fifty francs," he says in bewilderment. But I think we can wear him down and away from his fixed ideas and get something out of him—with T. doing most of his work and letting him sign the papers for law's sake.

Another thing that puzzles and secretly shocks him, and Otto, and Mme. Doellanbach, and so on is that we're not planning to have a *homme*. They look at us crosswise and try not to smile when I say that I like to cook and prefer to have a charwoman occasionally.

While T. went up to Le Pâquis to make some sketches, Al and I inspected the apartment with the agent, noting nail holes and so on against the day of wrath six months from now. We looked down at the market, in full swing, most of the flowers white for Le Toussant, under the white snow air and the whitening mountains. And as we crossed the marketplace, later, I spotted a little walnut chair like the one I bought last week (this week? time is out of joint), and we bought it for four francs and put it on Al's shoulder and took it back to the apartment. People smiled at us.

Then we went to Mme. Doellanbach's for a market-day *petit salé* and a glass of wine and a little angling (successful) to see if she knew of a charwoman. To the pension to find T. in a cloud of smoke, his eyes blurred and his smile vacant as a thousand house plans surged in his head. He had drawn a picture of the facade just as we want it to be. Now to get an architect to make it possible!

After lunch, he drew, Al took one of his ever-surprising cat-naps under the afghan, and I wrote. They're gone now, to buy toothpaste and breathe fresh air.

Oh, I will be glad to settle, even for six months. Too long on the wing.

I am tired from nightmares, and the day is cold. Perhaps a bath and the chaise longue and supper here in my room? I want to write to Anne,* though, to tell her why I like *Golden Wedding*. I've never written before to an author to say that. Perhaps it is better not to. But if I ever wrote a book, I should be glad to know what some people thought of it.

2. xi. 36

This morning we went to the apartment, where a mildly friendly little man was making ready for the advent of our stove tomorrow and putting in light bulbs. All was clean and fresh. We felt even more anxious to be there—chez nous. I never thought I'd feel that way about a rented apartment, but I do.

Then while Al saw the agent about a stall for the car, Tim and I went to a brush shop and bought many brushes—scrubbing, dusting, bath. And a doormat. And coat hangers.

The coat hangers are a little demonstration of the only rub, so far, in our domestic relations—a very small rub, but I note it because it may be interesting later to remember. It has many developments, all contradictory—the thin life Al and I led when T. knew us in Laguna, the same life he led on Fuller Street in Hollywood, our mutually careful but more decent existences in 1934–35. Then came last spring in Europe, when I traveled with T. and his mother, always first class and reveling in it after so long second and third, all of us spending money rashly and unthinkingly in a mixture of rank sensual enjoyment and desire to keep Mrs. P. comfortable. Then came this summer, when Timmy with Anne bought bicycles and rode them five days and then gave them to

* Dillwyn's sister, a novelist in the 1930s and 1940s.

agreeable hotel servants, furnished their private sitting room with lamps and left them because they were too hard to pack.

The result, showing daily in small and so far very safe ways, is that Timmy is afraid of my sybaritic tendencies, and occasionally, when I talk of liking linen sheets (for instance) enough to make a tentative list for the next fifty years for Le Pâquis and of giving it to Otto who could get us a 15 percent discount, he tightens his face almost like his mother and gives a vague speech about disliking to borrow money, Anne's generosity and our probable abuse of it, the need to live simply and fittingly as peasants in the peasant Le Pâquis.

I, on the other hand, when he and Al suggest staying at the Compote or the Gare for dinner, think resentfully of the meal already paid for here at the pension and almost unconsciously add up the five-franc pieces that we would be spending on linen sheets instead of cotton. Or if T. goes into a shop, heads straight for a rack of coat hangers marked "1–4 francs," and gathers together two dozen of the most expensive, I automatically say, "How about these at 2.50?," and when he as automatically answers, "Very nice, but I want the four-franc ones," I feel a faint sure prick of resentment that he can imply my extravagance without noticing his own.

As a matter of fact, we are all three of us fairly sensible people about money, and I feel confident and safe in thinking that such puny contretemps are without menace to our peace. Each has some whim or foible, far from serious and easily passed over. *Ça ira.*

Last night T. read us some of his Cornwall journal. It made this very poor stuff. However, I shan't try to "write," simply because he has succeeded in doing so without any apparent effort. What I'm putting into this book is meant, basically at least, to tell us later a few of the early occurrences. I doubt if even that simple purpose will be fulfilled. I'm afraid, really, of the personal. And how to write of three people with complete impersonality? The result will be a stiff chronicle of vegetables bought, charwomen paid, meals consumed. Or it will be a pseudo-personal gossiping, skirting with timid words the truly important relations and instead relaying small "bright sayings" and amusing anecdotes. T. has a happy touch with flowers, with a priest picking clover, with sea-gulls. I feel heavy and obvious in such company—now, at least. Perhaps that is because I am in a state of inward puzzlement. When I can answer my own questions, I shall be able more clearly to ask them of others, and more firmly, too.

3. xi. 36

Nine o'clock of a sunny market morning, and I sit in the window of what will probably be our salon, waiting for goods to arrive from the station, where Al and T. and Otto are identifying them.

The electrician just blew a fuse, and I heard him clear his throat quickly as it popped, very much as a man does who inadvertently belches or breaks wind in church or at a dinner table.

It will be good to cook again. This morning I felt eager to begin, as I walked along the edge of the market. The flowers were crisp and beautiful, and the cabbages and salads and all the leeks and leaves and colored things were like the flowers. The bread in piles, onions woven into necklaces, the potatoes, the rumps of all the patient standing horses were warm and gleaming and clean. The people looked sturdy and quietly spirited.

12. xi. 36

Some days later, and I am sorry to see what a poor bluff I am at keeping a journal, even while I say sincerely that it might be better to cease trying. We have been installed for a week now. The apartment, large, light, filled with chrysanthemums in pots and vases, is very impersonal and pleasant. We continue to acquire pots for the new electric stove, lights for our bedsides, chairs to sit upon. We consider a fine Valaisanne table, inlaid and carved. Tradesmen's faces emerge from their first anonymous fog, and the unctuous clerk at the Bel-Bâle gives me presents of chocolate. We have thirty bottles of wine in our cellar, bought in a mixture of diplomacy and enthusiasm after Al and T. had tasted it with the vintner-mayor of our *commune de St. Saphorin.*

A wind has blown down most of the wide coarse leaves from the plane trees and several times has sent the swans scuttling into their haven at the edge of the market. The gulls have tossed themselves valiantly into every slightest breeze.

One day the mountains, the water, the houses in the town looked as tiny as a Christmas tree ornament and at the same time very fierce and as if chipped from cold pewter.

It is cold today. The mountains are near and high.

Otto came. I wish I could write his remarks about weeds and plants. He says I must have an herb garden, with "all the best cures for all troubles of all the interior, automatically." Of them I remember that three days of drinking an infusion of dried chervil stems cleans the whole body, "just like the espiragasses [asparagus]." Peppermint tea after dinner helps digestion. The brewed roots of nettles, mixed with alcohol and "two to three drops perfume," form a fine hair tonic.

Also he says to pick a few onions, dandelions, cabbage leaves, any meadow grasses, and nettles and brown them in a little butter and make a fine soup. "If they did not *pique* [sting], all those nettles in the world would by now be *détruit* [destroyed], on cause they are so good for curing sick animals which would automatically *mange* [eat] them all."

It grows dark. In the kitchen T. cuts little pears from Le Pâquis into a saucepan. Al is out, buying a brioche for his breakfast. I lie lazily on the couch, feeling well now but still scared from a mildly unpleasant bout with what I think was my forgotten enemy the appendix. All goes well now, and I am puzzled as to what caused this morning's trouble. Certainly my life could not be called debauched. My only excesses are mental, if they exist at all.

We have bought the beautiful table. I am glad. It will be good in the grand salon.

Our plans for the house are almost decided on, and Jeanneret now makes the detailed drawing. Then it must be exposed for two weeks in *la maire de St. Saphorin,* that our neighbors may see what we plan to do and say if they do not approve. Then we can begin. We hope for good weather.

We have rented a radio, which crackles constantly and painfully. Where are the fine programs of Europe that are discussed so nostalgically in America? So far, whatever we have been able to hear between crackles has been mediocre "safe" music, the kind that makes old women in respectable pensions say, "Ah, Beethoven! Ah, Brahms!"

15.xi.36

The night of the day I thought for a few hours of appendectomies, I had eaten nothing. Al mixed a very good martini before supper. We ate well of vegetables and milk and then went to see the latest movie version of *Michel Strogoff.* We had a small beer in the entr'acte. The movie was mildly entertaining, as familiar as *Uncle Tom's Cabin,* with Michel's mother as obscenely objectionable as are all cinema mothers—even worse than most actual ones.

When we came out the door, wind blew violently against us, rain flicked us, and we all tried to suppress the instinctive hysterical laughter of humans when a girl's hat blew off and rolled madly down the street, with her scuttling after in a mixture of embarrassment and anxiety.

By our door the overhead lights from the *place* were wagging wild shadows. It was too exciting to go home. We clung together and pushed on down the *place* to the Lion d'Or. Four people played cards there. When we asked for grogs, they smiled delightedly and scuttled in four directions, the game waiting with the hands laid out like fans. Rain ran across the floor from the two doors, and we felt warm and falsely safe from the violence outside.

The grogs were simple and crude but hot. We drank them slowly and watched the white flick of cards at the reassembled game table.

"This is the night for a fondue! We've never tasted one! Oh, they are delicious! Yes, this is the night! Too late? Never too late for a fondue!"

We all felt very gay as we whirled up the *place* toward Mme. Doellanbach's. Al had a few misgivings about the lateness, but I felt very careless and happy and pretended to ignore them, and he really didn't care much, I think.

Le Vieux Vevey was crowded and smoky. Four boys I have seen in every café were playing cards. One of them has been trying to flirt with me—dark, gaunt, with sunken hot eyes and the stretched smile of a corpse—and all evening I was afraid Al would ask them to have fondue with us. They had almost no money, and we wouldn't finish the fondue—but I didn't want that cheeky boy at our table.

It was fun, dipping the bread into kirsch, into the thick pungent cream, up into our mouths. We drank a little white wine. We chattered. I felt very gay, pleasantly drunken although I had drunk little.

On the way home, the rain seemed wilder. We went quite silently to bed, where T. worried some at my foolishness in eating and drinking in such silly ways after a bad cramp, where Al tossed miserably and for the hundredth time swore never again to eat cheese at night, and where I, unjustly perhaps, lay in a pleasant Gruyère-flavored wakefulness, puzzled still but conscious of well-being, warm and listening to the wind.

The next day, free for some reason from appointments, we drove up the Rhône valley. At first I was timid in the car but soon grew used to it. It is a good car, I think—smooth, easy to handle, powerful, and very comfortable. We all drove. We ate dried beef and a large sausage with bread and *fendant du Valais,** and bought a rocklike chunk of the beef to eat before dinners with aperitifs. We drove up a narrow coiling road to Leukenbad, where we drank bottled beer and were watched by two pretty little girls, and then we looked at the beautiful pine pews in the church. It was there, too, that we looked down a narrow steep street at a flock of white sheep with black muzzles, and suddenly between us and the mounting beasts appeared first a twig broom, then a ladder, and then a chimney sweep carrying the broom and the ladder, and all of them of the softest, heaviest, most profound black that we had ever seen. We had walked on past the mouth of the little street before we realized how black, how odd, the sweep and the troop of beasts had been. Then we began to talk and laugh excitedly,

* A slightly effervescent white wine from the Valais.

feeling that we had seen something witchlike at least, and perhaps not even so. All of the pitched village of Leukenbad immediately swung into unreality in our minds.

We passed another fairy story—two steep peaks, close as two fingers of a hand, with a high chapel on one, a crenellated castle ruin on the other. St. Maurice was nice, and Sion, and one little town had a square lined off with plane trees that reminded me of Tarascon.

Yesterday we went to the Bel-Bâle and down into its cellar, where we tasted discreetly of several things and bought twenty liters of Châteauneuf du Pape '29, two liters of twelve-year fine champagne, three liters of Malaga, and five liters of old Jamaican rum. Next week we go to try sherry.

The young manager, who tasted with us, took one sip or perhaps two and then tossed the rest of his glassful back over his shoulder against the wall. It was plain that he enjoyed this gesture, although he looked nothing but nonchalant. Once, too, he insisted on showing us how strong an uncut rum was by filling his mouth with it and then blowing it into the air over a lighted match. It made a great tongue of fire, but even that did not bring any apparent happiness to him. He had a good time, I know.

Our table has come. It has been a week since T. and I first saw it, dusty and covered with other furniture, in the dark shop of a Jew. We told Al. He and T. looked again. Al chatted with Ebenezer (M. L'Ebèniste), and then after much visiting and parleying with Otto, finally he and Otto bought it, for 250 francs instead of the 300 the owner demanded and the 600 to 800 everyone declared it was worth. And at that Otto was somewhat hurt that Al hadn't let him haggle the price down to 230. Now business is done, and we have a beautiful table. It is long, high, narrow, of dark walnut, very crude. The ends are simply carved, chisel work. The two sides are more elaborate, with a queer running border of acanthus, grape, stipple—a mélange but pleasant. The top is fine—inlaid crudely with the letters, numbers, and a religious symbol cut in. I am very pleased by it. I like to think of Le Pâquis with this table in it.

Last night we talked to Jeanneret (with Otto, of course) for the last time. The plans are good. Main change is that I now have the upstairs room in the old house, Al the middle room in the new, and Anne the end room with a little fireplace. Their rooms have the balcony, mine the fountain, theirs the bath, mine the old stairs. I hope they'll be as content as I.

It is midafternoon of a Saturday, and I am newly amazed to see that the *place* is clean and bare again after the morning's ordered beautiful bustle of market and after the scattered cabbage leaves and straw of noon. The little men who creep under the horses' tails with buckets and brushes have gone with their rich gleanings, and all the wine has been washed into the lake, and not a single forgotten carrot top shows where three hours ago the whole countryside's hunger was given its weekend's satisfaction.

A letter from Sis says she is troubled about Christmas. I knew that would come. Mother *demands* that she come home, with all the pathetic horrible maternal demands: pathos, trembling, all. Anne feels desperate. I know why. I think she should not go, but I think that in her place I would submit as she probably will, and in a vain essay try to make Mother feel strong, important, protective again. That's what Edith is searching for and clinging to—any sign that she may still be the young vital woman who led, who taught, who directed the four loving children. Things like Christmas trees may, she still hopes, give her back some of that dissolved importance. And how hard I've worked, and all of us, to give to Christmas even an atom of its old festivity. Every year, as we all grow older, less needful of Mother as she longs for us to need her, more desirous of our own kinds of living, we drink more and more to keep up the bluff. Doesn't she see that? Perhaps she will not. Now she is using Shaun as a wedge—we must give Shaun the real family Christmas. Can't she see him, the shy quiet child, tired from travel and crushed with attention and too many presents, the only young one in a circle of bored, half-drunken old people? No, I think she can't. I hope Anne stays in San Francisco. It will be hard for Edith and Rex. Many things are harder, though.

16. xi. 36

A good day today. We rose late, after a few dances at the Trois Rois to a poor but interesting orchestra, and after coffee strolled to the park of La Coupole, where we drank sherry and changed a bill. Then we went by funicular to Mont Pélèron.

The funny music machine was still there in the little slanting station, with the same many-pockmarked disk of le Beau Danube. We played it. It is very off-key and so silly and nostalgically gay— we'd like to buy it.

We walked along the ridge of the hills to Chexbres. The curves of the land seemed very sweet, and we wondered at them, near as they are to the cruel upsweep of the Alps. Little brooks ran swiftly through them, little boys raced over them on a vague paper chase. On the road all the Sunday walkers greeted us politely.

We were hungry by the time we got to Chexbres and ate cheese, local ham, and bread with the wine. Le Lion d'Or was full —a rather noisy but pleasant reunion of young men with lavender chrysanthemums in their lapels, several families, a few old men. One small-faced old one with good blue eyes sat by us and talked pleasantly with Al. He knew our neighbor at *faverges,* but not very well, since he had only been in this district forty years! He missed his dead wife. I heard him say, "Oh, my son is far away in Geneva

—but, of course, I still have several more left!" When we went, he shook hands and wished us luck, health, a welcome to Le Pâquis. We went down the hill.

Le Pâquis was beautiful. With all the leaves fallen, it was easier to see the curve of the earth and to imagine the bulk of our house. It is a good spot, and its life is worth any personal ennuis that may occur, I think.

Some day I should like to own, or even rent, the ridiculous little hut and the dwarfed dignity of La Roche Ronde, with its ten-by-twenty vineyard and its little balcony. I should like to work there, by myself. I could even live there—cook and sleep and work in the two rooms, bathe and live otherwise at a hotel in Vevey. It's a silly idea—but such a complete fine little place seems very desirable, for a few weeks or months of the year anyway. But Le Pâquis, too, is good. I am anxious to be there.

6. i. 37

Late in the afternoon I walked with Timmy along the esplanade. Gulls whirled and coasted like black ashes in the pewter sky. The snowfields in the great crease of the Grammont were warm and radiant, but all the other snow was as repellent as frozen flesh. Air moved freshly across the smooth surface of the lake and blew in sweet rainy puffs against my face. I felt very happy. We looked down into the water, in the little port, at the flashing minnies nibbling around a chain. They were like live stars, mostly invisible.

7.i.37

Otto told T. that homosexuality is alarmingly on the increase in Switzerland. He says it is because there is so much unemployment, with all its slackness and dissatisfaction, and also because so many depraved, ill, and wealthy foreigners stay in this country and influence the Swiss. I had thought of the first reason but not the second. They both seem reasonable. Certainly most of the Englishmen I see here, especially the younger ones, are a sad set of tubercular alcoholics.

On the fourth of this month, we started to dig into Le Pâquis, to build our house. It was a cold bright day. We drove up there early in the afternoon and found several men at work. They wore soft blue clothes and dug and wheeled earth with the slow thoroughness that seems characteristic of all labor here. They spoke politely to us. A round man with a sheaf of blueprints seemed to be completely bewildered and looked quite overcome when he found we were none of us the architect. Schyrr *fils,* round, too, but much larger, a sturdy pleasant man, was directing the disposal of the dirt. He showed us the outlines of the terrace, which will be large and beautiful.

I liked the way the men were cutting the turf very neatly and piling it to be used again, instead of mutilating it heedlessly as they probably would have at home. I was glad, too, to see that the primroses have started to bloom in the grass.

That night the long clear spell broke, and rain started—the first of much, I am afraid. I hope it won't slow the work too much.

The next day, or the day after, we trimmed the willows along the wall and the brook and cleaned our side of the brook. It was fun. We felt very happy then, too—got quite scratched and, of course, were stiff the next day, especially Al who had chopped some of the great pile of fruit-tree wood.

I had not been to Le Pâquis for several days, and they told me that at last the snowdrops and crocuses were in bloom, the ones we planted last autumn. Mine, down in the open space beyond the garden, were in a wide ring, very gay, and Tim's were thick along the brook slope. Yesterday we went to see them, but all were gone. Some lay broken on the grass, and a few of the bulbs, hacked across with a sharp knife, lay like white mushrooms. But most of them were quite disappeared. It was sickening. Timmy and Al thought it was vandalism—some resentment from a neighbor or a peevish child. Otto spoke soothingly of the dandelion hunters. My explanation was best, I think: I remembered the countless pots of meadow flowers for sale that morning in the market and was sure that a hurried thoughtless vagabond, sure of selling a few francs' worth, had spotted our flowers and roughly pried them loose, discarding any hurt ones. It is too bad. We'll put up a sign asking people not to pick the flowers.

There were (and are) still primroses thick as stars, and many daffodils and daisies, and a few violets. The tulips have not yet come—perhaps they won't. By two years from now I want to have many more daisies and daffodils.

The walls are going up. Unlike Al, who seems capable of standing for hours watching the snail-pace of the work, I cannot enjoy it. It is ugly. I know it will be thoroughly done, since it is Swiss. There is no aid I can lend. So I prefer not to see it in its present cluttered hideous form. I think I seem unsympathetic to Al. I am sorry.

There is so much wood that we are going to have Jules, the vigneron, help us cut and pile it.

We saw old man Schyrr this week and have pretty well settled the garden for this year. I think we can handle it. He will plant strawberries, *asperges* [asparagus], tomatoes, and eggplant for us. We'll sow the rest. I am very glad that we decided against the hothouse this year—it would have been too luxurious. We'll get along very well, and as soon as we're settled will lay one or two *cloches** up near the road wall.

Every time we go up there we bring back a plate of primroses, with one or two daisies and a little clump of violets in them. They are lovely, especially when we put them on low stools and can look down on them as if they were still growing in the meadow.

If I continue this journal, it will be almost wholly about Le Pâquis. I can see that. Other things, in spite of what I'm afraid seems my lack of interest in the building, are unimportant. I eat, sleep, dress, bustle about paying bills. I live my several lives. They are evanescent.

3. iii. 37

Today is a beautiful blue day, with white glitter in the air near the mountains. It is cold outdoors but warm here in the sunny bedroom. I drink slowly at a bottle of beer. On my windowsill, to catch the rare sun, is my little garden—two pansies, a deep blue cineraria, two pots of spindling morning-glory sprouts I hope to raise. In the courtyard of the École Préparatoire, across the street, some twenty children hop to the clapped hands of their exercise teacher. Timmy writes at the dining room table. Al is at Le Pâquis chopping wood and then going to Chexbres to eat soup.

* Bell-shaped covers for plants.

At the moment I find it difficult to write. I have some things to get out of my head, but I wait to hear from Mr. Saxton about my next move: will he like what I sent, does he think I should try for a Guggenheim, and so on? I cannot settle down to anything. I am, as often, tempted to start a personal book, *mais à quoi bon?* I think my present life is a strange, complicated, interesting one. But my deep distrust—or is it timidity, cowardice even?—of such self-revelations will, perhaps, always prevent me from thus relieving myself. I don't know, though. As I grow older and farther away from the first effortful amenities, I feel myself, nevertheless, more dispassionate, more able to see myself with all the other bacteria squirming on a culture slide. So instead of writing or of loosening my self-censorship, I'll put down what I know of Mme. Chapuis, my cleaning woman.

She was recommended to me by Mme. Doellanbach, who owns Le Café Vieux Vevey and knew Timmy ten years ago. Mme. D. did not know Chapuis but had been told by a client who employed her that she was good and needed work. I left my address at the Vieux Vevey and learned that she would come to see me at a set time and day.

I was a little nervous—I had never before interviewed a servant. When I saw her, I was surprised at her slender, tall body—I had thought that all cleaning women were short and stubby creatures. She sat on the edge of a chair, fussing nervously with her purse. She was dressed neatly in a half coat, a black hat, a knitted scarf. I was anxious to get the thing over with. I tried to speak good French. Her voice was rather high and nasal. When I said, in a terse, scowling way, that I wanted only two things, to have absolute cleanliness in the bathroom and kitchen and to pay her one franc an hour instead of the usual eighty centimes, her voice wavered in a singsong effort to keep from crying. I felt even gruffer and much moved in a petty way.

I ended the interview. She went to the door and stood fumbling in her purse for two or three envelopes. "You see, Madame," she said, pulling papers from them and spreading them before me, "I have very good, *excellent* references. I am not used to work. But everyone has been satisfied with me."

"Good, good. I am sure . . ." and so on I muttered. I realized that I had made a blunder in not asking for her references before.

I set a date for her to start. The door was almost closed after her. Then she turned to me and said rapidly, "I should tell Madame that I am divorcing my husband." I could see she was being very frank, that she expected me to say I didn't want her to come.

"Good, good! Come tomorrow at 2:00, Madame. Good-bye."

The next day she came and literally tore through the apartment, not breaking anything but cleaning with a kind of frenzy. She told me her husband had been taken from her after eighteen years by another woman, that she had a son nineteen who was with the father and who had not even visited her for three years, that her sixteen-year-old daughter was with her and was a naughty girl. But mostly she worked, and very well.

I went through a period of figuring many kinds of fantastic schemes for employing servants. In them I pretended I was deaf and so on. The best one was to hire through an intermediary, who would say that I was harmlessly insane and wished to hear absolutely no details of any life but the one the servant led as a duster and cleaner in my house. *Why*, I thought, *why* must I always know the cavernous agonies of the cook's mother, the travail of a café waiter's wife or sister, the flat feet, the divorces, the earaches of everyone who is near? Why can't the functions of society be performed without interrelation?

But I did nothing. Occasionally I ask Chapuis how she is or something like that, because I am human and humane. I hate to hear. I want to do all I can to help her, but I do not want to hear about it. She was sick for two weeks: I visited her, I helped her financially, I sympathized. Now she is working again, and I do not want her in any way to overtire herself, to do what she should not, but I do not want to hear about her.

She is given to female details. I discourage them. I told her when I hired her that I did not want her ever to do too much during her periods. I should have added that neither did I care to hear about them. (I ask myself if my extreme distaste for any mention of female disorders is a small sign of homosexuality. I am almost sickened by any talk of such things and care nothing for details of pregnancies and confinements and less than nothing for talk of other women's sexual experiences. Once I thought it was because I am childless, but I notice that other childless women are quite avid for such conversation.)

Chapuis says she has a vaginal catarrh and is going weekly to a doctor in Montreux, for three months, to be "cauterized." She probably has gonorrhea. I feel very sorry and am horrified at her being so treated and so duped into an expensive torture. But I do not wish to hear about it.

She talks (it sounds as if she jabbered constantly, and as a matter of fact she has learned from my noncommittal replies and my long silences to say almost nothing) . . . She talks some of her daughter and asks me for advice, which I never give. The girl is finishing high school. She is well developed and highly sexed. Chapuis, who likes her bit of fun, refuses to let the girl go out, and when she herself is out at night, she locks her daughter into the rooms. She seems hurt and surprised that the girl resents this. At Christmas the girl went to her father and stayed without warning her mother until time to commence school again. The mother was cross and more so later when she found that the father had deducted two francs a day from the alimony for the girl's keep.

Chapuis is thirty-eight. She is, as I said, taller than I and quite slender. She has a low brow over small close-set eyes, and a rather loose mouth badly colored with lipstick. Her hair is beginning to turn gray. She goes every Saturday to have it washed and waved. Her clothes are always neat and simple. Her rooms, which she earns by being concierge of a building near here, were very clean and fresh when I visited her during her illness. She is polite, deft, quiet in her housework, and seems quite intelligent.

For some reason I do not like her.

8. iv. 37

Tonight, while Al and Timmy play Camelot, drinking beer, muttering now and then, or breathing heavily, and while I sit on the couch feeling agreeably tired after a day of curtain making, I'll write a few things about the house.

Last Saturday we gave our "bouquet"* for the men who up till now have worked there. We had waited far too long for the signal, a little fir tree nailed to the new rooftree by the carpenters. Finally it was there, a lopsided tree aflutter with what Otto calls "robbins" of colored paper—streamers of red and white, large bright magenta roses, and Italian colors on the tip, intentionally or not. The men pretended not to watch us as we first looked at the tree, but I could see them beaming.

---

* A celebration that occurs when the tree, or bouquet, is attached to the rooftree.

We had planned things fairly thoroughly already, but there was still some bustling to do. Otto was very useful, the epitome of bustlers. We bought forty-five little glasses, mustard, colored paper, and twelve kilos of sliced ham and meats at Uniprix (after some argument, for I disapprove of those chain bazaars. Their high quality and their undeniable cheapness won. I continue to feel unfair to small tradesmen, though). We had a pound of bread for each man, and three little cheesecakes, ordered from the corner bakery. We commanded sixty bottles of 1934 *faverge* from our neighbor Rogévue. And Friday afternoon, after the workmen had gone, we decorated the upstairs, still one big room, with red and white for Switzerland and blue and yellow for Vevey.

Saturday was cold and mizzly, after several blue days. We were sorry. It was not anyone's fault. We put on several layers of clothes, and at 11:00 Al and I went up to Le Pâquis to cover the tables with white paper and arrange things a little while T. collected Otto, little Anna, and the cheese pies.

We had wondered if anyone had warned Jules, the vigneron, to be there, but he had felt it in the air. When we said hello, that we were glad he was there, he looked rather embarrassed and said that he was just happening to stop in to see how the building was going. "But you'll stay for the party, won't you?" He pretended great surprise, and said, Why—why, yes, I'd be very glad—thank you! And he went lumbering across the road to help carry the wine, with a pleased grin on his face.

The foreman, a deep-voiced handsome blond man who never looks upset, even when we discover that he has left out an essential wall or put in an impossible one, was laying planks for two long tables. Soon we had them covered with white paper. Then Anna, T., and Otto arrived, with the cheese pies steaming on a great tray wrapped in lap robes, and a big basket of bread. We put bottles, glasses, mustard pots, bread, piles of ham and sausage in a line down the middle of each table. The cheesecakes fumed. Otto and Al pulled corks. We all bristled.

I went out for a minute onto the windy balcony. It was noon. I looked down by the fountain, and there were all the men washing themselves, wetting their hair, even tying fresh handkerchiefs around their throats. They were quiet.

They came upstairs in several groups. The young ones walked right in and sat down. The older ones stood shyly for a minute before they went less surely to the tables. As soon as we could, we filled our glasses, said, Santé, drank, and went upstairs, where we had taken some of the food and wine.

We could hear everything and see a little through the hole where the stairs will be up to T.'s room. Things were rather quiet at first. Men drifted in—excavators who had hurried from other jobs and so on. There were about thirty-six, I think. They ate and drank earnestly.

They were quiet partly because Schyrr *fils* was there. He should not have been, because he is a contractor. I am pretty sure he was sent there by his father to keep an eye on his men, who alone of all the workers had to go on with their jobs. I saw old Schyrr the day before, and when I mentioned the party, he acted quite surprised, although he knew about it from Otto, and then he told me, in a grudging grumpy way, not to give his men too much to drink. I said that that was something the men would have to tend to but that I didn't think there would be any orgy. He looked very disapproving. (Rogévue told us that old Schyrr had a few words with him while the Schyrr laborers were working on the excavation—accused Rogévue of enticing the men into his cellars just to make them drunk, and so on.) Anyway, there was young Schyrr where he shouldn't have been, and I am sure his presence kept the men quiet, although they like him.

It was cold. We ate the delicious hot cheesecakes and some bread and meat, and drank the white wine, and kept moving to keep warm. Otto jumped around like a little flea, and so did Anna, who was helpful and for so young a girl very efficient. (I think she and Jules had the most fun at the party. He was the only one who showed any signs of being drunk. He had a beatific beam on his ugly good face all during the meal. I could see him discussing politics with the whole table, a piece of bread stuck on the end of his knife, two slices of ham dangling from the hand that held his glass. By the end of the party, when I gave him a package of meat, a bottle of wine, and some bread for his wife, he was a bit glassy-eyed and could only open his mouth especially wide for a thank-you.)

We saw Baublebottom, the private fool, the jolly idiot of a workman who always gets the dullest simplest jobs and always does them wrong. The man who casually causes all the accidents by doing things like tipping a barrel load of rocks into a cellar full of workers—we saw him pick up the tray of cheese pies and spill the whole thing onto the dusty floor. The men roared. He grinned nonchalantly, shoveled the pies back onto the tray, blew some of the cement off them, and carried them to the tables.

Suddenly all the men began to sing, and sing as Swiss all can, sweetly, truly, rather sadly: "Sur la haute montagne était un vieux châlet." We kept very still. Timmy's face got very red and crumpled, and he cried slightly, looking so much like his mother for a minute that I was startled. Al smiled and looked up toward the mountains. Otto and Anna and I all looked quiet, probably.

At the end we clapped. The men sang some more, not so well but pleasantly. When Anna and I went down with tobacco for them, they started a song about "Lift your lovely blue eyes"—but Schyrr shushed them at his own table. It was nice of them.

One young man came upstairs, thanked us very politely, and

excused himself to go to the practice of his *sapeurs-pompiers*. A few others left. Finally Schyrr went. (I know one reason he came was to drive his men up in the truck—otherwise, they could never have walked and got back to work. But he was sent by his puritanical father as well.)

Things grew noisier, but because of the cold, the wine had less effect than I had expected. Of course, I didn't predict any riots, but I thought there would be more singing and shouting. About three o'clock we went down and told the men to take what bread was left to their families. They were pleased. Soon after, they had gone. The tables looked strange, because almost every man had cut a half-circle of the paper in front of him to wrap up what he didn't eat.

Little Anna washed the glasses in the fountain, while we talked stiffly to Jeanneret, who had wandered in with his shy silent wife and her little niece, who looked like a child's drawing: round eyes, stiff bobbed hair, a wide mouth, colored with blue, yellow, red Crayolas and utterly blank.

Now Al and Timmy have finished their games and their beer. I have finished my white wine and soda. It is about midnight. Tomorrow I must sew hard, and I want to go up to Le Pâquis, where this week we have done a lot of work in the garden. Perhaps it will rain, though. Well, that will be good for the seeds we have put in—peas, carrots, lettuce, onions, and flowers.

In the meadow now are violets and buttercups. The crocuses are gone. Daisies and primulas are almost gone as well. On one slope the double daffodils are in full flower, and some yellow vetch shows.

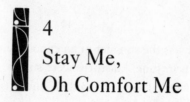

4
Stay Me,
Oh Comfort Me

There is an urgency, an insistent beauty, about words written while they are hot in the mind, soon after something has happened to make them burn there. I wrote that way the morning after my last meal with Rina. I sat in the gentle sunlight, just inside the great open window of a *brasserie* on the Champs Elysées, and the words flowed onto the letter paper like melted stone, swirling in strange shapes and mysterious shadowy meanings that I can never find again. I kept the sheets of paper for a long time, without reading them. I knew that what I had written could not yet be talked about or even looked at. And now that I feel it is all right, the paper is gone. I shall have to tell this from recollection, and it is a kind of consolation to admit to myself that I can do it in tranquillity, the way the poet said it might be.

That was the summer of an exposition in Paris. It was supposed to open in June, but there were strikes. At least, that is what the reactionary newspapers said . . . and it is true that when you went on the riverboats past the autoworks on the little island, the men leaned from the windows and yelled and raised their hands in the clenched worker's salute.

Some of the exhibits were ready to open, incredibly neat and even beautiful behind the rubble in the half-finished pathways, and the cafés were full of foreigners come to Paris to work in the fair or to see it. They sat gaily in the June sun, drinking their native drinks, or *citron pressé,* or even champagne, waiting for things to begin.

I was in Paris because my father and mother were coming from California. I was excited about that, but I had used them as an excuse to be by myself. Nobody knew this but me, and I was not ashamed of it. I had to be by myself for a few hours, so I lied a little, where I lived in Vevey, and came a day earlier than the boat was to arrive.

I do not think I knew, on the way to Paris, that I was going to see Rina, but as soon as everything was in order at the hotel, I called her.

The next morning, as I sat in the sun and wrote about it, I still felt sickish. It was almost like a hangover, but I knew I had not drunk much the night before.

When the waiter first came, and I asked for paper and a pen, I told him I would order later. I felt a little strange, alone in the big place. There were only a few people at that hour, and although the tiny tables and the trim wicker chairs on the sidewalk were in twenty neatly impenetrable rows, the back part of the *brasserie* was still dark and smelled dankly of Javelle water from its late scrubbings.

There were a lot of places like that then, high priced and badly served, along the Elysées: big tawdry rooms, usually with balconies at the back and windows that slid away so that the wide *trottoir* and the interior of the café could be one establishment on any sunny day or warm lovely night. There was always either a "gypsy" orchestra or a "ladies'" orchestra. Sometimes it was called *"orchestre de dames tsiganes,"* to be thorough. They were usually pretty good, too, in spite of the contortions of Romany abandon that their contracts apparently called for. The leader, always a violinist, was the prettiest, and winked and wiggled her way through night after night of Liszt and Enesco without ever quite forgetting that she had almost been first at the conservatory in Lyon or Clermont or maybe even Paris.

And there were the beautiful German girls that summer. There had been a few for three or four years, but that summer they were in full strength. I had noticed it at Easter time, when I went to Paris to decide a few things, but now that the fair was to begin, it was even plainer.

I sat at my table, writing fast and then resting, watching people, and as the chairs on the terrace filled, I thought that I had never seen so many beautiful German girls. I knew, without much surprise, that they were there for a reason—to show all the hungry, thirsty, excited tourists that they were the most beautiful in the world and the happiest, being the most German.

It seemed like a dirty trick to play. I remembered the fat girls from little Prussian villages, and their dowdy muckle-dun suits, and the way their eyes squinted and their hair smelled, in the classrooms when I was going to the university in Dijon. Those girls had won scholarships and worked like slaves at their lessons. After

1933 you didn't see them anymore. And now Hitler's machine was sending these lovelies . . .

They were tall, slender with the lithe flatness of youth. Their skin was firm and beautifully gilded—not burned brown enough to look un-Aryan but gilded to show what you knew anyway, that they could sail and ski and dance. They all had rather shaggy hair, bleached a little in streaks so that you were to be sure the sun had done it. It was startling and lovely, after the neat tourist hairdos and the elaborate whorls of the French women, and the girls would stand hatless, tall and young, beside the tables of their acquaintances and shake back their hair softly against their shoulders, like sensual colts. And they all wore beautifully tailored gray flannel suits, casual but as artfully revealing as any Hollywood extra's, and white shirtwaists open at the throat.

They never worked together, but there was at least one at every big café in Paris that summer. They would stand up and call out to people they knew or stride from table to table—anything to make people see them and know by their accents that they were German. They all used that seemingly childlike, voluptuous soft way of speaking that is supposed to be Viennese, so that the French would not possibly think of them as Boches.

An Alsatian *brasserie* was just across the street. I knew it was supposed to be a Nazi hangout. I saw two or three of the girls come out of it and then head for their next jobs, up and down the boulevard. I felt very bitter suddenly, and when my waiter came slapping and scowling toward me, I asked him to bring me a double porto-flip. He looked sourly at me and probably was about to tell me that the barman was not yet on duty, but I said very firmly, "Double, please, with two egg yolks . . . and the best red port."

I loathed port, and raw eggs, too. But I had left the hotel without breakfast, and I knew that it would be silly to drink an aperitif and then feel even stranger than I did already. Soon my dear parents would be in Paris. . . . I must meet their train and be young and happy and untouched by evil.

After I drank resolutely at the sweetish, creamy eggnog, I felt steadier in spite of my resentment of it and began to write as fast and as impersonally as I could about the night before. I wish I had not lost those papers. This would be much easier. . . .

It doesn't matter whether I meant to see Rina or not when I went to Paris early: I did see her. I kept saying to myself, or rather my mind kept saying, the way a mind does when a person is trying to ignore too many facts at once, Flagons and apples, flagons and apples. My mind would also say things like, Involution, convolution, trivo-intro-spinolution.

But as I sat in the hotel bedroom and knew that flowers were in vases and mineral water was ordered and English novels were on the bedside tables for my parents and that all was in order at least a day too soon, my mind was saying, Flagons and apples . . . oh, stay me with flagons, stay me with flagons and comfort me with apples, for I am tired of love.

Was that it? It was in the Bible. Did it say tired or sick? I was tired. I wanted love, but I was tired of it, wearied by its involutions, convolutions, its complex intraplexities. I had fled from it, leaving there in Vevey the husk and the bud, the empty and the refilled, renewed, revived, recrucified. . . .

When I tried to write a letter to tell my husband that I was well and happy, I knew that running away had not helped us at all. I loved him too much to lie, although not enough to live with him . . . and it was the same thing again: Stay me with flagons, for I am tired, sick, tired, tired of love.

It was then that I decided to call Rina. She was the answer.

She would be like cool water, I knew it. I felt younger and suddenly freed from all the wordy anguish of the last weeks. Rina knew everything about love. She knew so much and for so long that she had left it all behind. I felt sure of that, convinced of it.

Rina had known every kind of love in the world, and by now she must have left it all behind, she must have. By now she must be a woman beyond purchase, dispassionate at last because she had known all passion, cool at last after all the fires. I wanted terribly to be with her for a while, to rest my weary self with her. I knew now why I had come so resolutely, so slyly, a day early.

It was five years since I had last seen her, perhaps, but everywhere she went she sent me her new address, as if I would be likely to find myself, or her either, in Berlin, or Minorca, or a Baltic fishing town. Now I even had her telephone number in Paris.

My heart was beating hard, partly from the nervousness that telephoning always brings to me and partly from a strange physical reaction, the way it might if I had been lost in a dark cave and had suddenly found the exit.

A maid answered, and then I was talking with Rina. Her voice sounded low one moment and then high and foolish the next, and I realized quickly that she was saying things to me, the usual things two women say after a long separation, but that through me she was talking to someone in the room with her. She was trying to impress someone.

It annoyed me. She must know that after so many years she could not impress me, but doing it to another person was important enough to her to risk my scorn before two minutes had passed. I listened to her voice, lush with affectation and little laughs and murmurs, and wished that I had stayed in Vevey.

There was some nonsense going on about a Packard. "What do *you* think of them?" she demanded lightly, and then before I could answer, she said, "But that's exactly what I say! You've never driven anything else! That long gray roadster . . ."

There was a lot more like that, and I kept thinking, Oh, to hell with it! I've never had a Packard in my life. Long gray roadster!

Rina's accent grew more and more British, and I felt cold and bored. She . . . they . . . just leaving for the Riviera . . . she must see me . . .

I looked around the sterile little room and thought of eating alone: any table in Paris would be one at which my husband or my own true love and I had sat . . .

"I'm leaving, myself, early tomorrow," I said politely. "But I'd so like to see you. Can you have supper with me tonight?" I heard my voice, almost as silly and affected as hers. There was more chatter: I was to come first for a cocktail. . . . I said yes and hung up, bone weary, almost empty of the fine hopes that had leapt in me.

It was a charming afternoon, though, light and limpid, the way Paris can be. There was a big chestnut tree in the courtyard, and a few of its white candles, nearly burned out by now, moved in the pure trembling light against my balcony. The walls looked silvery, not gray, and the dingy mustard plush curtains were golden. I took a long bath and lay on my bed drinking slowly at some brandy and water, and when I finally got up, I dressed almost as carefully as if I were meeting a man I loved very much, instead of a woman who by now should be past such things.

I remembered that I had always dressed with extra care for Rina. She wore very conventional clothes herself, like a rather horsey Junior Leaguer from Pasadena or Milwaukee, but she always made other people want to be extraordinary, to tie a scarf as it had never been tied before or wear one pink glove and one black one. I was satisfied with myself, Rina or not: my dress, the color of a green almond, was like a good dressmaker's idea of what human skin should be, with all the tucks and gores just so instead of as God put them. That was two or three years before women began to wear veils, and I had a big green net that held on my black priest's hat and tied under my chin.

I gazed at myself coolly for a few minutes with great pleasure, as I put on my black gloves in the sweetly dying light. I was slender, chic, with a face as smooth and almost as meaningless as a doll's, and my mind felt quiet again. The bath and the brandy and then this agreeable vision of myself made me put far out of my mind the weariness after my talk with Rina.

By the time I was in the taxi I was excited again, thinking that perhaps she would be as I wanted her to be, wise and rich and dispassionate. I needed someone like that, someone far past sexual wonderings, like a mountain, like a true priest. I needed to withdraw from the lists, to stand for a few minutes away from the battle.

Rina's name was printed on a card for the sixth floor. The apartment house was quietly swanky, somewhere off the Étoile, and I went up in a tiny elevator. A middle-aged maid with a mean face opened the door, and then I was standing in a big room at the top of the building, meant for a studio. Light still glared hotly in through the huge tilted window so that I was dazzled. Rina always liked darkness, I thought. She must hate this.

There was a pleasant fragrance in the air, like full-blown roses.

It seemed as if I waited several minutes. I stood motionless near the door, noticing and thinking several things at once, like any animal in a new place. I still heard the maid saying, "The young lady will be here soon." That sounded queerly insolent when I repeated it to myself; she should have said Rina's name, she should have asked me to sit down. Something rang false as hell.

The room was attractive, surely, in a way that had been made banal by French decorators: white plastered walls, several good pieces of peasant furniture, hand-blocked heavy cloth on the low couches and the chairs. The floor was darkened to look "provincial," and there were good rugs. It is queer . . . I don't believe there were any pictures at all—the walls must have been quite blank.

But it was a pleasant place, except for the loud glare of light —and, except for that, completely characterless. I felt surprised; Rina always took possession of wherever she lived, and I could see nothing of her here. I began to feel very curious about her, in a detached way—what she would be like, after so long.

I took off my gloves and then started slowly to put them on again, knowing without caring that she was going to make an entrance. That at least would be in the right tradition, I thought, not maliciously but almost with relief to find something still left.

The last time I saw her, what did she look like? It was in the rain, in the station at Dijon. I was catching the midnight train for Paris, to go back to California for a few weeks. She stood with her arm through my husband's, and I thought he would probably fall in love with her. Men always did, helplessly. She would do him good, I thought.

I stood in the train window, watching the wet lamplight on their faces turned mutely up to me, and probably I felt a little noble to be so fatalistic. Rina was beautiful, so thin from China and fevers and Leningrad that the bones showed everywhere in her, yet she still looked strong. Yes, it would do them good, I thought, looking down at them as if I were already a thousand miles at sea.

(But he did not fall in love with her. Instead, she gave a disease to our best friend, and when she found out about it, two years later in Berlin when she was having an abortion, she wanted to kill herself. She wrote to me, but by then there was not much I could say.)

I thought of all these things and probably more, and when Rina finally came through a door at the other end of the room, down near the big glaring window, I stood without speaking for a moment.

She put her hands behind her, in a strange childish gesture, and said, "Don't look at me that way. Don't, don't!"

Now, I was not looking at her in any way at all, unless maybe past her, and her low violent pleading was planned. It was a deliberate command to look at her and to be shocked and speechless. I know that my face, which can be very stolid, showed nothing. That was to reprove her for trying to make me gasp or turn away, as she wanted me to do so that she could suffer more.

I sat down on a couch and took off my gloves again without touching her. "Hello, Rina," I said, and she began to talk in a high affected voice, twitching all over the room, moving ashtrays and pillows and such, asking questions too fast and too silly to be answered: how was I, how was the trip up from Vevey, did I like Gitanes or Gold Flakes?

She seemed much shorter, probably because she was so fat and because she wore beautifully cobbled brogues. Her stockings were exquisite, and she still had fine legs, and her tailored suit and shirt and necktie were fine, too, as I had known they would be. But it is true that I never would have known her.

I had met several women who looked almost exactly as she did now, in Hollywood mostly, but it had never occurred to me that Rina would ever resemble them. I suppose it is a glandular condition. She was fat in a certain way, with compact hips and very heavy, almost bull-like shoulders. Her head stuck forward, making her neck look shorter still, and there was a roll at the back, like a caricature of a German burgher, so that the close-cropped hair made unattractive bristles. It was thin at the temples, like a middle-aging man's.

Her face was the strangest, yet I knew it well . . . on other women. It was dead white, with the close-pored vaguely dirty whiteness of an alcoholic's. Her eyes had grown very small, it seemed, and were timid now, instead of large and deep blue and gravely intelligent. She had no eyebrows left at all but only a thin silly penciled line above each puffy socket. And her mouth was small and carefully made up. It looked like a baby's, covered with lipstick, meaningless and nasty.

Perhaps I was less stolid than I thought, for Rina suddenly stopped fussing at the books on the big oak table and came over and took my gloves away.

"Don't put them on again," she said quietly. "You're nervous, too, aren't you? Let's have a drink." Her voice was natural, the low almost harsh voice I remembered. I could smell a heavy scent —she had always liked them.

She pushed an electric button in an elaborate little cloisonné thing on the table in front of my couch, and because neither of us had anything to say, we waited silently. She rang it again. She ran her fingers back over her thinning hair. "It's because *I'm* ringing it," she muttered, not looking at me. "She knows I'm ringing it. She hates me." Then she pushed crankily at the little bell several times and said in the affected English voice, "Servants are so difficult, what with the Exposition . . . I'll simply have to do it myself."

She laughed like something in a drawing room comedy. "A sidecar. You do want a sidecar, don't you?"

"No, thank you, Rina. May I have some brandy and water, please?"

"Oh, but I make such heavenly sidecars . . . Well . . ." She put her hand on my shoulder, the first time we touched, and said, still in that foolish voice, "Just like a little boarding school girl: please . . . thank you, no; thank you, yes . . ."

Then she went hurriedly out of the room. I could hear her heavy flat footsteps go down a long hall.

I was shaking a little all over. I didn't know why, then, but now I think it was the same way a cat shakes after she gives birth to a kitten. I had got rid of something, some burden inside me, and it was a physical shock. For fifteen years I had known Rina and, without words, had believed that she sometime would be my comfort, my very present help in time of trouble. I had lied for her and condoned her eccentricities, her cruelties to people who loved her, without ever loving her myself but because I believed that someday she would save me. And now I knew that she never would. I pushed all that trust away from me, and it was like reliev-ing myself of a great burden, like a birthing of something I had thought was dependence and was really my own freedom. That is why I trembled, but I did not know it then. I just wondered a little.

She came back soon with two tall lovely glasses, the kind that should have flowers in them and are too heavy full of drink. My highball was thin but good. Rina was drinking barley water.

She sat down at the other end of my couch and began to talk rapidly, as if she wanted to tell me everything before it was too late. I listened without speaking, very coolly, as to a tactless stranger.

There was almost nothing I recognized: she was still a snob, but her old small references to social position had become crude boasting about titles and hunting lodges; she was still conscious of money, but her old mannerism of pretending that it was too base, too vulgar to talk about, had turned into a long financial whine.

She seemed to feel misunderstood now and persecuted: Tanya the Polish cook sneered at her, her uncles had cut down her share of her rightful inheritance from a sixth to a thirty-sixth of the estate, Moira always rented places with studio windows when she knew what torture the light was, she went to doctor after doctor and they deliberately hoaxed her into taking medicines that did no good, Moira was wonderful but wouldn't let her help in any way so that she simply felt *kept*. . . .

"Who is Moira?" I asked politely, knowing that she must be Rina's mistress.

She looked oddly embarrassed, as if I were too young to be told. I grinned to myself, thinking of when we were in boarding school together and in college and of all the girls who had hated me or tried to hurt me or wept in my arms because Rina was cruel to them and loved me better. "Do you love her?" I asked as if it didn't matter, which was true.

Rina frowned peevishly. "We . . . I live with her, if that's what you mean," she said in a stiff way. "Her name is Moira Bentley-Wivers, *Lady* Bentley-Wivers. She is an exquisite Irishwoman. She will be here soon."

And then she was off again on her monologue: Moira's dog was more important in the ménage than she, the doctors took her money and laughed at her behind her back, Tanya did, too, and told Moira lies about her. . . .

Rina got up two or three times to get more barley water for herself, and when she came back, she smelled more strongly of the heavy perfume, so I guessed that she was drinking brandy or whiskey and trying to hide it. She asked me each time if I wouldn't change and let her make a wonderful sidecar, but I said no and nursed my glass. I did not feel like drinking anything at all, or even breathing.

"I fixed those flowers for you," she said, interrupting herself as if she could no longer stand the sound of the high silly voice. She sounded like my old friend again but pleading, not proud. "Do you like them? They remind me of you."

I saw that behind me, almost hidden in the angle the couch made with the wall, was a copper kettle filled with pink peonies, the pale bruised gray-pink color that only peonies can have. It was their subtle roselike fragrance I had first smelled. Now it was lost in Rina's crude perfume.

"They are lovely," I said politely. They were, but I felt bored and mean.

"I fixed them for you . . . that color against the copper . . . I knew you would like it . . . ."

"I think pewter would be better," I said, and as if my small cruelty had broken open a wound, she cried out harshly, "Oh!"

And she called me a name that only my husbands and my family have ever called me. It is a short ugly little name, but nobody else has ever dared call me by it because it is completely private. Rina had heard my sisters say it, of course, and my brother, too. Now it was more shocking than I can say to hear her use it. It was past impertinence, past importunity, like seeing a father show his idiot son for money, and it was sad in the same ignoble way.

"Oh!" Rina cried again, again calling me by that name, and she was like someone in hell, praying to the last god on the list, beating on the last closed door.

I put down my glass on the low table and thought as coldly as I could, This is probably a game she has often played, often rehearsed. It is the usual masochistic whine of a once proud, once strong and beautiful human seeing herself, whimpering in self-pity for her perversities.

But when I looked at her, I saw in her blinking pale little eyes that she was there, the old intelligent Rina, perhaps for a few seconds but truly, and I had to answer.

"What can I do, Rina?"

"You are the same. You haven't changed." She turned her

head away as if she could not stand to have me look at her eyes and said, very low, "Take off your hat. Take the pins out of your hair. Let it down so that it will be the way it used to be just once."

I had to, I felt so full of pity for her. I put my handsome little hat and the fine green veil beside me on the couch and took out the pins so that my hair fell softly down my back.

Rina looked at me without smiling, but I could see that she felt better. She leaned a little toward me, and I tried not to smell the heavy perfume on her breath.

"Oh," she said, using my private name again, "is there anyone who can help me? Do you know anyone? Look at my hands!" She held them in front of her as if they stank: pale, puffy, trembling, with bitten nails. "You know how I used to be! Is there anyone to help me?"

I remembered her firm strong body, and the way she could always do anything, *anything* at school better than we could, and how she was more exciting and brilliant than any student had ever been so that the professors feared her and girls wept for her and men stopped breathing for wanting her. All that grace and wit, all that strange electricity had been mine for the taking. But I had taken nothing. I had waited too long, and now I felt a deepening remorse in me. Perhaps if I had been more generous . . . it was too late now to tell anything but the truth.

"Rina," I said, beginning to shake again a little, "there is a man in California, an endocrinologist. It might kill you, though. You're rotten. There'd be no liquor, no love . . . no drugs. . . . I don't know whether you have the guts."

But she did not hear me. The little elevator was humming. The doorbell sounded, and then Moira and her dog were in the room, and me with my hair down and my fine hat on the couch. Tanya half-followed Moira, her hard sly face full of pleasure, and then pulled back like a snail when she saw my disarray.

Rina stood up and began fussing at ashtrays and books as she had when I first came, but I sat still, not knowing what else to do, while the tiny dog sniffed circumspectly at me and Moira stood in the middle of the room, as I had stood, slowly drawing off her gloves. I liked her, and she liked me, but we were wary. We recognized a mutual knowledge of what time could do and of our fleeting unimportance to each other.

She was a tall woman, about our age or perhaps a little older. Her torso was solid and mature, and she had lovely legs and a small head rather like mine. She wore very high heels and a subtle hat, and although her suit was tailored like Rina's, it looked female, not male. And she did not wear a shirt and cravat, but a soft silk blouse with a cairngorm shawl pin at the throat. Her hair was short, too, but not like Rina's. It was tawny, and all her clothes were the soft colors of toasted bread, warm and clear.

I cannot remember anything about her face except that it was all right—good bones, noncommittal—and that the corners of her wide mouth were as pointed as an adder's tongue and as sensitive.

All this time Rina was fidgeting. I left my hair the way it was, and I knew Moira was looking coldly at my hat and veil there on the couch. Rina had introduced us in her incredibly affected voice, and then she said, "Oh, darling . . . the embassy has been calling frantically . . . and there are flowers for you from the *vicomte* in the kitchen. Tanya wouldn't let me open them. And did you get the Packard, Moira, darling?" Like that, on and on.

Moira pulled her hat off and threw it with her gloves on the big table. "Let's have a drink, shall we?"

She smiled at me and began to talk politely about the weather and what a pity it was that the Exposition was late and weren't the peonies exquisite this year. I felt back in school again, taking a deportment lesson and saying, Yes, Miss Moira, No, Miss Moira, with my ankles crossed. And yet, as I say, we liked each other.

Rina came back in a few minutes with a shaker and three glasses, and the perfume in a cloud about her.

Moira said, "But, Rina . . . I always drink whiskey."

Rina laughed shrilly, as if Moira had made a great joke. "Darling! But it's all gone . . . I hate to say this, but Tanya looks . . . Oh, well, for once, Moira, drink one of my sidecars. You *know* how good they are . . . and we love them, don't we?"

She leered archly at me from under her crazy penciled eyebrows. She was a stranger, and an unpleasant one. I took one of the cocktails. I never tasted it, but I knew Moira did not care, any more than she cared when Rina clinked glasses elaborately with both of us and said, "First drink today! I've been a good girl today, Moira . . . nothing but barley water. Of course, Tanya would love to tell you another tale!"

"How did you two get along today, dear?" Moira spoke dutifully, like a nice husband home from the office.

Rina laughed again, like a parrot. "Beautifully," she cried. Then she turned to me. "As Tanya so aptly puts it, Moira got all three of us the same week. We all get our pay, too. Tanya cooks for her, and the Pekingese amuses her, and I ——— her."

And she used a word that I have never been able to say. I had never in my life heard Rina say anything like it. In school, she had never even goshed and helled and gollied, like the rest of us.

Moira went on sipping at her drink, and I started to put the pins back in my hair.

"M'ing!" Rina called. The little dog raised his head. He looked like a Chinese carving, there in his basket under the table. He stared for a cold second at her and then closed his eyes.

She laughed again and said gaily to me, "Do you remember

those wonderful hunting dogs your father used to have? I've told Moira about them."

Of course, my father never had any hunting dogs . . . just one old broken-down hound that wandered to the Ranch and stayed there until he died. But I murmured yes to that and some other equally outrageous things that Rina knew I knew for lies, and then said I must put on my hat. I stood up.

Moira said quickly, warmly, "Oh, but we're having supper together, aren't we? You *must* have supper with us!"

I was surprised at her urgency. And I had forgotten my invitation. I wanted more than anything in the world to go back to my hotel: I felt sleepy, the way you do when you go up a high mountain and then come down again all in one day, or one hour.

"Oh," I said, "I had hoped that you and Rina would have supper with me. We could go to Michaud's or Daniel's—they're nice—"

I saw Moira look strangely at me. "No, no," she said. She sounded almost cross. "No, we insist, don't we, Rina? You *must* have supper with us. We have a favorite little place . . . so quiet . . . and tonight is Tanya's free night or we'd all stay here . . . but I know you'll love this little place. It's very near here." It was queer to have Moira suddenly so eager. The room was almost dark, but I could see her looking at me, insisting with her whole body that I stay, that I be their guest.

"Thank you . . . I should love to." There was nothing else I felt able to say. After all, it was my own fault. I would leave early. . . .

"Rina!" Moira's voice was sharp, and Rina spilled some of her drink as she stood up heavily, clumsily, from the chair she had finally settled in. "Rina, I must call the ambassador—no, I'll write him a note, and we can post it on our way out. Will you please show Mrs. Fisher our room? She wants to rearrange her hair, I'm sure."

She's a smooth one, I thought admiringly, as Moira sat down at the desk and switched on a light beside her, and Rina went ahead of me into the shadows under the big window.

I fixed myself in the bathroom and then went into the bedroom, where Rina stood quietly by an enormous mirror. It was like the window in the other room, except that now the light on it was very delicate and somber. Rina turned her back to me, and we stood looking at each other in that glass for a long moment, not really saying anything but feeling the only peace we were ever to feel again together.

Then she laughed shrilly, and turned back, and said like a boastful little girl, "This is *my* dressing table."

It was covered with large bottles of very expensive perfume, and there were boxes of powder and several lipsticks, more like a movie star's than this pathetic woman's.

"And this is my armoire. See?" She pulled open the doors, and there were more beautifully cut suits and piles of fine silk and linen. It was like a finicky man's wardrobe, and yet not like it. "And there," we turned about-face, "are Moira's dressing table and armoire. And there is our bed."

How narrow it was, I thought. It seemed impossible that two such large people could sleep together in it, night after night, every night.

The room was like a big setting, like a sardonic Ziegfeld parody of a boarding school bedroom: matching furniture stage right and stage left, bed upstage center . . . and then the great mirror where the audience would be. Perhaps there were chairs and such . . . oh, certainly there were . . . but I really remember only that ridiculous little bed and the mirror.

We went back into the studio. Moira was writing busily under the light at the far end. Rina and I stood for a minute looking out into the soft beautiful Paris night. The horizon behind the chimney pots was like Venetian glass, lemon clear, but stars showed, and underneath there were lights, more and more.

Rina was talking, not too loud but loud enough for Moira to hear if she wished. "Now I can live. It is dark now. This window hurts me, kills me. She knows it. Everywhere we go we live in a glare like this. It tortures me . . ."

"Oh," I cried, and at my voice Rina stopped breathing, just as I had, to see flaming against the dark glassy sky a kind of torch. It was gold, and it glowed but was solid, too. Suddenly it had leapt into the night there, perhaps a half mile away from us across the roofs, and it stayed, instead of flickering away again as such strange things should rightly do.

"Rina! What is it?"

"What does it look like?" Her voice was low, impatient. "It's the statue at the Soviet pavilion—a man and a woman on a pillar."

"A man and a woman!" I laughed. "But it looks like a seal from here, with a ball on his nose. Yes, I can see it better now. It's a seal with a ball on his nose." I felt silly and almost happy, like a child. The golden thing there in the sky was magical.

Rina said something very distinctly about balls. She said it the way an old man will murmur a rhyme to a little boy, watching him to see how many of the words he knows.

"You don't think that's funny, do you?" she asked softly.

I could see by the way she swayed that she was abruptly drunk. I have watched that happen to other people who drink the way Rina did: they stay coldly, deliberately steady for almost any length of time they want to. Then, perhaps because they cannot fight their own secret demons any longer, or because they are bored, or because it is dusk or high noon or they hear someone singing in the street, they are drunk. They are drunk in the middle of a sentence. This is how it was with Rina. She was all right, in a pinched hard way, and then, standing there beside me watching the golden torch, she was suddenly very drunk.

"You don't think that's funny, do you?" she said again, loudly.

"No."

Moira came quickly to us and put her arm through Rina's. For the first time she sounded Irish when she spoke, soft and cajoling.

"Supper! Forgive me, both of you! I've kept you, and it's time for supper, surely now."

She led Rina into the bedroom. In a minute they came out, Rina in an awful hat not quite a man's but never meant for a woman, Moira smooth and cool looking, with only a finger or two on Rina's elbow to guide her.

When we got to the elevator and held open the door, it looked too small for even one of us. I said, "Please let me walk down. I hate elevators." I wasn't being polite; it was the truth.

Rina lurched away from us. "No," she said violently. "*I* hate elevators. *I'll* walk down."

Moira tried to seize her arm. "No, Rina," she cried, and her voice was full of anguish. It was the only time I heard her talk with any love. "Rina, please! It will be bad for you. You aren't well . . . your heart . . ."

I thought what a pity it was that this fine tender woman, so full of compassion, should not have her own children.

Rina laughed sneeringly, like a man who is mean drunk. She pushed Moira hard into the tiny elevator and then, without touching me, started down the first flight of curving stairs.

I got in as quickly as I could, closed the door, and pushed the button. Moira stood leaning away from me, all drooping, like the leaves on a broken branch in the hot sun. She said, "Oh, God," quietly.

"Are you unhappy?" I asked it without thought and then knew that I had been wrong: she raised her head, and her eyes were cold and the fine thin corners of her mouth trembled like adders' tongues.

"Why should I be?"

"Is she . . . are you used to this then?" I felt impertinent, like a brash child, and glad that there was no more time to be rebuffed, for we were down already.

The elevator door rolled open. Rina stood there, trying not to pant. Her face was an ugly red. She must have run all the way. It made me shudder to think of it.

"Rina! That's wonderful," Moira said warmly, and Rina's face lit up. She laughed and pulled off her horrible hat, and we went out and got into a taxi, and Moira gave an address.

Rina sat next to me. I thought for a few minutes that she had stopped being drunk, but when Moira got out to post her letter, I could tell that she was perhaps worse. She leaned against me a little, needlessly, and breathed in an excited way. It was mechanical, like a prostitute pretending, or an old man.

It was as if Rina did it because all women that close to her expected her to, but I was not all women—I was me, her longtime friend, who knew her too well ever to love her.

I made no sign of anything, and when Moira came back and saw Rina so close to me, she looked sharply at me, but I still made no sign of anything. You should go along the Elysées, I thought furiously, and get yourself one of the German girls. Yes, go along the Elysées, with some of Moira's money. Go anywhere. But *I* am *me*—

The restaurant was small, the kind that is a café during the day, with a little bar beside the cash desk and wavy mirrors behind the marble-topped tables around the walls. It was like the Roy Gourmet, if you remember that, except that it was just one room instead of two, and it was mediocre instead of good. There were waitresses, big taciturn girls. The patrons were big, too, perhaps young lawyers and functionaries and store people, with their wives and a few middle-class whores. When we came in past the row of tables under the open widows on the sidewalk, everybody stopped eating and talking and looked at us.

Now, every woman who holds her head up and looks as if she has known good love has at times made a room quiet when she has walked into it. There is something silencing, even for a few seconds, about her. It is not because of beauty or her vestments or the people with her; it is a kind of invisible music, or perfume, or color that surrounds her and makes people stop their usual thoughts and motions. When they pick up their forks, they may not even know why they put them down and may never think of the woman again, but for a time she has touched their lives, usually without meaning to.

This had often happened to me, of course, because of my bony structure and the fortunes of my years, but I had never been made either comfortable or uncomfortable by it. I had probably taken it as part of being human.

When we walked into the little restaurant, though, and all the heavy people in their black office clothes looked at us, I felt as if my skin were being pulled off. I saw their eyes slide with amazement over us: Moira so cool and disdainful, with her mouth thin and tight and her mature body tight, too, under her beautiful clothes; Rina all puffed and bullish, like a monstrous caricature of a creature neither man nor woman; and I so obviously not a partner to either, I like a slim and modish cuckoo in this ex-normal nest. They looked most at me, wondering about my green dress and my green veil probably, trying to place me in their vocabularies of behavior.

Moira and I sat against the wall at the last small table, with Rina facing us. A waitress brought us the usual blurred menus and then with a smirk took Rina's hat and hung it on the rack by the cash desk with all the other heavy dark fedoras and straws.

I was ravenously hungry—I had only eaten some cold chicken and salad that day on the early train from Vevey—and besides being empty, I felt a sort of hectic need in me, as if I had rid myself of something enormous, and all my bones were now crying for new nourishment. I wanted a meal to satisfy me, a real meal chosen with thought, a long good meal with the right wine or two.

The menu looked fairly promising. But Moira was already ordering for the three of us. She spoke French correctly but with a rather scornful flatness, as if it were a language not worth sounding out, which reminded me more of an English than an Irish person. The waitress stood looking down at us, her face blank and her eyes wearily entertained.

"The day's specialty . . . that sounds all right," Moira said. "It's too hot for anything first, of course . . . or would you like something first, Mrs. Fisher?"

I felt annoyed that such a seemingly well-bred person could be so careless, and I was disappointed, too: I had thought Moira would be more intelligent. So I said, "Yes, I would, thank you. I am awfully hungry. I'd like some pâté . . . it says *pâté d'été* here . . . that will taste good."

"Madame will take the *pâté d'été*," Moira said to the waitress in her flat insensitive French. "We will have the entrée at once and . . . and a bottle of the restaurant's *champagne nature*."

"No salad, no vegetable for the young ladies?" the waitress's voice was subtly insolent, the way Tanya's had been when she told me Rina would come in a minute.

"No. And hurry, please."

I looked at Moira, and suddenly I realized that she was terribly anxious about Rina. She wanted to get food into her as soon as possible; Rina was swaying in her chair, and her poor pale eyes were glassy. I felt ashamed of myself for changing her orders, for interrupting the quick functional flow of food into belly that this meal must be. How stupid of me to think that with a person like Rina at the table a meal could have any grace or ease or pleasure in it. It must be a feeding, that was all—a sort of sponge for extra alcohol, which was to be swallowed as quickly as possible.

Why do people like this ever eat in public? I wondered. They should take food as they take physics, in the privacy of their bathrooms.

I looked at the menu: the specialty of the day was *coq au Chambertin*. It would be ghastly with *champagne nature*. It would not be made with Chambertin either. I could tell by the looks of the place. The pâté might be all right . . . probably veal and spices with a little cubed ham discreetly through it, but cold and savory.

"Rina, some bread? Here, split it with me." I held out a big piece to her. She pushed it away.

"Rina hates bread," Moira said, "Don't you, darling?" But Rina did not answer.

Moira sat stiffly against the cheap cloth seat, and I felt that she was forcing Rina with every muscle in her body to stay conscious, to sit up, not to fall over or be sick. Her face was almost as expressionless as mine.

The waitress brought the unlabeled bottle of wine. It was very crude, but we all drank it thirstily. It seemed strange to me not to click glasses, no matter how perfunctorily, the way we always did in Vevey. It was very sour with the bread, but I felt starved.

The people, except for an occasional shrug and almost surreptitious look at us, had gone back to their own problems. Rina sat without speaking. She held her glass in both hands and drank in small rapid sips, as if the wine were hot consommé. Moira was talking to me about her house on the Riviera. She and Rina were joining her parents there, she said politely, as if either of us could be interested. There would be other people there. Did I love to swim?

"Tell her about Raoul," Rina said suddenly. Her words were almost impossible to separate one from another.

Moira looked upset for a second. "Oh, Mrs. Fisher doesn't know Raoul," she said. Then as she saw Rina open her mouth again and scowl, she went on, "Raoul is our dearest friend, our . . . father confessor, really."

"Show her his picture," Rina commanded brusquely.

Moira shrugged and without saying anything took a little leather folder from her purse. There was an old-fashioned photograph of a man in it, a slender delicate face, the hair long, the eyes rolled up, one finger of his bony hand pressed against his temple. It looked like a cruel parody of an 1890 aesthete. There was nothing to say about it, except perhaps "Oh," which I did.

"We are very fond of Raoul," Moira stated flatly. "He spends a great deal of his time with us."

"Moira keeps him. Moira keeps Tanya and M'ing and Rina and Raoul. Moira is kind, isn't she?" Rina muttered.

I could feel Moira praying desperately for the day's specialty to come. I looked at the picture facing Raoul's. One of the women was Moira, in a bathing suit. Her figure was beautiful. The other woman, sitting at her feet on a beach, was in slacks and had a heavy long mop of bright blonde hair, and for a minute I did not see that it was Rina. She looked very beautiful, too, the way I remembered her except for the hair.

"Let me see," Rina said, and pulled the folder out of my hand. She shut it after a quick look. "That's me. That was last summer. I dyed my hair. I thought it would change things." She pushed the folder back toward Moira, and I sat wondering how any human could be so different within so few months. I didn't look anywhere but ate little pieces of bread and drank my wine.

Then the waitress came with our plates piled up her arm. "Messieurs-'dames," she said insolently, and put down a casserole, and then my pâté, and the serving spoons in front of Moira. "Or does Madame prefer me to serve?" she asked. Moira picked up the spoons quickly.

"What's that?" Rina asked loudly, and looked up at the girl.

"Coq au Chambertin, as ordered."

"Coq?" And very distinctly, without smiling at all, Rina said something completely obscene about a cock in clear and perfect French. The waitress drew back, frightened, I think, and then flushing, and people around us stopped everything, the words heavy in their ears.

"Thank you, Mademoiselle . . . I can serve," Moira said, and there was something so dignified and suppliant about her voice that the girl hurried away, instead of screaming or striking Rina as she might have.

Moira put quite a lot of the chicken stew, for that is what it was, on a plate for Rina and filled her glass again. She began to eat, too, watching Rina all the time.

Rina ate a little, but she was dreadfully clumsy and kept getting bits onto her fork and then watching them fall slowly off again, the way I had seen old drunks do in hash houses on skid row in Los Angeles. There were already several smears of the dark sauce on her suit. She looked as if swallowing hurt her.

I was still very hungry, in a detached way, but I couldn't eat. The pâté, as I had thought, was far from disreputable. It was simple and savory, just what I had wanted. But now I couldn't. I tried to eat the chicken. It was fairly well made but too heavy for such a summery night. I wanted a salad—but I knew that if I had one it would not go down my throat. I drank some more wine.

Moira was talking, and perhaps I was, too, when Rina suddenly stood up. Her chair squealed against the floor, and people looked at us again, a kind of alarm now on their faces.

"Shall I come with you?" Moira asked softly.

Rina shook her head without speaking and walked unsteadily out the door and past the sidewalk babies.

We all watched her—all of us, even the waitress. The men shrugged, and the women leaned over the tables toward them to whisper strangely excited little questions, and I kept seeing long after she had disappeared down the dark street the heavy shoulders, the thin black hair on her temples, the neat hips and slender legs.

But more clearly I saw the other Rina, the proud sure one, the reckless handsome woman who had gone like a flash of lightning through so many hearts and bodies.

"The water closet is down the street," Moira said casually. "It is really too hot to eat anyway, isn't it? We should have stayed home and raided Tanya's kitchen. But sometimes Rina thinks Tanya is trying to poison her."

"And I leave so early in the morning," I lied. "I should really go back to my hotel and pack."

It seemed silly to keep up that kind of bluff, but we both did it. Rina came back. She looked a little soberer and ate some of the cold sauce on her plate with a piece of bread. She drained her glass and then said, "Pay the bill, Moira."

"I wish you'd let me," I said. "You know I asked you this afternoon, Rina . . ."

"No. Moira always pays the bill, don't you, Moira?" And Rina laughed shrilly, like a parrot again, without looking at either of us.

In the taxi we sat without talking, after I had told the driver my address. It was as if we were too tired to say anything. Moira sat up straight, but Rina was bent and sagging, like an old person. We had to stop often: the crossings were crowded with people strolling slowly, the way they always used to in Paris on warm summer nights. I felt an almost violent impatience to hurry, to end all this.

Moira shook my hand in a polite, detached way when I finally got out. "Mrs. Fisher is going now," she said to Rina.

Rina roused herself. "Good-bye," she said, and she used the name that nobody ever uses but my family and my husbands. This time it did not sound importunate or brash but only final, so that I could not resent her.

"Good-bye," I said, and went into the hotel without thanking them.

I took another bath and went to bed as fast as I could. It was as if I had a rendezvous with something in my sleep. I rushed to meet it.

And this is where I regret the lost pages I wrote the next morning in the *brasserie,* because I wrote mostly about the dream. It was a long dream, one of the most vivid I had ever had, and I woke from it panting and shaking with a kind of abysmal horror such as I had never felt before.

This is all I can remember now: I was on a high wall, watching a long stretch of beach where little blue waves edged with white curled symmetrically, as in a Chinese embroidery. And down the beach raced a great roan horse with a golden mane. He reared back at the wall, and then, time after agonizing time, he hurled himself at it in an orgy of self-destruction. It was terrible. Time after time he leapt straight at the wall with all his strength, and there was a sound of breaking sinews and flesh, and everywhere there was his blood, bright imperial yellow blood, while the little waves rolled silently, symmetrically. . . .

I awoke, and it was as if I were drowning in horror. Then I went to the bathroom and was sick, and put cold water on my face and brushed my hair very hard. I went to sleep again, and everything was all right, as if I were a little child.

In the morning, as I have said, I felt strange. It was as if I had been poisoned and then violently washed clean of the poison. The porto-flip finished the job and made me feel warmed and fed again. I drank it dutifully, not liking it but knowing its reason, and paid my bill and put all the sheets of paper in my purse and walked out into the sunlight, past the filled noontime tables on the sidewalk.

People looked casually at me as I went by, as I would have done in their places, and suddenly, because of last night and the stares and shrugs there in the little restaurant, I felt as shy and ill at ease as a young girl. The thought of going alone to lunch, *anywhere,* was impossible.

But my father and mother would not be in Paris until late afternoon. . . .

I walked slowly toward the Tuileries, gradually getting used to humanity again, like a soul sent back to earth. I stood in the sun for a long time by one of the round fountains with the fat glass pigeons.

In the gardens under the plane trees I bought a ham sandwich and sat on a chair eating it and watching some little boys sail their boats across the pond.

By the time I had to go back to the hotel I was young, untouched by evil. I was ready to be with my dear parents, and I was ready to meet love alone again, not asking for another person's comfort, nevermore to thirst for any flagon but my own.

—Paris, 1937

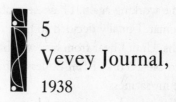

5
Vevey Journal,
1938

The purpose of any diary I might keep in this book, when I started it over a year ago, was to tell what was happening with the building of Le Pâquis. It was soon plain to me, however, that any such chronicle was beyond my talent as a writer and that even a poor compromise between the house and its builders would be impossible. Things went too fast and inevitably toward an undreamed conclusion. The house was built, and much we had built or hoped to see grow in it was forever broken. What grew in its place, in our several hearts, it is too early to identify.

For a long time it was better to write nothing than the stiff comments I permitted myself. Now I feel easier, but I admit that today I write this simply because I want to write and am too lazy, too mazy, to work on something that needs more thinking. Here I can write some, at least, of the thoughts that drift in and out of my brain. A story or an article would need construction.

I am in a high-tide pool just now, waiting for the cold impetus to send me working again. I have sent off some stories to London, to the woman I finally decided to have for my agent for a trial of six months. Until I hear from her, which will probably be after she returns to New York, I feel do-less. That is one way of trying to vindicate my laziness.

I have several new books for research and a fat envelope of notes, but I have an aversion to doing anything but vague mental nibbling at the Quaker story for a while yet. Laziness again, partly.

I have been back from America for sixteen days now and have done no work except a short introduction for Jake Zeitlin. My whole existence has become more completely physical than ever before in my life: I eat, sleep, listen, even cook and read with an intensity and a fullness that I have never felt until now. I am completely absorbed in myself—but myself as seen through Timmy. It is a strange life, and one that cannot last long probably. I am abandoned to it now—and probably this need to write in a journal is one sign that it is almost over. I know it can never end completely. It must shift and change, though. I know enough to know that, at least.

After the monotonous dry perfection of the climate at the Ranch, this weather is as stimulating and exciting as a new symphony or a play. I stand at the windows or lie in my bed, watching and wondering about it: what does that round brown cloudlet mean? Will it be clear tomorrow, or in half an hour? Where do the feathers of snow go after they drift down so surely? They go on through the earth's surface—and then where?—like ghosts through a closed door. Do I see burgeons swelling the lilac twigs? No. Yes.

At night my ears hear the fountain as easily and constantly as a mother hears the blood-beat of her child still to be born. I awake to its changed rhythm and know in the second before I sleep again that one of our winter lettuces, bought days ago and kept fresh in the cold water, had drifted under the stream spouting from the short bronze spigot. Or perhaps the extra beat I hear is Lou-Lou from across the road, slaking a midnight thirst with thick slaps of his tongue. Or even a quiet wanderer is there. I am not alarmed, as long as the rhythm is resumed.

The days are growing longer. I like the long days of summer, but I feel cheated, resentful almost, that this winter I missed all the short ones. Last summer when we were working so constantly on the garden, I'd think, When winter comes, there'll be no long lighted evenings so good for watering and picking, and I'll go into my warm dark hole like an animal and write and think and listen to music.

But this winter I was in America, more occupied with time-bound things than I have ever been, and now it is almost time to start digging and planting again. I have another excuse for not writing, and feel relieved and disappointed and ashamed.

Occasionally a car goes by too fast. I hear it coming up or down the hill, and almost before I can look up, it is far past the window. Horses are different, slower and easier to hear. They still wear their winter bells. (I wonder why not bells in summer?) Sometimes two men are on one cart, and then I hear the rough low voices. In another month, they will be singing.

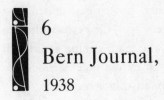

6
Bern Journal,
1938

One thing about writing is that it takes time. This last month I have thought of perhaps a thousand things, to estimate conservatively, that for some perverse reason I should like to write about —sights or smells or sounds, or occasionally ideas. This last month—

It is 9:14 at night, a queerly noisy night, with at least two radios blaring from somewhere over the Kornhaus Bridge, and many people walking past the hospital, and trains racketing with extra fervor from the stop by the theater across the Aare to the Kursaal. I can look out and see the lights slide along the wet black bridge and the dull shapes of two floodlit towers push up into the sky.

I finish a glass of brandy, and want to write about this month, and know that I am too sleepy. And then I wonder why I do want to write about it, because I despise talk, and the people who talk, who tell others about themselves, and the dreadful necessity that pushes them to such confessions. They must talk. They must expose themselves. It helps them, and more horribly, it helps others.

That is what bothers me. I hate this need. I've never done much of it, and I despise it in others. But I know that I am more articulate than some, and I think, Well . . . my God in heaven! If what I've learned about pain or food or the excreta of the sea snail can help even one poor human, I am a rat not to write. Then I know I am wrong.

And now, at 9:23, I am writing, for the first time in more than a month. My eyes are sanded with sleep, and my back is numb against the two limp Swiss pillows.

I look up at the mirror above my washstand to see if there is light reflected from Timmy's room. We tried two pills tonight, which did no good, and then gave the old faithful shot of Analgeticum at 8:00. He is asleep, heavily, with his mouth dropped askew. I am fairly sure that by 12:00 he will call me. Then it will be Pantopon.

I can't understand so much noise from town, but, of course, people are still celebrating that there's no war. It would have been today. Yesterday Switzerland would have had general mobilization. Of course, we are all glad. I am, and so is Timmy. I don't like the idea of those bombs the Germans tried on Barcelona, which are made of aluminum filled with liquid air. I wouldn't mind being killed outright by one, but I am sure that the people who were a quarter mile away and were stunned by them had dreadful headaches.

I hear the cathedral clock strike 9:30. It always rings first. I have tried to listen to one certain hour to see if all the clocks ever make the same pattern, but even at 3:00 in the morning they never strike the same way twice. Sometimes they make a beautiful sound. I heard that Shostakovich regretted using so many themes in his first symphony, because he had so few left. He should come here,

to the Viktoria Hospital—the night bells across the dark Aare
would tell him many new ones.

2.x.38

After three days of rain it is really hot in the sun. I sit on Timmy's
balcony in a green skirt, a white sweater, and his gray coat, which
I'll soon take off. Through the crooked glass I see him, distorted
as one of his own drawings of pain, being bathed by Sister Irma.

Yes, I must take off the coat. As I wriggle out of it, I smell a
faint musky hot smell that almost reminds me of something, about
something, we once did together. Was it walking up a hill? Or was
it something about a sea pool, with us bending over? No, I cannot
say. I feel as if some sound or smell had almost recalled a dream.
There for a second was the dream. But what dream? It is too late.
Perhaps again sometime it will almost be clear again.

I smell rather rummy, too. I am sure that I've read of people
who put wine in their pipes to burn out the varnish or some such
thing. So with the awful-looking pipe I bought yesterday, because
Timmy has decided that now is a good time to learn to smoke one.
Sister Irma and I have been playing with it for the last half hour.
It wouldn't light at all at first, and the nasty pinkish rum kept
dropping out of the mouthpiece, and finally it sputtered a few
times. Now I stink worse than the pipe well, I know, in spite of its
being a cheap shiny one. I wish I could remember how Al liked
his—he did it so well and lovingly.

Anne left this book, which is hard to write in. It's the one she
meant to keep a journal in. She told me that this was the first
summer for twenty-five years that had passed without her filling
several notebooks with diary. A good thing, I think. This time last
Sunday, or perhaps a little later, she and Timmy and I were lis-

tening, by his open door, to the earnest singing of ten Swiss. They came, dressed in their church clothes, to sing to a member of their club who is ill here. Their voices were strong and sweet, and a yodel came up like bells through the hideous hospital corridors. We were truly thrilled, and Tim's face looked quiet. So I put twenty francs in an envelope and wrote on it that someone wished the singers to drink to the world's health. Irma took it down, protesting that such a thing had never been done and beaming with excitement. And then there was a great scuffling and stamping of thick shoes and a whispering, and there was the *Sängerbund* outside the door. They sang and sang, with that rather forced lugubrious hymning that creeps into all Swiss songs but with a yodel that never missed the tone, like a true bell. We were pleased by that, and I at last was bored by the chapelish verses, and then to our surprise all the singers shuffled in and shook hands with Timmy, Anne, Irma, and me. They got in a great tangle of crossed arms and embarrassment, and I, too, felt quite self-conscious, saying, *"Merci, danke schön! Merci bien,"* to ten stiff young men.

I was sorry David and Noni weren't here to listen—they'd have been excited and amused, and Dave jealous of the yodeling. It was my fault that they had not come early. When they left the night before for Die Pension Schmultz, Noni had said, "When shall we see you—9:00, 10:00, 10:30?" And I'd said, "Oh, tomorrow's Sunday—let's all sleep." They had looked a little disappointed, I thought. And then how sorry I was, in the morning, that I'd said that!

But still I dreaded to see them. At 8:00 in the morning, Dr. Nigst came in while I was drinking tea, and when I asked him how things were going with Hitler, he lifted his arms and let them flop against his sides, and said, "I really don't know. I cannot feel war near, but—yes, it looks bad." That was the first time he had said that. And then in about ten minutes came a cable: "Arrange children sailing have written Edith." I read it to Tim and for a minute almost cried, thinking of their disappointment and how much more excited Noni was about the accordion lessons than the German ones. But I knew Edith and Rex wouldn't ask them to change all their plans for a hasty thoughtless reason. So I began to gird myself to tell the children they must leave Europe and us and go back to American schools again. I watched for them to come across the bridge and rehearsed how I'd tell them. When I saw them striding along, with the rather shambling deliberate steps of all tall people, I felt sad and nervous.

They were quiet, of course. Noni cried a little, not with sobs but with silent tears that ran down her cheeks and made her blow her nose. Then I told them to . . .

3. x. 38

A cold hard night, the first really cold one. It is only 8:30, but I am tired and in bed. Tim sleeps motionless as a tiger. These nightly bouts of pain are dreadful. I don't know how many more of them either of us can stand. He had Analgeticum at 8:00. Last night Nigst tried a mixture of Pantopon and scopolamine that made him cry out and weep and babble in the few hours of sleep it gave him. His nerve is finally breaking. He shakes and cries when he feels one of these bouts coming. I am weary and so often frightened. And what must he be?

There is a fair in one of the squares across the Aare. Its melodeon annoys me, faintly, like a gnat. It reminds me of the fair in Vevey.

But I'll write about that another time. My brain teems with memory, but my eyes are heavy. They always are now. I know things will change soon. They *must*. Almost five weeks of ceaseless agony—

This morning the handsome tall postulant came to make my bed, and I went into Tim's room. In a minute there was a small crash. I wondered what—perhaps a vase, or the blown-glass chicken filled with curaçao that Anne and the children had brought me. In a minute more, I went in to get a handkerchief. The postulant was whiter than ever, and the brown circles under her eyes were almost black, but it wasn't until tonight that I noticed that the bedside lamp with its glass shade was gone. Now I have an unbelievably old-fashioned thing in a discreet wired skirt of faded cretonne, which throbs with misdirected electricity when I come within two inches of it and gives, with the mellow generosity of a drunken miser, not quite enough light to write by. It was so silly, like a Rube Goldberg invention, that Tim had to stop his strange yelps of pain to laugh at it when I took it into his room.

I am drinking what is left of a bottle of bad champagne, now slightly warm, from a toothbrush tumbler. I like it.

When I opened the windows tonight, Bern looked like the more than beautiful backdrop in a heavenly Orpheum Music Hall, with bogus lights on all the towers—cathedral, clock tower, market, parliament—and lights pricked fakily all along the Aare and then up the funicular beyond the town to the high hotel.

I can think of a lot of things to write about. Almost any sentence starts a long string of—not thoughts—of reminiscences, impressions. For instance: today an enormous box of really exquisite pale powdery gold chrysanthemums, on long stems with intense dark leaves, came from those inane pale stupid people, the

Beutlers. Immediately we thought of how she had been so ill and we had not even asked what hospital she was in. Of course, we hardly knew them then—but still— And then I remembered her truly warm sincere note, after Tim came here—the schoolgirl language, so banal, and how nicely and thoughtfully and dully they had entertained us in their new house. I remembered the good bad paintings and the Third Symphony that nobody really heard but was still played from a something-or-other kind of cabinet that had been copied from one in the Palace at Avignon by Freddie's cabinetmaker. And then the queer people—the pudgy misunderstood genius of a bank clerk who dribbled his way egotistically from Chopin through Brahms and on to Grieg, with none of us daring to break the rapturous spell of Real Music.

The little fair across the river bellows out its silly gramophone records. It makes the sight of Bern at night even more theatrical—and sometimes I can hear the measured racket of a coaster machine, and the occasional scream of an excited girl, or a man's hoarse shout.

I had tea yesterday at the Nigsts'. It's a queer apartment, with a dressing table all laid out with silver-backed toilet things in the hall so that the patients can tidy themselves before or after they see the doctor. A shy little maid stood by helplessly while I wrestled with my rubber boots. Then I went into the salon, which has very bad, very modern paintings on mulberry damask wallpaper, and an elaborate, shiny-as-only-Swiss-furniture-can-be-shiny set of furniture upholstered in "rich" blue damask, and a table with some flowers on it and the kind of Japanese china tiger—scarlet—that could only be won in a shooting gallery at home.

Tea was strong enough to trot a mouse on, served from the kitchen already poured in after-dinner coffee cups, and a huge basket of delicious hot stuffed croissants (we each took one), and then a huge tray of rich cakes (we each—three of us—took one), and then dry vermouth for the doctor and me, and cigarettes for us all.

Coming home, the doctor got around for the third time to his vacation and how he'd be alone and dining out, and finally said (I felt like the innocent girl being asked to come up to see some etchings), "But do you never go out anymore for meals, now that your brother and sisters are gone?" Hell, I thought to myself. "No," I said sadly. "But why not, Miss Parrish?" We swerved wildly down the street. Well, he's asked for it, I thought. "Because I really don't like to eat alone," I said with a brave, sad, resigned look—I think. "But"—and we swerved a double swerve—"may I ask you to dine once with us? We have—we eat—I mean to say—" "Oh—but how nice of you, Dr. Nigst! Of course, as you know, if my husband does not go well—" "Oh, but Miss Parrish, I *promise* you that all will be most successful and content!"

I have a half-inch of flat mock champagne still to finish. The mock music grinds flatly on. I think with sharp poignancy of my poor Rex, Edith, torn by the first doubts of old age and their own impotence, of Anne ground between the wheels of self-knowledge and self-dramatization, of David and Norah all too quiet and too knowing. I think of Tim, lying rocked in the dark opiate arms of Analgeticum, lulled by the weariness of a shot of Pantopon. I think, vaguely and not too close, for safety's sake, of myself here, there, drugged or alive or dreaming or hysterical—

Schwester Irma left a vase for the Beutlers' chrysanthemums in front of a pot of small white garden blossoms. From my bed I cannot see that the flowers are not springing, cut off and lovely, from water in the vase. But I know that it is empty and that they are growing in the earth, behind it.

8. x. 38

I t is reluctantly that I write, and truly I don't know why I bother. Shall I write in that book tonight, I have asked myself several times today, or shall I have a whole day without a duty letter or a letter home or even a scrap of bread cast upon my own literary waters, even a note thrown to my own future?

Now it is 20:20, and I am in bed, and I have a more than moderately amusing detective story, in a green and white paper cover, called *Obelisk at Sea,* and a brandy and soda. And Timmy seems quiet, with the *piqûre* earlier so that Irma could go have her heels straightened before the shoemaker closed shop.

But I am tired—and dull. Last night I slept a long, disturbed, wretched sleep, filled with half-waking dreams of puzzlement and stress. Tim only called three times, and I slept until 8:00 this morning—but God, I am tired. I look well. I *am* well. But sometimes I feel weary, weary, weary.

This morning I woke stuffily, heavily, to realize that the winds of the night had probably blown, too, for Anne and the children, a few hours out of Liverpool. I thought of them with love and pain, pain for them all but especially for Noni. And I was thankful they were gone, at least by distance, from my immediate life.

I hurried to wash and put on a little lipstick, Vaseline on my eyelids, two faint lines of brown eyebrow pencil, two swipes of blue eye shadow to match the blue stars on my scarf and my blue flannel bathrobe, and then a little powder. I brushed my hair and put a ribbon around my head—a blue ribbon, of course.

Then I fixed Tim's coffee. He was dreamily cheerful, after the best and the longest (six hours) sleep for over five weeks. (It's five weeks today since he had the second operation, and I lay here wishing he would die.)

Then I came back to bed and drank my pale tea and ate an

unusually tasteless bun, with butter and synthetic apricot jam. I had a faint nagging ache in my belly.

For a change, I got up before Tim's bath, and dressed, and then held him by his beautiful blue-white hair while he bobbed helplessly about the tub of saltwater. Sometimes he is really very funny. I cackle—I can't help it—and so does Irma—and then we sound so funny that he laughs, too, even in great pain. I couldn't possibly say what is funny, but I find myself really *cackling*—and then when he begins his careful, high, cautious half-laugh, I am helpless. I know he has to do it, so he won't budge his side—but it is funny still.

Then there were massages and so on, with Nigst coming in in the middle, moving very carefully with what I suspect was a hangover from his wife's leaving last night, and then Irma and Schwester Agnes Ina almost driving Tim crazy trying to clean his leg with benzine. They dabbed balsam juice of some kind on the two places in his leg that look bad.

Then he had a raw egg, and we each drank a little brandy highball while I read a story by G. B. Stern, an obvious, facile, and very entertaining one in a book called *Pelican Walking,* I think.

Tim dressed for lunch, and we ate in my room—always his wretched bouillon with a bromide tablet in it, sweetbreads with aubergine (not enough), a roasted pigeon with rice, a glass of St. Emilion 1929, some strange vegetable-marrowish-looking vegetable we didn't taste, a bite of the watery Bernois salad, and some surprisingly good plum tart.

Afterward we put on a few more scarves (the hospital is still far from well heated) and walked across the Kornhaus Bridge. We stopped at the bodega, the Café Zu Den Pyrameau, and drank a sherry. It was a bad sherry, but it is a sympathetic little bodega, and the waiter and the pudgy proprietor are nice—so quietly thoughtful, without drawing attention to us.

We hopped on down the cold street, with people looking nicely at us or not at all, and Tim doing things with his usual meticulous grace. I have a horror of his putting one crutch into a grating, but I don't think he ever will. He is so well balanced that the vision of his ever crashing over fills me with a nightmare terror. But he won't.

We went to the Café du Théâtre, where the chasseur and the waitress were nice and brought us English journals full of diagrams on how to build a bomb-proof shelter or where to run in Hyde Park, and two café-cognacs—with free cookies! We wondered if anybody but us remembered the fine meal that Timmy ordered there, a few minutes before he felt the strange cramp in his leg more than five weeks ago. We'd often cogitated about going to the Théâtre, and then when we finally decided to, Timmy couldn't until today.

We walked to the taxi stand by the casino, and a kind ratlike man drove us slowly to the Viktoria. Timmy managed the getting in and out beautifully.

For almost half an hour after he got into bed again, it looked as if he'd fool them this time. But then, after one swallow of hot tea, he was almost out of his head, with the teacup rattling on his chest and his eyes wild. It was a bad siege. He whispered craftily to me, for the hundredth, the thousandth time, that *now* was the time to help him die. Then he yelped and chattered, like a hyena.

Irma, her eyes red—that, too, for the hundredth time—gave him two Pyramidons with a solemn impersonal face. And somehow, with radio and Rachel Field's new book and me and so on, we lulled him on until 6:00. I lay down for a while, weary and feeling a little sick. But supper, except for his fretting, tapping fingers and an occasional strange look in his wide eyes, was fun. And then soon after, he washed himself and undressed, and we gave him the little glass of heart drops, and the swig of Niyol, and the tea with a Urotopin tablet in it, and finally the shot of Analgeticum.

And now he is quiet, and I am tired, and I think I'll read a few pages of my green and white book and then sleep. My brain is almost bursting—Noni, tomorrow, Adelboden, La Tour—but I know that before midnight Tim will need me—

17.x.38

"D'you know something about my leg?

"It's that, from where it was cut on down, I can't remember *one goddamn* distinguishing feature!

"It was just a leg.

"It had an ingrowing nail on the big toe—on the inside, I *think*. But I'm not sure.

"Isn't it queer? Simply another leg."

Probably there is in all intelligent people, of whom I consider myself one (perhaps mistakenly, I add without any apparent coyness), a constant warfare between innate delicacy and reserve, and the desire to talk, to Tell All. I am often conscious of it, and oftener than not I refuse to indulge in my natural itch to write because of an overfastidious fear of what may be scratched into being, into the light of paper. Often, at night, I don't want to go to sleep when I come into my bedroom from the last business of tea and injection and pillow smoothing with Timmy. I say, Now I can write in my book! Then I add, What? Then quicker than is decent, I add, But what? What can I, what *should* I say? Why in hell, why in the name of Edith, Rex, and all the host *should* I write *any*thing? Why should anyone write anything? And so the old hackneyed twice-cursed thrice-monotonous wheel turns once again.

Next week we go to Adelboden. Already I eye the eight weeks' collection of books on my bureau and my table and count the number of cakes of soap we may need. Of course, there'll be an adequate and probably, during the ski season, a highly sophisticated pharmacy up there, but my pioneer instincts are still adamant, in spite of some thirty thwarted years. The hearts of all my white chrysanthemums are turning brown. I was thinking I'd give them to the little scullery maid with pale hair and hectic cheeks, who came shyly to play the guitar. But they are no longer lovely.

Tonight we went to Doetwylers', and unfortunately it was mediocre. Going up the stairs I spoke, without turning or loosening my grip on Timmy's arm, to the shopwoman, and Tim very neatly fell back a whole step. It upset him, and me, and the shopwoman, and the busboy who leapt up and practically carried . . .

A little whimper—

"What's the matter, darling?"

"Those goddamn mice!" in a deep voice, like Chaliapin.

. . . carried him to our table. None of us raised an eyebrow. Later Timmy said that his leg suddenly seemed to grow six feet long and to search frenziedly all about for a step, like the gigantic proboscis of a moth feeling for nourishment at night.

23.x.38

Today, after almost three weeks of fine blue autumn days, it is cold and darkly gray. I am listless, moonstruck. Timmy is in greater pain than usual, feverishly ill at ease. We go out, and after peering into several steamy cafés, whose floors, cluttered with dogs and cigar butts and spittle and a few children, spell disaster to crutches, we go to the Schweizerhof for beer and a gin-vermouth for me.

Home in a taxi, and while I watch Irma massage the smooth white curve of his hip, I am quietly horrified to see a purplish blotch above the bandage. It seems slightly smoother. Is it a bruise from trying on the temporary peg, day before yesterday? I am appalled and go away without speaking.

24.x.38

The first four hours in Adelboden. Yesterday was bad, because of weather, and what is probably a bruise from Timmy's trying on a prosthesis, and so on. But last night was fairly good. This morning Irma was like a little excited brown badger, and I became amazingly vague, wandering between the two rooms with my hair down and pieces of packing in my hands. Finally she got us all into boxes and sacks and bundles, like refugees. Tim and I fled to the Café du Théâtre for lunch. We had each planned secretly to order caviar or perhaps oysters and champagne, and we both ordered grilled steaks with *pommes* chips and a good old *bourgogne*.

I drove up to Adelboden. Nigst's friend, the Colonel Garagiste, who may be buying our car, sent us a monkeylike little chauffeur in very good livery, who worked hard and well to get all Irma's bundles arranged and then wedged himself into and under and over them beside her on the backseat. She permitted herself her sole ribaldry by saying, "Oh, Madame, there is not even a package between us, and I doubt if there is any danger—but one never knows!"

I drove up, under, and through, and then suddenly above a

milky October fog, and occasionally saw in the mirror the wan simian face of the chauffeur. He leaned his head with complete relaxation against my gray coat, which was wrapped around the dreadful *prosthèse provisionneur* [temporary prosthesis], a thing heavy and rigid with plaster and black wood for a peg and wretched canvas straps. Now and then he dragged languidly at a cigarette from one packet Timmy had given him and looked with slow mischievous eyes at Irma.

Up here all was ready, even to a gay bunch of blue and yellow flowers in the sitting room. We bustled. Timmy and I drank, between suitcases, a flat brandy and water. We kept looking at the mountains, the nearest and most beautiful I have even seen. Near their tops they are like the mesas in the West, hard and sculptured against an infinite blue sky.

Now, after a good supper, Tim sleeps precariously from Analgeticum, and I sit in my narrow bed, under the strange high feather puff. I hear the slowed autumnal rush of water far below, and even past my balcony light I see the hard prick of the stars. My cheeks burn; my eyes, too. I am excited and yet half-asleep, eager to wake early to watch from my window the sun upon the mountains.

27. x. 38
13:40

In a few minutes I go down through thick milky mist to the pharmacy, along the straight sleeping street lined with closed shops and pensions. It is cold. When I look out the window, here in the warm room filled with the staid strains of Handel's Concerto Grosso, I might be on a ship, fogbound to the sound of invisible cowbells from below, or in an airship, as well as in this snug Swiss hotel.

I cannot permit myself the doubtful luxury of thought. I am too close to frenzy, to a wild anxiety.

The first day was not bad. The second day, after only Timmy slept well, thanks to Analgeticum and Pantopon, was exciting. The Nigsts came. We had drinks on the terrace and then went down for lunch, with Nigst clucking like a hen over Timmy's agility on the stairs. Timmy overate, to please him. Later the local doctor, von Derschwanden, came for café on the terrace. At first he reminded me of a wretched sordid little snob I once knew from Manchester—not so much his manner, which was brisk behind his English pipe, but his mussed and pudgy English slacks and brown tweed coat. (Now I like him, even more than Nigst, I think. His hands are sensitive and investigatory, and he thinks of everything.)

That night was not bad. Yesterday was wretched, with fever for the first time above 37.5 degrees, and the right leg very painful. Last night was all right—injections, of course.

This morning the doctor came. I could see he was worried—congestion in the main artery of the right leg, general low condition.

Timmy lies for hours with an open book or journal before him. Occasionally he turns a page, but he has read nothing. Slow tears slip down his cheeks, and now and then he shakes violently and clutches me and sobs.

I must go down to the pharmacy.

I stay in the sitting room because I think I upset him a little when I sit in his room. I keep thinking, He may die—other people do—and then I will be sick at the thought of the times I spent here when I could be there. I'll try to begin a book today.

Whenever I start to write, I seem to think of nothing but sadness. Perhaps it is because I never talk of it. Tonight I am almost intolerably depressed. I don't know quite why. I'm not one to be downed by weather that is usually thought to be mournful. But all seems wrong. Of course, the main thing is that Timmy is not so well. I try to tell myself—and him, when I have to—about the effects of altitude and so on. But I cannot convince myself that all those things could make such a difference in him—fever 37.8 ½ degrees now again, and surely higher at 8:00, and pain in the *other* leg, and this general withdrawal from me and life. He looks at me and seldom sees me. Everything he must save, all his various strengths, to fight the weariness, to hold at bay the bouts of pain, to keep himself on the right side of hysteria. I can see it all.

I stay near but away, where he can see me but not have to look at me. Often I keep the radio going. (It plays now, and it almost drives me frantic.) I tried to write, this afternoon, but I couldn't—Irma, a nap, talk, Tim calls me, so on.

I try to play the phonograph. That, at least, I have thought all along, will be wonderful, this wonderful. But it has something wrong, a grinding sound that creeps above everything but jazz. I tried to play "Es ist Vollbracht." It was terrible. And even with that grinding, it made things seem too sad. Then, when I said, "Do you like that, Timmy?" he answered, "What?"

I found that my favorite album is not here, the Sibelius concerto, and I paid for sending them all from Le Pâquis only today. Others are missing—and now it is too late to reclaim them.

And the man called about the car, to sell it at 2,700 francs. I said yes, probably unwisely. But it will be one less thing to worry about.

Of course, we have often been low before. Occasionally things seemed so bad, at the Viktoria, that I wondered if we could stand it. We never spoke about it. And then in the morning all would be well—a decent night, a blue sky, a good letter—

The strange faculty I developed, during my last years with Al, of shutting myself off has stood me in good faithful stead lately. It is only occasionally, as now, that it *almost* doesn't work. Usually I can shut parts of my realization, of my intelligence, off, rather as a ship's engineer shuts off various parts of a sinking ship. I can almost feel doors close—then—then. It is good, for the moment at least. I think it may have turned me into a duller person than I was—but at least I'm safer from myself.

There is much I can never write about. All this is superficial.

1.xi.38
Hotel Bärem Adelboden, Switzerland

Dearest Rex and Edith—

Night before last things looked very bad, so I asked von Derschwanden to call Prof. de Quenain in Bern. (He is the famous surgeon and diagnostician who did the first two operations and has been away for six weeks. I think he is much better than Nigst, who is really just a surgeon, although a very good one. Nigst is in Paris now and will be absolutely sick to find what has happened. Everything looked so well in Bern.) De Quenain told the doctor to call him again in the morning, after a urinalysis. He came up about noon. After a long consultation, the two men decided that a very bad case of phlebitis had developed, concentrating in the right groin and lower abdomen. They are completely mystified, not only as to what caused it but as to why it formed in the veins this time, instead of the artery. I asked them if it was a condition of the

blood, and they said perhaps—but perhaps also it could be a
paralysis of the walls of the veins. When I asked what caused *that,*
they simply raised their hands. They have never seen anything like
it, especially in a man of Tim's age.

It means from six weeks to three months of absolute mo-
tionlessness, and then all the walking to begin over, if he can. I
asked them if it would mean the right leg would always be dangerous, and they said no. But I think they are lying.

You can imagine what this new development has done to Tim,
who was already beginning to be dreadfully worn down by the
constant pain from the amputation. He has no desire to live, and I
feel the same way often. I don't know what will happen—he has
that terrible strong heart of the Parrishes, which has already pulled
him, against his wishes, through two things that should have killed
him. He looks like a ghost and has lost all of that spirit which even
in the worst days made him do very funny things with a perfectly
straight face. He lies absolutely still, of course, with his leg raised
on pillows, and seldom talks or even looks at Irma or me. He holds
a book in front of him and turns a page every hour or so. His one
interest is to get the first shot, about 8:30 at night, but he doesn't
even mention that anymore—just looks at the clock.

There are constantly things to be done—compress, drops,
injections, on and on. Irma is staying indefinitely—has given up
her case in Lugano.

Both doctors said that even if Tim could be moved, they'd
advise our staying here. I feel rather uncomfortable, because no
matter how nice the *Huldis* [hotel managers] are, a trained nurse
and all the hot-water bottles and so on *do* make a difference in a
small hotel. But there's nothing to do about it.

It's beautiful now—the snow is melting after two clear blue
days, and I can sit on the terrace for lunch.

Tim is still quite nauseated—de Quenain said it was because

the vein to the stomach is almost closed, which causes congestion —and has eaten only a little bouillon and cooked fruit for a week now. He's very thin.

We've ordered a hospital bed from Bern, or Lutenaken maybe, and as soon as his fever goes down, he can be out on the terrace.

All this is rotten luck, and I hate to tell you about it because I know how sad you'll be for both of us. It's really terrible to me to see Timmy without any spirit, because that has never yet deserted him. I feel confident, though, that if he lives through it at all, he'll get back his old life.

Thank God we have money enough to last for several more months. That would be the last straw, to have to be separated, with T. in a charity ward and me at the Y.W.C.A. or some such place. We're very comfortable here—and I sold the car for $575, which will help.

I must stop. Do write often, and tell me the news about everybody. Don't worry about me. This is no fun, but I'm taking very good care of myself—

2. xi. 38

I just posted, after much deliberation, an order for 115 Tanchnitz and Albatross and Penguin books. Aside from their costing about $80 and so becoming one of the most extravagant actions of my whole life, I felt from the first that they were an admittance of weakness in my nature. It is easy enough for me to justify wanting them, as Timmy said today that it was easy for any woman to defend her inability to eat less than she wanted. But the truth is that it is and will be much pleasanter for me to read book after book of silly "mysteries" than to make myself work. Of course, if

I were a real writer, predestined, dedicated, I'd work in the face of everything. (And even without that fate, I write constantly in my head—stories, paragraphs, phrases, sometimes the skeletons of novels.) But as it is now, I feel almost hysterical at the thought of concentrating on one thing. I am never left without interruption (here are the self-justifications!) for more than fifteen or twenty minutes, and when I am in another room from Timmy's, his door is always open so that I can hear what he does or says and be ready to interpret Irma's talk or help her. I've never held one way or the other with some creative souls' demand for absolute privacy, although Woolf's theory of 100 pounds and a room of one's own seems attractive personally—but I truly don't feel keen enough at this time to be able to put aside all thought of the present while it is moving and moaning ten feet to the left of me.

I notice two things about this life, since the first night at the Bärem: my increased fastidiousness and my equally increased *gourmandise.* Since I can remember, I've been very clean, but now I spend long serious minutes, after my bath, drying each toenail; I wash my navel or my ears as if they were Belleek china teacups; a tiny hangnail sends me hurrying for scissors, oil, all the minutiae of a complete manicure. And I have become almost piggish . . . not in my manners, for I eat slowly and daintily . . . but I eat too much. The food here is good, especially after the tasteless monotony of the hospital. But there is too much of it. Today at noon there was a rich clear consommé with egg cooked in it, ravioli with tomato sauce and cheese, roast chicken with puree of potatoes, brussels sprouts, and a chocolate cream with wafers. So rich! I eat in the little sitting room. First I have a small glass of vermouth with T., while Marta is setting the table. Then I take him a cup of the soup and the crust of a slice of bread broken into bites. Then I sit down, with a book—today, *High Wind in Jamaica.* I ate all the raviolis, with a glass of wine. Then I took T. a little chicken cut into morsels and a little applesauce. I ate the brussels sprouts, and drank another glass of wine, and then some chocolate pudding and three wafers. Then I ordered a cup of coffee and drank a small glass of cognac with it. Usually I eat a lot of salad, on which I put a spoonful of meat juice with a strange voluptuous solemnity. I am interested in this slowness and this solemnity. I suppose it is a desire to escape, to forget time and the demands of suffering.

Another thing is the way I dress: I've always been rather finicky about colors and so on, but now I find myself looking at my reflection in any mirror with a smug satisfaction, noting complacently the way my sweater, my socks, the ribbon in my hair are the same blue as the shadow on my eyelids, and how the black of my slacks and my sandals makes all the blues more beautiful. It is queer, and slightly boring, but I suppose it won't get any worse.

After a day part cloudy and part sunlit, light from behind the western mountains beams suddenly across the valley and brings my mountains close enough to lean against. The snow of seven nights ago melts fast, and cliffs I never dreamed of stand out with abrupt starkness from the white slopes, their rock sides cozy in the unexpected light. Lower down, the pine trees are oily green-black, clustered like plant lice in diminishing dots up the mountain. At the bottom, the foamy, dirt-white ice water rushes, with a steady hissing, to the warm valleys.

6. xi. 38

Before the light of the sun had quite faded from the mountains, the moon rose over them and cast downward its flat shadows, to make everything look like cheap scenery but beautiful, as such backdrops would look to a wise child.

I stood on the balcony and listened to the lazy melody of a

man's call in the far slopes, and the sharp excited bark of a child or a young dog in the village, and beyond all of it the quiet rushing of the river, full from thaw. As I walked toward the rooms, I saw Irma sitting beside Tim's white smooth rump, rubbing rhythmically, and the stiff ruffled curtains framing her in her white cap and pinafore, and then I saw my shadow, faint and clear in the afterglow of the full moon on the door.

7. xi. 38

This afternoon, after a half-night of wakefulness, I began to write a book. It will be impossible to show it to anyone but Tim . . . if I ever get it that far along . . . because it is about this last summer. Of course, all of us, and above all myself, are changed, muted one moment and caricatured the next, by my own licentious mind. If a person could ever be seen truly, it would be by himself. But that seldom happens. Or perhaps, is that rare inward vision of oneself what explains the look of rapturous amusement on a dying person's face, which is always interpreted by good Christians as the first peer at heaven?

A letter to T. from his mother, fairly spitting and steaming from the envelope with rage that Anne, who had been two weeks home, had not yet come to Claymont, whereas *she* had defied nurses, doctors, and hospital to get home to welcome her errant darling . . . ten days too soon. I can understand her chagrin.

A quiet and prolonged scene with Schwester Irma today, solved finally by petting, cajoling, babying, playfully teasing her into a good humor. God, these complicated middle-aged nitwits who feed on attention! Am I headed for it, too?

After two years of having experts try to fix a gradual crescendo of whir and squeak in our extremely expensive and completely pleasing gramophone, the fumbling, puzzle-witted local radioman came in this afternoon and arranged it as it should be. Of course, I don't know how long it will last, but I enjoy it meanwhile. This afternoon I played a few things, and then the Brahms Second Concerto. The third (?) movement of it, I thought . . . my favorite piece of gentle music . . . it will soothe us, it will solace us. But I almost didn't hear it at all, so busy was I trying to keep T. from looking at the clock and crying wildly at the filthiness of a life that is only endurable with *piqûres*.

It is 10:00 at night. I'll try to stay awake until T. calls, about 12:30 to 1:30, to give him his shot. Irma has fussed so about how badly she feels that I'm bitch enough to want to fool her and do the night work myself for once. It's a shot-and-a-half, and I hate the idea of it, but I'm sick to death of her nobly stifled yawns in the mornings. I hope I can work it. *Piqûres* make me sick still, but not actively, as they used to.

It is satisfying, in a queer way, to have written the bones of a book today. I'm puzzled by it and feel quite doubtful that I can do it as well as I want to—but at least I'm working. As I told T. today, I've been proving with so much conversation that I'm through with the lost cause of literature that at least I can go to work now with the courage of my convictions.

8. xi. 38

It's become almost impossible for Timmy and me to talk anymore, except now and then when he is almost human after an injection and I'm not too sleepy. I find myself, after almost eleven weeks of encouragements and quiet words of good sense or jaunty or plain goddamn cheerfulness, so sick of myself that I can't help feeling that he is, too. Perhaps I'm hypersensitive. I know that I'm growing a little nervy: the last few days have found me several times cold with exasperation at Irma or even at the fact that no matter how Tim feels (always badly, but in degrees) or what he says, it is pessimistic. God knows I can't blame him, but lately I find myself wishing that when I ask him if he has slept, he will simply say, Yes, instead of Yes, but very badly, or Yes, but it was a queer muddled sleep. I know it could be nothing else . . . but I wish for once he'd leave it at that. And that shows that I am growing cranky. I feel very low today, partly because the few minutes I have had each day with Tim, since this started, have gradually become a listening to his crying and moaning and a fierce battle with myself not to break loose and tell him for God's sake to buck up, when I know that he has no strength left to do it with, and partly because Irma grows daily more cavalier in her behavior toward us, and such treatment always depresses me and makes me feel self-scorn at my weakness in putting up with it. But at the moment I simply can't have any more trouble. If T. were better I'd tell her to go. She's been very good, but she is haunted by the fact that she is in her fifties, and she is of a moody type that thrives on "hot emotional baths" and I can't supply her with them. She would love me (as would not how many other women in my life!) if I'd only weep upon her breast, or scream with rage, or sulk. But I can do none of these things with my inferiors. So *she* sulks and sobs in my place. Now she feels unwell, and I hear every detail of her malaise and heap coals of fire on her wordless resentment of the whole situation by seeing that she has extra fruit, extra rest, by not calling her even once at night, and all *impersonally*. That impersonality is what outrages her preconceptions of being human, of being warm and sympathetic. I regret it, as I often have before. I recognize it, as I should, after so many years of frightening people, of making them feel cheated by my lack of confidences.

For several days I've not had time to write, although I have thought a good deal about the book I'm working on. I think I made a mistake to talk with T. about it. Now that he knows, there may be less incentive to work on it.

I read to T. a lot every day and every night. The sciatica, which is being treated with an unguent made of bee venom that spreads a delightful warm incense in the air, has diminished a lot, and the phlebitis, although still increased in spite of ichthiol salve, is no longer painful. Temperature and pulse are normal, for the first time since September 1. But the theoretical foot is pure hell, reducing T. to a twitching hysterical wreck unless he can stay mildly doped. Today we gave him ½ cc. of Analgeticum, instead of the whole ampule, and although he was still in pain, he was somewhat soothed. He has been exposing his wound for five- to ten-minute periods to the sun, and that seems to aggravate the pain. The doctor is really deeply concerned and says that as soon as the one open place is closed, he can try injections of vitamin B-1 to nourish the cut nerves and so on . . . and that T.'s being able to move about will help. But in the meantime there is nothing he knows of, except injections. Last night T. told me he would infinitely prefer another amputation to this pain, if it would be able to retie the muscles or something. It's really terrible.

The weather is beautiful now. We eat lunch on the terrace every day.

I am stupid. I dozed along, half-dreaming, listening to Irma and T. whispering for my sake, until almost 11:00—the first time I've stayed in bed since early last summer. I've lost my skill at it, evidently!

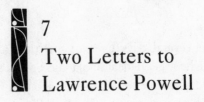

7

Two Letters to
Lawrence Powell

2.xii.38
Hotel Huldi
Adelboden, Switzerland

Unsent letter to Larry Powell

And Al . . . the "man almost crazy with grief" when I went home . . . did anyone ever ask how *I* felt? Did anyone wonder what my own grief was, when I waited and waited for Al to show, *in any way,* that he wanted me to stay with him when my mother suggested I come back to America for a summer? I was naive, of course, and unskilled, but I used every wile I was capable of to get Al to show, no matter how, that he would rather have me stay than go. I said to myself that he was proud . . . and this and that. Finally I went away, watching until the train left Paris for some sign that he would rather spend the summer with me than with you and Liger and Pierre Simonet and the waiters at the Café de Paris. If you'll look again, Ghuce,* you'll see bitter tears for the summer I

* Name used by Mary Frances in all her correspondence with Lawrence Powell. As a joke, he had inserted a footnote in his doctoral thesis attributed to "H. Ghuce, Docteur ès Lettres."

left Al. And all that about "killing the Ghost"—I've had it bitten into me until I'm tired of it. If a thing has life in it, it will live. The pain of absence, if it is a real pain and not an excuse for something else, will nurture beauty and poetry and music. That summer, it never occurred to me that Al could stand my leaving him, because the idea was absolutely insupportable to me. Then . . . and with what beaming relief! . . . he said, A wonderful idea! The two and more months I was away were the worst of my life, up to then. And when I came back to Dijon, Al looked better than ever and had made friends he was most unwilling for me to know, and in a kind of jubilant relief had stopped working on the Ghost. The first time I heard him imply, with that delicacy of which he is such a master, that because I'd left him a great poem had died, I was so shocked that I went home and vomited, for the first time in years. I felt as if my heart were being torn out, because I was still completely in love with Al, and I realized that in spite of his too-eager protestations, to everybody who would listen except me, that he loved me more than life itself, he did not. He loved what he wanted me to be . . . and more and more I wasn't that: the ideal he'd built in the East Adams Presbyterian Church of a girl who was well bred but who did everything he had been taught was not so: smoked, drank, wore lipstick, read T. S. Eliot, liked Picasso. Oh, what a sad mess, with such faults on both sides of the canvas! I regret it bitterly. But I am tired of being told that I "killed the Ghost." I . . . time . . . lassitude—who can say this or that thing was the culprit? And who ever wonders about what killed that part of me that may have *made* the Ghost?

Well, Ghuce . . . I meant to swallow all this . . . or at worst leave it until we met. Perhaps I should have.

As for the "haunting talks . . . when he told me hesitantly of the triangle of Le Pâquis"—oh, Larry, how many people have reproached me for that! How many women, drowned in the poignancy of it, and how many men, full of wrath at my cruelty, have written to me of those haunting talks! Go back to him, they beg. He has told me all! He has confided in me! You are his world, even if you *have* cut off his genius in its prime. He swears he won't hold it against you, because he *loves* you. Other people may blame you, because you are an adulteress and a nymphomaniac, but he promises to forgive you . . . and on and on. What does it all add up to, Larry! Certainly I am not "unconscious" of it all as you say. I wish to God I could meet Al as one human adult with another— but he has hidden himself behind a ghastly bulwark of The Woman He Loved and Married, an ideal formed when he was very young and Christian. I am not that woman. I never was. But when I was young and he was fresh from college, he thought he saw in me a proof to his omnipotent father and family that a woman could make up and read "daring" books and still be a lady.

Gradually he began to tire of that and want roast beef and mashed potatoes and chocolate cake for Sunday noon dinner, as he'd been raised to feel was concomitant with Marital Happiness. Gone were Proust and the grilled lamb chop and green salad. Gone were the nights when a few of us sat with some wine perhaps and talked and read and sang. Instead, Al and I went almost every night to a double-feature movie, and ate chocolate bars and came home drugged with bad air and drivel, and were too tired to "talk" —a thing he dreaded like poison, perhaps because his mother had tried to make him do so when he was young. . . .

Well . . . I think a great deal about it, because Al will always be one of the finest things in my life. And I will always have a feeling of unfulfillment about our life together . . . a feeling that his past came too soon too strongly between me and what I knew was there in him. I don't know how other women have fared with him. I hope that *something* I gave him (because I gave him everything I had) has held over, to make him easier to know and help and love

... and to make him easier with himself. All this may sound queer —I don't know because I shan't read it—but you are the only one I can say it to. You know Al better than anyone except me, and you and I are so much alike, in our male and female ways, that we know him pretty much in the same way.

2. xii. 38
Hotel Huldi
Adelboden

Letter sent to Larry Powell

Dearest Larry—

Before I forget it, this check is for a copy of *The Ghost* for me. Will you please keep it until I come? And if there's anything left of the check, I want you and Fay to have a little party or something you want: if you're not on the wagon, drink to me, and if you are, you can do it just as well in water. It's my last cut of the royalty from *Serve It Forth,* I think. (I was hoping that book would have a small steady Christmas sale, but apparently Harper's has already stopped issuing it—several people have written to ask where they could get copies, but of course I have none. Oh, well—)

I can't tell you how glad I am that *The Ghost* is finally to see light—and especially that you three are going to do it. I think you're doing it in exactly the right way, too. Of course, Al is convinced that he has no interest in the project, but you mustn't take that too literally. Unless he is an *entirely* different person now, he is really pleased and excited by it. I don't need to tell you how strange it makes me feel to have something so intimately a part of my life now going on as it should, with me no longer having anything to do with it—except to stand helplessly on the sidelines and ask to buy a copy. That's a bad sentence, but you know what I mean. Anyway—I'm sad but I'm not jealous, and I'm glad you're doing it.

Thank you for writing me such an interesting and good letter. (Timmy thanks you, too, and says he knows he's lucky to have me here, as you said. I hope you're both right!) I was truly fascinated by what you told me of Al's visit with you and the things you had heard about him. (Incidentally, it was a fine piece of direct narrative writing—wrong of me to notice in a description of Al's conduct probably, but I couldn't help being moved and impressed.)

I should like very much, sometime, to know "the whole story, from Al's viewpoint." As I told you, such astonishing tidbits have come back to me, from various sources, that the only decent thing I can believe is that Al, a born romancer, must occasionally have got carried away. Certainly he is reported to have told things about us, and especially me—in strictest confidence, of course!—that no person who had ever met me could possibly believe. Probably if he heard them, he'd never believe that he himself had said them. If he did. Of course, Al has always been thoroughly convinced that he is the most secretive and noncommunicative of souls, whereas a matter of fact he is a friendly and almost garrulous person, willing to talk intimately to practically anyone. That is one reason why he's an almost inspired lecturer, especially to young people.

I'm sorry, in a way, that he knows I told you of his sexual impotence toward me. It's not a thing that any man likes to have told, and although only you, my father, and Tim know about it, Al must wonder how many others there are.

Of course, nobody saw more clearly than I how difficult it would be for Al and me to go to Switzerland with Tim, and in letters and in countless conversations I did all I could to convince him. But he loathed Occidental and his profession—or thought he did—and he remembered how happy he'd been in Dijon, young, in love, free. Tim and I, too, felt that it was terrible for a man as fine as Al to be so miserable as he felt he was, at Occidental. So— We all went to Switzerland, and before we'd been there five hours Al knew that even my exaggerated tales of how difficult it would be were not wild enough. He was stuck in a prim, stuffy little commercial town, no longer young, no longer passionate, isolated from any erudite colleagues. You know Al really believes that he is the lonely philosopher, who needs only his pipe, his books, and an occasional evening of Bach or a solitary roam over the hills. But have you ever known him to do much more than talk about such an existence? He is an extremely social, gregarious person—he *loves* people, and life, and movement—parties, gossip. I don't say this at all bitterly—but I do regret terribly that I didn't realize it before. You remember the constant moviegoing we did in Dijon? We were *never* settled down—it was always with some good excuse: our accents or something—but we were always restless. And then in Laguna, I really think Al almost went crazy with boredom. We had absolutely no money, so we couldn't entertain—but he'd roam off down to the public beach, or visit people, preferably alone—and every spare nickel we got went for movies. By that time I knew his real need for more variety and movement than I could provide (especially on the $32.50 a month that we managed to live on), so I was glad when Stelter gave him a job.

You know how Al protested, constantly and bitterly, his loathing for that job, and indeed for teaching in general. I wonder if he always will? I really believe he loves it—he loves the attention of adoring students, the intrigue and conniving among the faculty— even the occasional weighty research and the occasional publication of an erudite little book on some obscure Greek epigrammatist. But I doubt if he'll ever admit that. He is one of the most thoroughly self-fooled people I've ever known.

You ask if I really thought I could live in the house with two men who were in love with me. (I seem to be going in for Confessional—don't let it bore you, and please realize that it's not my general habit.) It probably seems as strange to you as it does to me, now. But for so long I had throttled all my sexual needs (it took me a long time to get used to living side by side with a man whom I still loved passionately and who was almost actively sickened at the thought of being with me) that I was pretty sure they were well in control. And I had proved that I could be with Tim without setting off any bonfires. So, as far as that part of life went, I truly hadn't a qualm. It was certainty that Al would be bored that worried me—but when I talked about it, he would always assure me that the only thing he really wanted in the world was complete solitude, time to *think*.

As for my leaving Al for Tim, it is quite untrue. I have told Al that, and I think he knows it, but no man likes to admit that a woman has left him for any other reason than another man. If I had been going to leave him, though, it would have been some six years ago (for Tim, or any other man). It is true that I am with Tim now and will be as long as he lives or wants me—but I would never have left Al for him. I am sorry that Al won't admit that.

Yes, I've gone ahead with the divorce. It will be granted some time in January, probably. It is very unpleasant to me to be the theoretical wife of a man who has not even seen me for over a year —it's distasteful and dishonest to me at least, and I should think would be to Al, too. I can't understand his wanting things to stay that way—except that being legally married is a kind of protection to him, perhaps.

And that leads me to what you tell me of all Al's talk of needing a large measure of ripe flesh. It is rather difficult to talk about. I wish I could tell you how deeply I wish that Al really would *take* some ripe flesh. He *does* need it, and *want* it. But I am fairly sure that he has little of it. Of course, he pinches and pokes and leers and strokes—and above all he *talks*. Al is a master of implication. He can (and does) imply the thousand affairs of a rather pedagogic Don Juan.

But what are they? They are wish-dreams, almost all of them. Al was twenty-six or twenty-seven when he married me, and still a virgin. He was, and still is, frightened and repelled by the actual physical act of love. Even at his freest and happiest, he had to condone it and make it acceptable by quoting what Plato, and Bertrand Russell, and Marie Stopes said about it. And it was disappointing—partly because he was inexperienced—and frightened by years of churchly training from Y.M.C.A. leaders and a father who after thirty-five years of parochial life could still talk solemnly and sentimentally of "the sweet mystery of love and life"—that is to say, sexual intercourse.

Al was, and still is, horribly frightened by the thought of venereal disease, which has made him take out his urges in the more or less safe forms of pinching and writing schoolboy notes. God—I hate to admit all this, even to myself. I'm proud of Al and want him to be a full, happy *man*. Of course, it was hard on my female pride, for a while, to realize that I had failed to make him one. Then I hoped desperately that his getting away from me would help him. But I don't think it has. Teaching in a girls' school, always having to be circumspect and cautious, certainly doesn't help—but there *are* men who can do that and still live vigorously and wholly. And now I hear, not only from you, that this damnable half-life of flirting and giggling and tickling is still going on, stronger than ever. I am sad.

You are right about Al's letters—they are not the best side of him, inclined to be sententious and humorless. That's not a new development, although I think it is exaggerated at this time by what you rightly call the "spiritual chip on his shoulder." I hope, and very very much, that some day he will allow himself to be loose and easy and free with me. I rather doubt it, though—it will take the warmth and completeness of a life with a real woman to bring that about, and Al is stubborn and self-torturing enough to prevent himself from ever enjoying life. He is capable of living forever now on pinching-and-telling and the idealized vision of his life with me. (Even before he left, he was almost sleeping with a picture of me when I was sixteen which he'd found at the Ranch. He so hated actuality that he had made a dream of what I was then some five years before he even met me! It was a kinder, sweeter, weaker Child Bride he loved—one he'd never owned.)

Well, dearest Larry—I remember the first time I ever met you, at a dance at Orr Hall, I said that you had something of the father-confessor in you. Certainly I've proved it today—and for the first time, as far as all this goes. I was too unhappy and sad to talk to *anyone* when I was home. And, of course, I am quite alone with Timmy, who knows most of this from having been so close to both Al and me. Let it stay in the confessional, and think no ill of any of us.

I am so glad about the Newell boy. Please tell them.

Jean Matruchot could never say that what I'm writing now is *"charmant, délicieux."* It is so terrible that I reread one chapter and was almost sick. I doubt if I will ever try to publish it—no point in rubbing people's noses in their own filth. It's good for me, though, and hard work—different from anything I've ever tried. If I finish it, I'll probably ask you to read it.

The change to high altitude that was supposed to help Timmy recuperate almost killed him, and for about three weeks it looked bad. Fortunately I had a good nurse. I am convinced that he should be at a lower level, and as soon as he can be moved, I want to go down to Vevey, for a few weeks at least. Then he must get used to walking again, and then we'll probably go back to America. He is almost recovered from the phlebitis that occurred when he came up here, but the theoretical foot and leg cause him such agony that he has to be kept doped most of the time. It's no life for a man, and at times he's hard put to it not to despair. So am I. But we'll see what going down does. Of course, it may be even worse than staying here, but we're willing to risk it—*some*thing must be done, and we've tried almost everything (including injections of cobra venom! They almost sent him off his head, among other reactions. It's terrible to be so trapped: I *know* what blundering dolts most doctors are, and yet when one suggests something that may help this agony I see before me, I can only say, Yes, yes, anything!).

Please write, and to *30 rue du Château, La Tour-de-Peilz, Vaud, Switzerland.* If I don't write before Christmas, this sends you and Fay and the beasties my loving good wishes for then and all the New Year. Tim, too. I hope we'll see you before the year ends. Please don't be afraid at my sudden burst of confidence—

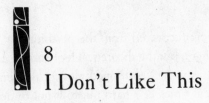

8

I Don't Like This

Tonight I looked at the cover of a current issue of a weekly magazine all about peace and war. The picture was of an angry mother in Texas or Israel or Beirut with her two hot-eyed sad children clinging to her proud heavy body, and I said firmly, I do not like this.

Then I was thinking about the word *like,* and I remembered one time when I was looking down at the poor anguished body of my love, while a group of young doctors and nurse nuns stood about the famous doctor who was using him as an object lesson of some kind. Tim lay in the cold Swiss light. There was a thick ring of faces above him, around the bed, trying to be dispassionate but still sad for him. His one leg lay firm and beautiful and naked, and the stump beside it twitched helplessly now and then and was open and angry, with yellow in the middle of the gaping open end. The doctor was speaking stolidly, elegantly, and the younger nurses hummed little sounds as he paused. He looked sternly at me, standing there, and asked, "And what does the lady think?"

I said in French against his German, "I do not like it."

There was a long pause, filled with shock and an almost physical disapproval. The ring of sympathetic cooing little nuns drew back, and behind them the young doctors stood like sentinels, alert and ready. The doctor looked straight at me, and then shrugged and smiled and said to the circle. "Madame does not like something, eh?"

He laughed shortly, and they all twittered in obedience and waited. I stood there and did not look down at Tim, who lay like a drugged beast—a small neat beast, like a fox perhaps, but still drugged and unknowing. The doctor laughed again, looking full into my open face. "Madame does not like this," he murmured as if to himself, and he bent over the open bone end of what had once been a fine leg and rubbed at it with a long swab. Every face drew closer, and I pulled away, forever outside of that or any other circle.

Tonight I do not like the faces of those three people who have no home. But what can I do for them? What could I do that time for Tim? We had no home, either. Still, I think these sad angry-eyed children may survive, just as their mother has, and perhaps as I have, too.

I am warm and I have, temporarily anyway, a place to call my home, and they do not. But the mother knows that there will be something more, I suppose, if she thinks about it at all. Perhaps she does not. I did not think any way at all when I said flatly to the great doctor, "I do not like this." The mother does not like what she sees now. But there is no arguing about it, except to make it clear that it is not right.

That is what I keep trying to do. I doubt that anyone listens, but I keep on saying it. I do not *like* this. It stinks. It is hideous. It is a filthy trick. It is a cruel trick. It will lead to intolerable suffering. It is ugly and twisting.

That day in Bern I stood while the doctor mocked me, and neither I nor the man drugged on the high white bed blinked an eye when all the little nurse nuns and the student doctors gave out a kind of exhalation of amused consent as the doctor bent over the stump and twisted expertly at some gauze, reverting into German as he continued, "And although she does not *like* it, she will have to see that the inflammation increases as the general state of vascular deterioration . . ."

Yes. Yes. Where can we sleep tonight? Will there be any food? Where will it come from? Will we live or die?

We do not ask. We say, if asked, that we do not like it—war or hopelessness or hate or love or or . . .

—*Glen Ellen, California, 1991*

9
Bareacres Journal,
1940–41

18. iii. 40

I am beginning some two months late to keep a kind of record, diary, journal, about Bareacres. I have meant to do it ever since the first day we saw the place, because the few times I have found parts of such records they have been really interesting to me and to Timmy. This one will be written for the two of us, quite frankly, with the idea that some time far from now it will interest us again. Of course, such a record is often dull and almost as often embarrassing, but surely by now we are old enough to be tolerant. I can remember finding, some ten years later, a diary I kept when I was fourteen and being so sickened by my adolescent prig-gishness that I felt actively nauseated. Then I decided that I should keep those few pages, as a kind of token that change is right, for I was sure that even with my faults at twenty-four, I was better than I had been at fourteen. I run across them occasionally, and al-though I never read them—that would be too difficult—the sight of those ruled pages stiffens me a little and makes me hope to God that another ten years will change me again. I remember how uncomfortable Al was about his diaries. He hated the thought that I had read them, the ones he kept in high school, and once I made a great mistake, when he said something about always having been unusually tolerant, in quoting something or other from one of them. He never forgave me, and soon after the diaries disappeared. I don't think he destroyed them, since he wanted to keep things like that for his biographers—but he made sure that no contemporary eyes would fall on them. It was too humiliating. I know a little bit what he felt . . . but I believe that he should have been proud to admit how he had matured and how he could still change.

This is not about Bareacres, directly at least.

Mrs. D. moves from there sometime before this Friday, which is Good Friday. Yesterday we were there, and I tried with blatant "goodwill," the kind that made me smile too much and be too gracious and then feel ashamed when she responded so hungrily to my false food . . . when I tried graciously and smilingly to find out when she planned to leave, she could not tell me. Tim and I both felt annoyed, but there was nothing to be done about it. At first we were afraid, some two months ago, that she might refuse to leave . . . have the old man go to bed or some such common trick. She was very unfriendly. But now we are pretty sure she will get out on the twenty-second when she is supposed to. Once we were sitting up under the eucalyptus tree, and we heard her say to Dad, the old man, "Well, we'll only have one more week here now." We could not tell by her flat, high voice whether she was glad or sorry. Another time we went up there, and she was putting small boxes of stuff in the back of her nephew's car. So I think she'll go sometime this week.

I feel rather ashamed of pretending to be so friendly toward her, since I find her very unpleasant. I am friendly simply because I don't want to antagonize her in any way. Tim and I are almost desperately anxious to move up there. We go over often now when we should be working here, and sit on the hill looking around us.

Yesterday we took the little radio over, and sat in the bushes against a rock, and listened to the *Emperor* Concerto and a funny Mozart concerto for clarinet, from New York. The sky was milky, and occasionally a cool wind would make us pull coats around us. Then it would suddenly be too warm for them. There were several kinds of wildflowers around us, and the ground was covered with tiny white forget-me-nots. We were comfortable. I gave T. a good shot, so that he looked better, and we drank some beer (I drank vermouth, because I am trying to lose eight pounds before summer) and ate celery and radishes and I an artichoke and he some peanut-butter sandwiches that I willfully ignored. Then after the concert we read some Bulldog Drummond, which we have decided is a model for thrillers. But the main thing was being up there in the sweet air and looking around at the wild rock slopes and down toward the little house. Bareacres was ours.

While we were there, Arnold Elliott drove up to look at the spring and stopped to talk to us for a minute. It was surprising that we were so well hidden in the sage bushes—he had difficulty finding us, although we could see him clearly and were waving and calling to him.

He told us that he had opened up the other spring and connected it to the main pipe—"all the same job." That was a good surprise, although we are a little puzzled as to why he is suddenly being so altruistic. He also told us that looking after the two springs went with the job, which we hadn't counted on, and that if anything went wrong with the exit pipe from the tank, he would replace it himself, and that he would keep his eye on the leaks, if any, and patch them free of charge. As I say, we are puzzled but grateful. Probably the reason for his sudden and almost protective interest in us is that he feels that he is much better as a workman than Miller, who graded the road for us last week and, according to both Elliott and Timmy, did a pretty poor job. I think that might make Elliott feel superior and therefore generous.

He asked us if we wanted him to make some dining room chairs and a table. I don't think we do, but we were amused to hear about them. Some time ago, when we stopped at the pub in San Jacinto for a drink, Sherm Lewis, the proprietor, told us with what we thought at the time was not very commendable glee that he got Arnold Elliott to make his chairs for $2 apiece, when the wood itself must have cost almost that much. We looked at the chairs, which were good sturdy pine chairs, really handsome, and then we thought of Elliott and three children to feed and a wife, and then we looked at Sherm Lewis and thought that he should be ashamed. But yesterday Elliott told us, with the same amusement and a kind of proud self-ridicule, that he made the chairs for $2 and that the wood itself cost him $1.10. He seemed really amused at his own foolishness. We couldn't help laughing. They are good chairs, and we might get some later or give some to somebody.

What we need now is some more comfortable furniture for the porch and eventually the patio. We bought two chairs from Mrs. D., mainly to grease her skids, but I don't think they are especially suitable for the porch, even if we paint them. We got a rather nice little footstool from her, too. I'll probably scrape the varnish off it. And a low fat bureau, which Tim insists will be good-looking when he paint it. We do need more drawer space, especially in the kitchen ... and although I think the bureau is hideous, I have great confidence in anything he says about furniture and furnishings. (As well as everything else except maybe me, and, of course, he is very prejudiced about that.)

We have to go to the Ranch tonight and will bring back some hammers and saws and so on. We ought to be able to take them over to Bareacres and start puttering by the end of this week. The thought of it makes me feel quite trembly.

I never thought I would ever be that way again. To tell the truth, I always had reservations about Le Pâquis, in spite of thinking it the most beautiful place in the world . . . but we put so much of our lifeblood and our inner love and misery and strength into it that I felt sure I would never again be able to do it about any other place. And now, some three years later, I am even happier about Bareacres, because I truly have no reservations about it.

It is a little like marrying for the second time. I could not understand how Gigi, who was living with John, was so positive that she would never marry him after she got her divorce from Tim. She did, after a year or so. And then when I was divorced from Al, I was the same, even though I was deeply in love with Tim. I felt an active aversion toward marriage with him or with anyone. No, no, I thought, it is better to stay clear. You hurt people when you marry them. I'll never marry again. And now I am married and would not have it any other way.

We have to go to Hal Bieler's* tonight. It will be extremely dull and uncomfortable. I used to like to go there and listen to records and eat some good vegetables. But now he serves only muffins and milk and plays the piano instead of the gramophone, demanding constant praise and worshipful attention . . . and, of course, Tim is antipathetic to him (is that the word? I mean that Hal makes Tim's hackles rise) and cannot smoke. So I hate to waste an evening there. However, we have an appointment at his office at 5:15, and he has asked us to go home with him afterward.

I want to talk to him strongly, but I don't know if I will. The

* Doctor and friend to both M.F.K.F. and Larry Powell. His approach to medicine through nutrition had a strong influence on Mary Frances.

last two weeks have been harder than usual for Tim. It may be spring. Anyway, he's had two really terrible bouts of pain and nausea, and I have had, most unwillingly, to increase the shots of Analgeticum. I hate to do that because it shows retrogression on his part and because we have not yet heard whether the last order has been able to get through from Switzerland. If I don't have to increase the dosage any more and if there is no accident to our supply, I have enough to last for about fourteen months. And then, Tim says, if he still needs it, the jig will pretty well be up anyway. (And that is where I am counting on Bareacres to give him strength and more courage and will to live.)

We have lived pretty much as Hal prescribed for about nine months now, and he says that he sees great improvement—weight, urinanalysis, and so on. I see some, certainly . . . but this constant fight against pain is unfair. After all, it has been over a year since the last amputation. Eighteen months of what Tim has had are more than any one man should have to face.

Of course, I haven't a leg to stand on, really, in my criticism of Hal of Tim's condition, because we have not followed his diet to the letter. We drink a little whiskey and beer, and Tim smokes, and occasionally we have coffee, and we eat pepper. So I can't complain to him, of all people. It is mainly my fault that we have slipped in our rigorous following of Hal's directions. But I know him pretty well and have watched many people under his care, and I know that it is inevitable that all but the most sheeplike of his patients end by adapting his advice to their own natures. Probably they are wrong . . . but it is inevitable. And I know Tim, and since he does not have some actively painful condition like a cancer of the stomach, which would have an immediate reaction to food, I cannot help feeling that for him the monotony of Hal's diet would do more harm than an occasional divergence from it. I hope I'm not too wrong . . . because if I insisted, Tim would do his best to live by the law.

I must manicure my nails before lunch. We start soon after. Tomorrow I have an appointment with Dr. Kelsey. I have always been a little coquettish about him and take more care than usual to look and smell nice when I see him. He is attractive, in a clean, dry way. He has also been very good to me, although he is very dull about everything but teeth and mouths. As usual, I am nervous about what he will decide to do. If it is, at last, time to renovate the work he did some twelve years ago, I shall be really discouraged. It will take a week of time that I could spend working at Bareacres, and a lot of money that we need.

22. iii. 40

In a few minutes we go to Bareacres, and I am really nervous. The woman is supposed to be either gone or on her way today, and if she is still lingering there, I feel that I'll perhaps cry or be sick or something. I know Tim is nervous, too. We haven't been over this week, as I remember.

As we drove toward Pasadena and Hal's, we began to get so hungry the other day that our stomachs growled and we "saw dark spots in the shape of hamburgers floating before our eyes." We thought of his ascetic meals of bran muffins and milk . . . nothing else to eat, nothing else to drink, no smoking. The nearer we got, the more we were haunted by an almost physical need for strong drink, food Hal would think vile, and cigarettes. Every time we passed a roadside stand, Tim's head snapped around dangerously to stare back at it. And finally we weakened and risked being late, and I forgot my dieting, and we went to a very swanky Carpenters' just outside the racetrack at San Marino and ordered beer and hamburgers. I gave Tim a nice shot, and we took a swig of whiskey from the flask and gobbled mediocre hamburgers with complete delight. Then we dashed on to Pasadena, only a few minutes late.

Later

It is about ten o'clock. I have just got out Tim's Speechless House-boy, as Mother calls the small rack called by the department store a Silent Houseboy.* (I rub his shoulder just behind the bone and wonder how much he notices that sometimes I have drunk too much or am preoccupied with cramps or an idea. Generally, the main idea is to give him a shot and give it to him quickly—to rub his skin hard with the wad of alcohol and cotton and to stick in the needle sharply. I think deliberately, always, of how to pick up the delicate little ampules most expertly so that they will not tip or spill. But sometimes I know that for one reason or another, voluntary, like drinking too much, or involuntary, like the twentieth of the month, I am clumsy, and I wonder how much Tim notices or if all he minds is how quick relief comes.)

Yes, I have just got out the Houseboy and sped through the little cold end room to pluck the three hot-water bottles from the end of the tub and the pee bottle from the top of the hot-water heater. I have filled a glass with water, and taken it and the pee bottle to the front porch, and put them on the blue-painted lug box beside Tim's bed. I have turned down the beds, and then sped back and filled the hot-water bottles and fixed one-half cake of yeast in each of two large teacups with hot water, to be drunk later

---

* A wooden rack to hold a man's jacket and trousers.

by us. Then, after writing a few words ostentatiously on this machine and wondering what Tim would think of me to start tapping suddenly after so long a silence, I have given him the first of the night's shots (I don't count the one at 7:00), and have told him as he went through the door that I would go to bed soon.

I am tired in a pleasant way, not like the night I came back from Los Angeles, when I was too tired even to get into bed and stood for a long time in the bathroom, not able to get undressed or even look at myself, feeling sick. Tonight I am very happy.

We went up to Bareacres about one o'clock. All the way we had been saying very casually that probably Mrs. D. would be there or probably she would not be there. Finally, as we jogged over the road, which is getting a little worse every day, I said, or maybe it was Tim, "Well, if there are still curtains in the windows, Mrs. D. will still be there tonight." (Because she is convinced that every night people stare into her window, and she keeps every one covered with curtains pinned together in the middle.) As we went 'round the final curve before we came to the gate, I saw that the windows were naked. I felt elated, so happy that I cried out. Mrs. D. was gone.

There was a gleaming nobbin above the edge of the terrace, either a vase that she had left or a man's head. Could it be her old charge Dad, the mild old man with senile dementia?

It was Septimus.* We were furious. He told us wheezily that he had been ill again for five days, that the new doctor thought it was probably ulcers, that the medicine seemed to be helping him. We smiled and condoled, and all the time we were seething with annoyance that here, now, the first time the house was really ours,

* Husband of Elsa Purdy, who later spent many years working for Mary Frances as nursemaid and friend.

we should be bothered by this ghastly old hypochondriac. We soon left, to eat our lunch farther up the hill. "You folks go right ahead," Septimus said graciously.

Later Mrs. Purdy came up to tell us that two friends and the children of one of them were there, too, having a picnic on our porch. We could do nothing but were somewhat gratified that she seemed a little apologetic. Finally, after we had gone down to the town, they left, and we had the house to ourselves.

We wandered through it, feeling suddenly tired and empty. It was not until, after taking many measurements, that we began to think on the way home. By now many things are clear, and Timmy has a fine plan for saving about $300 or $400 for a studio: lengthening the present dining room, thereby shortening the too-long porch as well. It looks fine on paper. Now we must talk to the carpenter, a gunsmith named Martin Lausen, a thin tall man with pink eyes whose even taller wife moves like an awkwardly graceful adolescent and talks with the slight accent that should belong to her husband.

We go over again in the morning to see the plumber, Louis Aden, the electrician, and Lausen.

This morning Tim took pictures of several of his canvases, while I filled flowerpots with earth and peat moss.

27. iii. 40

Sunday, Easter, we went early to Bareacres. The Purdys came, to our intense annoyance, and sat and sat. Finally we both had to excuse ourselves, since Ankum the electrician was asking questions, and then the carpenter came. Sometime later they left, after asking us if we wouldn't come down for a little meal and some beer. Neither of us wanted to, and in a rather shilly-shallying way

I said we'd love to, but since Timmy had to be back here for medicines soon after 6:00, we couldn't stay long. "But you'll eat a bite, won't you?" Mrs. P. asked in her soft voice, looking more than ever like a bright-eyed squirrel. "Oh, of *course,*" I said heartily, knowing that we were both of us (T. and I) too exasperated at them. Then I was sorry, remembering her life with poor rachitic, asthmatic, ulcerous, perhaps cancerous old Septimus.

Martin Lausen the carpenter is a tall lean man with red eyes, but quite handsome. At first he seems slow, but then you realize that he is thinking. And what he thinks, about carpentering at least, is solid and often ingenious. He is garrulous, but where Mr. Purdy's windy conversations set your teeth on edge, his are rather nice—quiet and sometimes funny. He told us of an accident when his knees got knocked backward so that his legs bent both ways and of various experiences with snakes (he is an amateur taxidermist). He and his brother have invented a machine run by perpetual motion! The brother plans to take it to Washington as soon as he raises enough money—which probably means as soon as we pay Mr. Lausen. (The tentative estimates for work on the house are $400 top for Lausen, $65 top for electricity, and $45, including a new toilet bowl, for Aden the plumber. Then the electric line has cost $48.)

We ate lunch rather late (I ate part of a green pepper, four stalks of celery, four large radishes, and part of a dill pickle) and sat around until time to go to the Purdys'. On the way down we decided to stay only a few minutes, and Tim was determined to be *"very distant*—by God, I don't *like* them at Bareacres all the time!" But a table was set by the fireplace in the little Indian house, and a special Easter supper of baked rabbit and baked potatoes and spinach and an egg salad—and beer, of course—and we were very nice and even enjoyed ourselves and did not leave until almost 7:00. As we left, Mrs. Purdy said very softly to Tim, "Ralph and I just think it was wonderful, kind of a good omen, that we could've spent this Easter with you folks!" Of course, we felt like rats.

About halfway home my stomach started to ache, and by the time we were here it had gone down to my guts. I drank some hot water and soda, but it did no good. Pretty soon I tried to take a small enema, but by that time it was almost too painful to move. I was frightened and discouraged, because I had all the symptoms of my bout at Sis's in November '37 and at Adelboden in December '38: distended belly, extreme pain, fever. I got to bed. By 1:30 my fever had risen to 102 degrees, and the pain in my abdomen was worse than it had ever been before, like white-hot metal filling my bowels.

Tim called Hal, who said to give me soapy enemas every two hours, even if I passed out, and (to our amusement) a shot of whiskey after them. It was a sleepless and very unpleasant night— pain, Tim's anxiety and hard work, no bedpan but a kitchen pot, no enema bag but a glass jar. But by morning I felt a little better, although I was still in the worst pain I have known. We called Hal, who said as soon as my fever went down I must be brought up to a nursing home. At that I cried—I could *not* leave Timmy, who has to be given six or seven shots a day and helped and who needs me, but hardly more than I need him. So Hal said he'd risk treating me by telephone if I improved. I was to take enemas of one part milk to two of water every two hours—nothing by mouth except cracked ice or a little whiskey—hot Epsom-salt packs or hot-water bottles on my belly. I ruled out the packs—Tim had too much to do already, even with Mrs. King's help mornings and at six o'clock each night.

(She is a well-made woman with a flat ordinary face, a hideous high rasping voice, and a really *good* nature, who comes from the next ranch to do what Mrs. Purdy did until she moved to Hemet. Mrs. King works harder than anyone I know—five hundred chickens, a cow to milk, pigs, corn to plant, a house to care for, two children in high school, a husband who works hard, too, for the Hendricks ranches. Maybe that is why she has such pretty legs and hips. But I doubt it.)

She took Tim into Riverside for his second of twelve roentgen-ray treatments, which so far have done no apparent good and have perhaps made his pain a little worse, and then yesterday to Hemet to get Mr. Lausen's estimate. It was more than we had counted on, but we decided to go on with it even if we have to borrow a hundred or so from the family or Uncle Boney. The five pairs of French windows and the large window in Timmy's workroom are the most costly things—about $75—but that idea of his is wonder-ful, since he will have a good, well-lit, well-heated studio right in the house, instead of building one in a year or so to which he would have to climb up or down. One hundred dollars now will save us five or six later.

Yesterday Hal cut the enemas to every four hours, with a quarter cake of yeast in half a glass of hot water every hour. (I give these details because I think his treatments are interesting.) By this time my temperature was subnormal, and the pain was less severe, although my abdomen was still swollen and extremely uncomfort-able. I could lie on my side, though.

Today he ordered two ounces of pineapple juice in four of water every hour, and to cut out the yeast—and only two enemas daily, thank God. He said I could eat some green beans or zucchini for supper if I wanted, and start tomorrow eating lightly of cooked vegetables (only the ones he approves, of course). I may not eat any tonight, if my fever goes up, which it shows signs of doing for the first time since night before last.

Timmy does too much for me and looks tired, but he takes pretty good care of himself. Today for lunch he had a large cold artichoke, some potato chips, and a bottle of beer. Last night he made himself some beautiful scrambled eggs and toast. In a way I suppose it is good for him not always to be on the receiving end of everyday bustlings.

28. iii. 40

I feel much better today and ate two artichokes for lunch, slowly, delightfully. I am still in bed, and tomorrow will get up for a little while. My abdomen is still somewhat tender. I have lost ten pounds, which pleases me, although I do not recommend the method.

Tim and Mrs. King went to Bareacres at 2:00, he to see what is happening there. (It is maddening to have to be in bed at this time.) Mrs. King had a long list of food to get.

Soon after they went out, the Purdys arrived. My heart sank —I wanted to work on a catalog I am doing of some of Timmy's paintings, to send to Anne. They stayed two hours, which was stupid of them, but were nice and solicitous. I had to listen to much talk of diet, hemorrhoids, ulcers, doctors, and so on from Septimus, while Elsie filled the back of their car with vases, boxes, and such for Bareacres. It was kind and helpful, and I was very glad to see them go.

I hope I feel like driving by next Tuesday—I want to see Hal, and I have an appointment with Kelsey, who found that everything was in good shape except my gums and wanted me to come back after I had used a certain dentifrice for two weeks. Tim and I were so relieved at his news that he made me buy a new hat. It is of fine black straw, shaped like a tiny curé's hat, with two black taffeta ribbons that tie in a rather large bow over my chignon. I think it is chic, and becoming, too.

This morning, lying in bed, we talked about politics and decided that we might vote for Roosevelt if nothing better turned up. We think Cordell Hull is good, in spite of the present campaign to turn him into another Lincoln—he is a trained statesman and believes in reciprocal trade agreements between nations. Timmy thinks an isolationist president would do terrible harm at the moment, and I think a man like Dewey would be bad, mainly because he is totally ignorant of statesmanship. A bad fault in America has always been our inclination to put a man successful in, say, journalism into a high political or diplomatic position and expect him to be equally successful. I remember talking with Paul Mourset, who was then attaché to Maréchal Lyautey, about the American ambassador in Paris at that time. He said the other diplomats scorned him for an arrogant bounder. He was a millionaire, of course (apparently that's necessary in such a position), and spoke no French nor any other language, and did countless things like referring to Frenchmen as frogs in the presence of other Frenchmen or announcing publicly that French apples weren't fit to eat and sending ostentatiously to Oregon for large shipments of American apples. It was sickening. Bullitt, in Paris now, is much better and even something of a trained diplomat—unusual in the American foreign service.

I seem to feel quite strongly on the subject of international relations. My first reaction is always to try to make people tolerant and understanding of "foreigners." I really think that America, in spite of her heritage of mixed bloods and nationalities, is even more insular and pigheaded than Great Britain in that way.

We turned down an invitation from the Moreno Valley Community Club about Switzerland. To our own surprise, we were sorry to, in one way: we both felt that it might be a way to make these few people a little less sneering and scornful of "them Yurrupeens"—a little less smug about being American and at the same time prouder and more thankful than they are.

8. iv. 40

Last night when we came back from Bareacres, the house was almost empty. When we turned on the lights, the sound of the switch was hollow. We were tired, and I had one of the few really bad, really terrible headaches of my life. And on the mantel was a pickle jar filled with deep red anemones and box leaves. It was so beautiful and so comforting and satisfying to find in this somewhat desolate place that we lay in our beds and looked up at it and felt that Mrs. King was one of the kindest people we had ever known to put it there. She is a contained person, without the beguiling sympathetic softness, the almost blurred gentleness, of Mrs. Purdy. She is not, apparently, sentimental. But she must be sensitive, because she knew how tired and how bleak we would feel, coming back last night to the nakedness of these rooms. And the flowers were beautiful. They are now.

I finally paid bills that have been collecting and read Mme. R.'s letter about the deaths of Papa Zi and Plume. We opened the letter on the hill behind Bareacres several days ago, and I was reading it aloud, and suddenly I felt too sad, so that my throat was full and my voice vanished. I had been thinking of Plume, of *le petit singe* [the little monkey]—and now he was dead. It was a shock, and yet right. His mother's letter was almost melodramatic and yet sincere. I was relieved for him to be dead, and yet terribly sad.

We move in three days. Yesterday T. got tired of the boondoggling of Lausen and his half-wit brother-in-law helper and issued an ultimatum or two. Today work was better. We may be able to close a few doors at least by the next weekend. It is exasperating to see men spend six hours fitting a piece of wood into a little hole in the floor that they and you know will be covered by linoleum.

5.v.40

I think it's some time since I wrote—I don't look, fearing embarrassment or boredom.

It is 1:30, Sunday afternoon, of a fine May day with blue sky and clouds. Behind me to the west I hear cars climbing and honking already toward the Bowl where the year's last performance of *Ramona* starts in an hour. A man sings in one of the cars. On the stone wall of the porch, Butch sniffs abruptly. A hummingbird whirls and chirps in the rangy tobacco bush outside the porch. It sounds idyllic and is—even the telephone that now and then shrills twice for the Bowl, asking probably for our tickets, and the afternoon breeze that already has started to pick up leaves and the magazine by my side and will probably carry off the actors' lines as soon as they are said, this afternoon over the hill.

I am alone, somewhat against my better judgment as a hostess and more so as myself. Anne Kelly and T. and Larry Bachman have driven in Larry's discreetly opulent Buick to Idyllwild, some twenty miles from here, to look at a summer camp for Shaun—T. because he had to move or go jittery with the pain in his leg, and Sis because she has to have constant if meaningless movement about her, and Larry—I don't know him very well, but I imagine from his thinness that he is in love and from his preoccupation that he has family troubles. I alone, in what Gloria Stuart furiously calls my "phlegmatic way," can sit by myself and assuage my own inward pangs by a sandwich of cheese and salami left from yesterday and a balloon of gin and vermouth, which makes me feel somewhat pontifical.

My excuse for staying here, besides the obvious one that three people are much more comfortable than four in a two-passenger car, is that I must, I *must* write to Aunt Grace* and my Cousin Harry. So I sit here, with my legs in the air in a deck chair on the porch, and I look occasionally at Butch on the stone railing and think how his eyes are like those of Albrecht Dürer's mother's, withdrawn and remote and impersonal, and I sigh and look down at my feet in their green socks and their striped cotton shoes with rubber soles, red, green, blue, yellow, and I think many things, including that the few men who have the energy to write whatever comes into their heads are very stupid.

7. v. 40

While T. takes a shower, I write some words. Apparently yesterday I was in a nasty mood. I remember it, but vaguely. I remember disliking myself. Today I feel much less preoccupied and am able to paint and eat and do smaller things like filing my nails without accompanying each with a silent running commentary of bilious and even masochistic self-deprecation.

We just finished painting the patio—cream walls with the lower fourth terra-cotta, and soft green on the doors and windows. We both think it looks extremely well, but, of course, we think everything about Bareacres is right, good, proper, and completely satisfying. It is fun to be so complacent about anything. It is true, though, that I have never lived in such an agreeable house. When people tell us about Captain Hoffman's unfortunately messy sui-

---

* An old school friend of Edith, dear to all the family.

cide, here in this room I know now as my office, I can only pity them for any hopes they may have to dismay us. If that poor clown's ghost ever waxed enough to come back this far, it would be too pleased to bother us. I think I have probably entertained other better ghosts and would truly not fear this one.

One reason yesterday was a bad day for me was that my secret worry about T. crept up on me. Today I feel stronger than it . . . but still I must admit it and recognize that behind all my pleasure and well-being about Bareacres is the miserable reality of his pain. What can I do? At times I am near despair, and how much more so he must often be. But what can I do? I see the supply of Analgeticum grow smaller, in spite of our fight not to use more than the absolute necessity, and I know that if the war goes on, it is most likely to be all we shall get of it. I read over in my mind the letters I have had from doctors, and I hear all the conversations we have had with them, and then I know that I could never blame T. for whatever he might feel that he must do to settle this problem that no one else seems able to settle for him. I am deadened by the very thought of it. And yet I must think of it with the same routine thoughtfulness that it takes to recognize hunger or peeing.

12. v. 40

I finally got completely fed up with this life T. leads (and I, too) and wrote Hal a sort of ultimatum, and as I knew he would, he answered at once. It is action at least. We go up Monday, first to an X-ray specialist who will take "soft" pictures, whatever they may be, to see if there are any swollen nerve bulbs in the leg. Then we go to an orthopedic man. Hal talked with him and tells me he is good. So many times we've thought that *this* time we'd get something done, and always the experiments have been useless or even harmful . . . but this time I really do feel that we'll do some good. It may mean hospitals and even another operation, but we don't care. Life must be sweeter than it is for Timmy to endure it much longer, even though we are so happy here together.

The weekend was hectic, in a queer controlled way. The Powells were here, with meals and so on, of course. Then, the night before they came (they wrote they'd be here for lunch and drove in casually at about 4:00 in the afternoon), Pizzi, out on the hill, let out an agonized wail, and there were heavy feet thudding, and she was gone. She was heavy with kittens, and I suppose easy pickings for a coyote or wildcat. Timmy felt badly . . . worse than I . . . but I felt badly, too. About 1:30 Saturday night, then, Butch went out into the patio to take a whizz or something and began to scream and moan, more like a person than a little dog. I ran out. I was scared, because I thought he would be fighting with a rattlesnake, and . . . I was scared. He was cowering by the old trunk, and when he saw me he dragged himself into the middle of the patio, still crying terribly. I picked him up, and Tim and I looked all over, but there was no sign of bites. His left front leg seemed stiff, but he was not biting at it. He hid his head under Timmy's arm. Finally we got him quiet and went back to bed. But in half an hour he let out another yelp, this time in the kitchen. We thought he was dying. We got him quiet again and pulled on some clothes and started for West Riverside and Dr. Walkerdine. The ride seemed terribly long. I took along what was left of a bottle of whiskey, but neither of us wanted any. Walkerdine got up, sleepy but nice, in pale blue flannel pajamas, and he couldn't see anything wrong with Butch, except that he was suffering from shock. He gave him a stimulant, and we stood in the little operating room looking down at him. "Poor little dog," I said. "His nose is pale." "Not only that," Walkerdine said, in his queer Scotch-Cockney accent, "but the little chap has an exprrrression of grrrreat anxiety." I left Butch there, and we drove back here, another forty-odd miles that seemed shorter than the way over. We slept for about two hours. Then I got up, hearing a queer sound that was more in my dream than in the air, and found Tawny just finishing having her sixth and final kitten in my typewriter stand. I was sorry I had not come sooner, as I've never seen anything being born, unless you can count an egg I once saw pop out of a hen. Things were quite messy. I helped her clean up and spent the rest of the day, it seemed to me, moving her and the litter about the house, looking for cool air. It was a stifling day, and I really think they almost died. She was too hot and weak to clean herself, and felt badly about it. Today is hot but better, and she's almost all clean except a little stiffness around her tail, and the six kittens are very much alive. In a little while T. is going to drown the three yellow and white ones, and we'll keep the three gray ones. I said I'd do it, and I would, too . . . but I was relieved when he insisted that he'd do it. He doesn't want to either.

The Powells stayed until 5:00 or so, although they had written they'd leave about noon . . . I sound terribly ungracious . . . and by the time they left I was in an interior dither of heat and messiness. I felt that the house and everything in it, especially me, was disgustingly dusty and grimy. So I gave T. a whopping shot and then spent quite a long time taking a shower. Then I felt very nice, and we had a good supper on the porch. T. ate two soft-boiled eggs and some Swedish rye crisp, and . . .

13 or 14. v. 40

Yesterday before we went to West Riverside to get Butch, who seems quite well after his scare, T. killed the kittens. Tawny tried to stop me when I picked them up and put them in a basket, but I think that was her only feeling then or now that anything was wrong. I dug a hole while T. killed them. He chopped each one twice, across the throat and across the skull. I climbed up the slope to take them from him where he stood holding them in a little bunch by their tails. "Poor little rats," he said. "What?" "I said, 'Little rats,' " he mumbled. He was not pale, but he did not look at me. He laid them on my shovel, and I went down to the hole. I slid them into the ground, and as they touched the cool earth at the bottom, they all three made one movement, the same they made when they nuzzled against Tawny looking for her dugs. I stood looking, although I knew they must be dead. T. called down, "Don't look. They're dead all right." I covered them up and put three stones over the loosened earth. As I climbed up again, I said, "I'm sorry you had to do that." T. didn't answer, and I saw him hurrying into the house. He went to the bathroom, and I thought maybe he was going to be sick, but he was crying instead. He took a long shower, and we have only mentioned them twice, when I said that Tawny looked much more comfortable and when he said that drowning was worse than being chopped.

Underneath everything we do or think, now, is the incredible knowledge that Europe, the part we knew of it, is forever gone. The actual invasions and bombings are less final than what is dying in the people. They will go on, naturally, and will build a life that will soon seem natural to their children and to them. But a part of their spirit, and a part of ours, too, is dead. It makes all of us zombies, if we are what we have been. I can smell my own decay. It has grown stronger since last September. I can smell it, my own and other people's, and feel it unsuspected in the air about young children and the most thoughtless ninnies, who do not know what is happening to the world and to themselves.

T. has just finished making another beautiful little cat door, this time in my workroom so that Tawny can go out at night while

Butch is shut into the kitchen where the other door is. This one is too small for Butch, much to his disgust. He can get only his head through. It has a little zinc panel that slides down and closes it against drafts in winter, and a curtain of fringed brown leather to keep out flies.

These boondogglings are good because they keep T. so busy, and he does them all so nicely. We'll be glad when they're over, though, and he can get to work again. He made himself a fine strong easel and has the studio pretty much as he wants it . . . but now we'll have to be gone for some days next week, and there's little point in getting into the swing of painting before then.

It is still hot. Occasionally an almost violent breeze sweeps through the house, blowing the curtains about and closing a door now and then.

17.v.40

The news that the Germans are within seventy miles of Paris sent Timmy, crumpled and terribly old, weeping away. I could not follow him. I felt that anything as actual as arms and kisses and tenderness would be obscene. I sat for a time and then played Tchaikovsky's concerto, that rather bangy silly piano thing, on the gramophone, and in a while he came in and I finished the album without looking at him and then went into the bathroom and found when I put on new lipstick that my mouth had gone all crooked and sideways, apparently forever.

28. v. 40

Many times lately I have had the time, and even the wish, to put something down in this book. But some of those times I have felt almost morbidly slack and in a way resentful of the way T. feels— resentful that this is happening to *him*. I don't want it to happen to anyone, of course, but especially not to him. And then other times have found me all at odds with myself so that I could hardly think in phrases, much less sentences, because of the things happening in Europe and even in this country. It is queer what a hopelessness has crept into all my thoughts. It is almost a slackness. Why be so economical? Why be generous? Why have children or plant trees? This time next year or next month or tomorrow—who knows what irrevocable change will have been made in all our values? Will we have soap to wash with, or a blanket, or even any spiritual honor? Then I am ashamed, as well as startled, and I know that I am dauntless, just as humans all over the world are dauntless. Pain and disaster and grim dreary poverty can never kill me and my inner self.

All this probably seems exasperated and neurotic. It is true, though, that at this moment the whole pace of existence, here at Bareacres as well as in fallen Brussels and in London awaiting its annihilation, has been sped up past reality into a state bordering on nightmare. We live fairly calmly here on the hill and have even sickened somewhat to listening to the radio news . . . but within us is the same dumb watchfulness, the same feeling of helpless inevitability, that soldiers and pregnant animals everywhere know too well.

The doctors could do nothing for T. The day was an exhausting one, and we were sick and dismayed when we saw that there was nothing. We had even welcomed the idea of more hospitals, operations . . . anything to change this half-life of pain for T.

One of the orthopedic specialists leapt agilely from his own field into psychiatry, with unbecoming haste, and talked behind closed doors of night dreams, fear of impotence, brooding . . . practically said that all T.'s pain was a foolish idea and no more. Hal prescribed rest, more B-1 pills, another visit to Pasadena in three weeks. Zubzubzub.

Bill and Jane Evans came down this last weekend and brought and planted a great many trees, vines, shrubs. It will be beautiful if they grow . . . and two days later they look very happy, thanks to good planting and fairly cool weather. Bill embarrassed me by not letting me pay him anything for them. So we gave them our album of Tahitian chants, and I'll find a nice plate for the plate rail in their new house. They are apparently quite absorbed in plans for that and hope to move in another month. The plans we saw seemed quite dull and usual, but then they are, too—dull, usual, and very nice. I think, after many years, that B. is a much better person than J. She is growing more and more like her mother, who is one of the two women in the world who completely shock and frighten me with their active repulsiveness. I was startled to find that J., who has in the past attracted me with her soft sweet ways, this time seemed merely affectedly "cuddlesome" and that her little body had grown stringy and old. *Tout passe* . . . and soon I, too, will be older than I am this minute, but I hope that I can remain nicer, to myself at least, than I think Jane is becoming. Of course, she may have no faintest inkling that she is anything that she was not ten years ago. Perhaps that would be better. But on the other hand, I would prefer not to have her wear such cut-down shorts and halters that I have to see her flat leathery puckered little belly and her hollow sharpened flanks. From my point of view, it would be pleasanter to have her realize the changes of time enough to cover up some of her body a little more discreetly. I don't know how old she is. To believe Gloria, who has always hated her guts, she is about forty. She may be thirty-five. Anyway . . . it is boring to have to avert my eyes, inwardly at least, from something that once gave me pleasure. And perhaps she feels so about me.

29.v.40

Time, whether good or bad, passes too quickly for me, and I am almost resentful that it is Thursday of this week and not Monday or even Wednesday.

We bought a rather pretty little sable bitch this week to be a companion for Butch. He was mooning toward the valley and growing capricious about his meals, and we thought it was loneliness as much as lovesickness. So now he is at the Rose of Sharon Kennels, being wormed and becoming used to his wife. I miss him. They'll be back in a day. I must learn more about coping with bitches in heat and all that; we don't want her to have puppies for about ten more months. Butch looks very funny and sweet now, with all his fur cut off. That horrifies Peke fanciers, but he was wretchedly hot. She (I don't know what we'll call her—she already knows "Brownie") has a much lighter coat.

The three kittens are beginning to play now and have their eyes open, like little shiny blueberries. When I bring them in by Tim's couch at night, Tawny makes a special show of being maternal. She is a good mother, as a matter of fact.

I start work today revising a book Tim wrote some twenty years ago. I may be wasting my time . . . don't know yet. I don't mean that it isn't good—parts of it are fine—but it may not benefit any from my effort, and I should be writing something more my own and sending it to Mrs. Pritchett while she still feels stirred up about "What Happened to Miss Browning." However . . .

30.v.40

Memorial—or is it Decoration?—Day brings out a special flood of emotional crap in the radio serials, which we listen to almost every day with a kind of ghoulish nauseated interest. Some of them are well acted and sometimes well written. Once when I was ill, I listened deliberately for several hours, and at the end I felt stranger than I have from any other drug . . . light-headed and terribly depressed, in an almost numb way.

I got to work yesterday on [Timmy's] *Daniel Among the Women*. I need to see a few popular magazines of about 1911. The local library has found me some old *Theatres,* which I'll look at tomorrow.

Tomorrow we go to get the two dogs. I'll be glad to have them here. We had the kittens on the porch during lunch today, and they were very diverting.

Last night T. asked me to hide the .22 bullets. I do not mention this from any martyr complex . . . Pity me, oh pity me . . . but because I think I had better. It is strange about suicide. I have always felt strongly on the subject. I remember arguing and then growing angry with Rex, years ago, when an old friend of his who was penniless found he was dying slowly and expensively of a terrible cancer and jumped out of the hospital window after arranging for some kind of pension for his helpless sister. "I never knew the judge was yellow," Rex kept saying. It was a terrible blow to him, to his idea of honor and strength. I argued with him that it took courage. I said that shooting yourself for exhibitionism or because you failed your exams or lost your job or your love was cowardly, usually . . . but not what the judge had done. But Rex kept shaking his head and saying, "I never knew the judge was yellow." Now I find that I have been living with the constant thought of suicide in my mind ever since September 1, 1938. That is a long time. I often think I am used to it. And then T. says something like his request last night, and although I answer quietly and do what he asks, I realize that in spite of all my thought, the actuality of killing oneself is hard to accept. Once in Bern I knew that if I left T.'s bed near the balcony edge, he would jump. He had talked of it often, begged me to help him, to carry him there, and I had argued calmly with him and asked him to give me one more day, one more week, three hours. But this time I knew, without any reserve, that he would do it. I wanted him to, with almost all of my love. I looked at him, and he averted his eyes and started to smile a strange crafty smile. I turned away, to leave him to what he so desired . . . and then I turned back, and pulled his bed away from the edge, and could not look at him for knowing that I had condemned him to more torture. And that sort of thing has happened several times. Once I found a razor in the night-table drawer at Adelboden, slipped cunningly under the paper lining. I took it silently and crept from the room covered with shame. But I could not leave it there. In spite of my love for T., my horrible primitive instinct to prevent suicide was stronger. I remember talking and talking about suicide with him and making bargains: wait seven days, wait six weeks, and when it is worse, I swear by Christ crucified that I will help you. We talked of ways. No drugs, although I had them under my hand, because it would make trouble for Soeur Irma. Not slashing wrists—so messy and so scandalous for the kind hotel owners. What, then . . . what? That sort of thing went on and on. And now when I hear a strange noise or when I hear too long a silence, I think, This is the time: it has happened, and I make myself call out in a quiet way or walk slowly, unhurriedly, heavily, to what I may find. The strange thing is that oftener than not I have a quick wild hope that perhaps this *is* the time. "Let us accustom ourselves to desolation," I find that I have scrawled on a scrap of paper, thinking about this war and how news that a month ago would make me weep now goes in my mind and out again as if I were rock. But I know that such a thing is not possible, any more than it is possible completely to accustom oneself to the acceptance of murder. I know how to kill T. and to do it easily and probably so that I would never have to be accused of it . . . but I know that I never will. But even after so long, I don't know that *he* never will.

I think maybe I am wrong to write about this.

I went to tea at Miss van Benschoten's yesterday. Three of the local gentry were there. It was pleasant enough, as such things go, but I came away terribly ashamed of myself for having managed to let them all know, in a charming gracious way, that Mrs. Purdy was my cleaning woman and not my intimate. God. Why did I do that? I wonder, feeling sickish. What the hell difference does it make? How could I lower myself to such peewee behavior and insult not only myself but my hostess? Well . . . I feel ashamed.

The first picture T. did when he started to work again last week, after so much time of carpentering and such, was fine; it is a portrait of four Mexican dolls, called *Les Fiançailles* [The Engagement Party]—very virile. Others have been good, but less good. He is working now but without wanting to. It is too hot to do any more of the siding that we started this morning. That will be wonderful—redwood, wide, already making the house look solid and much lower to the ground. It will cover all the cracks between the pine boards, too. We'll go out as soon as the sun is less hot. I must work on *Daniel* at least a few minutes before then.

5. vi. 40

I sit down, feeling I must say something that for one instant seems important, at least to my own scheme. And all I can think of is the soft trusting relaxation of the little dog, who lies put along the crease between the couch pillows, his legs bent whitely at the wrists, his belly bare to our whims.

My mind is filled with the enormity of people. It is two days now since our parochial visit, and I am still immeasurably disturbed by it.

Mr. H. is a tall man, with the face, at first glance, of a matinee idol like one of the Barrymores. He had a languid air, and he pops his pale eyes at times to help this illusion, probably—possibly—unwittingly. Now and then, *hie und da,* as the pathological analysis of Timmy's amputations says (I typed it this afternoon for a doctor who believes T. is stalling and fabricating pain because of a fear of impotence)—*hie und da* his finely modeled lips curve in an almost subtly quizzical smile as he speaks.

He speaks seldom. When he does, it is about the great number of books he owns, the "artist colonies" he has known, the people like Emma Goldman and Earl Browder he has heard . . . trying to show us that he is worldly and broad-minded.

Most of the time it is the woman who talks.

She is a coarse-faced woman, wearing thick-lensed glasses that accentuate her small mean eyes. Her coloring is crude. As I remember, she wears sensible navy-blue dresses and shoes with what look like built-in arches. She left a wretched printed silk scarf, black and white, and I think she did it deliberately so that either she or I must respond courteously.

Her conversation is typically that of a village minister's wife, with that ghastly tinge of whimsical baby talk that means that years of guild members have laughed at even the most inane remarks. She almost talks baby talk, and she has the same habit that Mrs. Lewis and one or two minister's wives show, of saying things with an air of irrefutable certainty. "Why on earth, my dear," meaning you poor ninny, "did you ever pay $16 a cord for oak?" and then it turns out that that is a very decent price and that she was thinking of olive and that it is really impolite not to have let her in on the bargain. But the first reaction is one of positive and noisy disapproval.

I'll write a little more about the H.'s because they made a strong and almost shocking impression on both of us, so that we found ourselves thinking many hours later of this or that about them.

They were very curious about the house, and I showed it to them room by room. His reaction was to hasten to tell us, in his vague dead manner, that he, too, was an artist, that he, too, had books and many more than we did. She chattered constantly and with her own strange ministerial impertinence, and fingered the curtains and estimated the number of pewter trays we had.

I made tea for them because I could see that they wanted it. All the time she talked and talked and told some anecdotes about Indians and so on that did not seem shocking until much later, when we suddenly realized that she had been boasting about fooling them and about being suspicious and stingy.

"What do you think about Leopold? How could he have done such a miserable cowardly low thing? Tell me exactly what you think," she commanded with what I'm sure she has been told is charming imperiousness. But she did not want to hear; she wanted to tell *us*. She did, at great length, and seemed to enjoy berating the king. Tim tried to say that it was hard to judge a man in Leopold's position, and I tried to say that one man alone might choose death rather than dishonor where he could not possibly do it for his whole family or his nation. But she did not hear us. In her chattering half-laughing way, she said some violent and cruel things.

Finally, after some other talk, she asked me, "Doesn't it make you simply furious to see ships of Red Cross supplies going to Germany?" "No," I answered, feeling suddenly sick. That actually stopped her for a minute. Her jaw dropped, and before she could start talking again and really before I had time to think and to realize how little good it would do, I said, "Germans bleed. They are humans, too. The Red Cross is for all suffering men." She looked surprised and perhaps even chagrined, but only for a second. Then she laughed gaily and said, "Well, perhaps you're right. Of course, of course. But all I say is, I wish they'd bleed a little more."

Her husband sat without talking, as usual, his pale eyes fixed on something above our heads, his pale hands posed before him, his pale lips twisted into a subtle smile.

She got up to go. As so often happens, I said good-bye and thanked them for their visit with more warmth than I could possibly show to anyone I liked. I was terribly disturbed by them and still am. I know that a priest is but the instrument of God, but it would be impossible for me ever to take communion from Hill. How could any decent man, and especially a man of God, let people talk as he lets his own wife talk? It is horrible.

I meant to tell about the little bitch we bought for Butch, but other things came into my head. She was a sweet-faced delicate little creature and clung to us, but when she walked her feet splayed out in such a weak rickety fashion that after only a few hours we knew that we couldn't stand to have her around. She had very bad table manners, too. So we took her back and refused to ask for any money back, so that our twenty-four hours with her cost us $12.50. We charged it to experience. She reminded me unpleasantly of a very good charwoman I had in Vevey . . . weak physically and spiritually, with a pretty face and a loose-moraled prudery about her.

7. vi. 40

Yesterday I was all ready to sit down and say that the French were holding the Germans and that T. seemed to be better. He does, still. I have been able to cut down a little on his injections without letting him know, of course. But the French are not quite holding the Germans, who are supposed to be about fifty-five miles from Paris now. They are going slowly, though, and even that is better than the blitzkrieg tactics of the war so far. The French are trying to exhaust them. I think they will succeed.

Here the term *fifth-column activities* is already so overworked as to be nauseating, and the air is full of spy scares and rumors of armed invasions. This noon we hear over the radio that the veterans of the last war are trying to raise a volunteer army of 100,000 men in Southern California to combat foreigners. It is sickening.

Two new air schools are to be started in the valley, it seems, to turn out a hundred pilots every ninety days. That seems a terribly short course to me, but I suppose it's not much harder to handle a plane than an automobile, and I'm pretty sure I could learn the mechanics of a car in less than ninety days.

The siding is almost up, and the house looks fine and solid, although much yellower than we'd thought. It will darken with time. I hope we're here to see it when it's chocolate black.

We heard this noon that Paris has surrendered to the Germans. My blood stops at the thought of what this must mean to the millions of people like Jean Matruchot and Connes and Jeanne Bonamour. But there was nothing else to do.

Tim is putting boiled linseed oil on the redwood and turning it a soft intense red color. It is beautiful. The porch now, with the dark red walls and the floor painted a soft green and the gay furniture, is one of the loveliest rooms I have ever seen.

I brought portulacas and zinnias back yesterday from our trip to the Ranch and planted them around the front door and in the patio. T. hates to see me get anything more to care for, and I really will stop now. Today the plants look droopy, of course, but I think tonight's watering will revive them. The plants that Bill thought would need watering only once a week need it at least three times as often, so I find myself carrying about thirty buckets a day to them. It worries T., and I am sorry about it, but I can't let them all die.

We are to increase T.'s doses of thyroid one capsule a day each week until he begins to have heart flutterings and headaches and then let Hal know. I think I see some improvement these last six or seven days . . . at least no bad cramps.

The worst thing about the relationships in my family now is the way Mother and Sis are about each other. They are malicious, sarcastic, and truly bitchy and seem to make no effort to be charitable or tolerant of the other's mistakes. The situation upsets me, but I do not know what to do about it. I hate to see Mother lose any of her dignity and find myself feeling slightly sick to hear her say some of the things she does about her daughter. I know, too, that she talks to other people about Sis more or less as she talks to me. It is bad. And Sis is the same way . . . or no. I don't think she talks about Mother much to other people. But she makes absolutely no effort to understand or help Mother and goes nonchalantly on using Mother's money and getting into debt and taking it for granted that the parents are damned lucky to have the privilege of supporting not only her child but herself. The weekends usually end either with a row between Sis and Father about money or tears and sarcasm between Sis and Mother about the discipline of Shaun. It is an unpleasant situation to find in a family that for so many years has seemed such a nice one to belong to.

Of course, the thing that has made both the parents lose their faith in us children as a group is the complete disappointment they feel in David. That is disagreeable for Tim and me, since without us it would probably never have happened that he would leave college and decide to become a painter or whatever it is he is. Their whole attitude has changed this last year. They are quietly bitter and in a strange way insouciant, as if it did not matter whether we stayed decent or even alive. I know it is not true, underneath their new callousness. I can understand them, too. But I regret it.

We are calling a halt on the work on the house, although we can still think of many things we want to do, like paving the patio and building a barbecue and so on. Timmy is painting again, and tomorrow I start work in earnest on *Daniel,* which I meant to do today. But this morning I went downtown. This afternoon I cleaned up my desk, and just as I started to pull the various piles of notes and papers together, the liquor man came with a case of beer and two or three bottles of whiskey to try, and then the garage man arrived with the Bantam, which was in the shop getting a new muffler and a generator repair.

We are trying to live economically, but today I have spent a lot of money. I went to the grocery store and bought a lot of canned things: a case of milk for the cats, a case of Pard for Butch, some salmon, soups, beans, and so on—$30. Then I went to a furniture store and ordered two beds for the guest room—about $60. Then I bought $30 worth of whiskey and beer. And the car cost $18.95. It is frightening when I put it into a paragraph. The liquor and the beds we could do without, of course. And, of course, they are nice, especially the beds, which Tim and I will use this winter, but which will be much nicer for guests than the cots I have had to make up in the guest room from the studio couch. The couch we'll put on the porch. And, of course, I'll have to get some kind of bedspreads. Oh, dear.

It is hot now, but we like it when we can live at our own speed. There is almost always air moving up here on the hill. It is delightful . . . the most beautiful place in the world, to me at least.

Later

I meant to get to work on the book, and then I thought about one or two things that I want to put here. One is that a group of women in Whittier is trying to witch-hunt Miss Ellis, the librarian. They say that in 1935 she personally frowned on a book that one of the group presented to the library . . . a wild book that attracted some attention, most of it jeering, called *The Red Menace* or something like that. It was endorsed by the D.A.R. and a few like organizations, and Miss Ellis accepted it for circulation but followed her customary good and often amusing habit of pasting a review or two in the back of the book. This hurt the donor's feeling, since one of the reviews was full of ridicule. She withdrew the book, with a scene during which she says Miss Ellis said that she was glad to have it out of the library. The woman seethed and went to some expense to have photostatic copies of the review made. Now, in 1940, with all this talk of fifth columns and spies and Communists, the group of women comes to Rex with a long story that Miss Ellis is a Communist and a menace and a subversive and that she should be hounded from her position. Miss Ellis, a prissy yearning virgin nearing sixty, is one of the least dangerous people I have ever met. She is boring and affected, God knows. She has worked hard and conscientiously for most of her life and supports an invalid crotchety old mother, and I am pretty sure her only sins are ones like feeling a slight flutter in what she innocently thinks is her heart when Alfred Lunt gets as far as Los Angeles in his current drama, and perhaps even suffering an occasional mental orgasm at some especially well-written bit of English prose. But the pack is after her now for being a dangerous agent of a foreign power and so on.

The other thing I want to note now, and I don't know why unless it is because I am in a rather soured state about humanity, is something Mrs. Purdy said the other day. She has a funny mannerism of laughing a little when she repeats anything or when she tells me something, some anecdote. She almost whinnies, very softly. She seldom gossips, since we have few common friends and I am not exactly encouraging anyway, and when she does she always laughs softly and says, "Oh I have some *goss*-ip for you." One morning, after she had been to a picnic given by the Moreno Community Club, she laughed that way and said that. "Oh?" I said. "Yes," she went on, still laughing softly, with her eyes twinkling, "the new tenant of your house in Moreno tried to kill herself the other night." "Oh, the poor woman," I said, remembering the strange distinguished girl, tall and faded, with her four children and her beautiful clothes and her queer dopey way of talking to me. I can't remember her name, but I always think of her as Mrs. Scatterbrain. "Poor Mrs. Scatterbrain," I said. "She must have been very unhappy." Mrs. Purdy stopped laughing for a second or two, and she looked almost startled, and then she began to laugh softly again. "Yes, she drank Lysol or something like that," she chuckled. "Maybe she had those children too close together, or maybe she has husband trouble," I said. "Well, I never thought of that. I suppose we shouldn't judge, should we? But still . . ." and Mrs. Purdy turned away, laughing again, "still, that's no excuse to act that way. Mr. Canterbury kicked her out of his place at 11:00 one night, and she was so drunk she didn't get home until after 3:00 . . ." I didn't say anything, because there was nothing to say —but I felt terribly sad to know that a woman as gentle as Mrs. Purdy, a woman who has lived a cruel hard life, could be so cruel and hard. I should think she would be understanding and full of compassion. T. says I am really naive, and I suppose this is a proof of it.

16.vi.40

I know what I must do with a rather confused chapter of *Daniel,* and indeed I have looked through it and even put the paper in the typewriter. But I do not feel like working on it.

Last night we broiled a steak on the temporary barbecue in the patio. I did it according to the *Sunset Barbecue Book,* and basted it with strong French dressing, and did not prick it with the fork, and we had made a fine bed of oak coals, and the result was good. The steak was truly delicious and made us realize that meat, a primitive hunger, is a primitive thing and best cooked as the cavemen did it, minus French dressing and some other refinements, of course.

We sat in the cooling dark courtyard, and Butch gnawed quietly at the T-bone, and now and then a lizard slipped clumsily through the dry leaves of the cottonwood trees. The moon, half full, was high in the sky. In my office the three kittens clawed occasionally at the screen door, and Tawny scolded at them.

The night, for me, was troubled with a steady dreaming of the war, as always now. This time I took care of Czechoslovakia, Poland, Finland, Estonia . . . I evacuated them, I reorganized the cabinets, I supervised the Red Cross.

At 2:00 I gave T. an especially good shot, knowing that he had not yet slept and that perhaps if I did so he would not need one at dawn. I did not tell him, hoping to surprise him with relief. But at dawn I opened one eye from my dreams and saw him looking at me. I turned over quickly and thought that if I showed no intelligence he would think, Poor girl, I'll not waken her, and then go to sleep again. But in a few minutes he was still looking at me. I pretended not to have seen him. Soon I heard him getting up, terribly cautiously. I knew that he wanted a shot but that he was trying not to ask for one. So I said nothing and went to sleep again, to settle, this time, the evacuation of Paris.

When I finally got up, about 9:00, we found that poor Butch had been hit by diarrhea and had made three shameful places. T. cleaned them up. Then, in the hallway to my workroom, there was a neat little pile of gut, probably from a gopher. I cleaned it. "There is a dead baby rabbit in your bookcase," T. warned me. But by the time I got to it there were two. They were sad little carcasses. I suppose Tawny brings them in to accustom the kittens to warm meat. They looked fairly neat, lying against the suitbox full of letters on the bottom shelf, but when I lifted them up by the ears and put them into the wastebasket, I saw that they were quite mussy. I cleaned up as much as I could of the blood from the new wood. There was a loathsome gray little thing, which T. said was a tick. It is hard to find burying ground for all these dead creatures in the hard ground. I put the two little rabbits under the irrigating ditch of the cottonwoods near the arroyo. The kittens had licked at their fur, and they looked terribly little.

T. had been painting and walking about the place. It was about 10:00 before we got through cleaning up the messes and the little bodies, and I got the animals fed. Butch would eat nothing and looked up at us like some sad sea monster. T. had already got himself a nip of whiskey, in the coldness of a dripping early-morning fog. So he had another nip and a prairie oyster . . . with seven capsules of Hal's thyroid mixture and a small *goût* of Epsom juice. I drank a pink gin and bottle of beer, and after T. went back to his painting, I sat in a strange alcoholic Sunday stupor and read an old copy of the *New Yorker*. I knew that I should work and that Paris was in the hands of the Germans, and still I sat there in the little bar, feeling the sun through the curtains and not even remembering what time it was.

Now it is after lunch. We ate chili con carne in a continuation of our matinal decadence. At 1:30 T. thought that it must be at least 3:30, and finally he broke down and asked for a shot. Now he is sitting on the porch, waiting for relief. He feels discouraged because he has not been able to paint anything good until maybe this morning, when he did a disturbing, chaotic thing about Creation, full of snakes and beasts and three or four men, full of pinks and greens and trouble.

Two of the kittens play languidly on the shelf spotted with rabbit blood, and one lies beside its mother but not too close. Tawny, about twice a day now, is teaching them to jump, to pounce, and bite the neck of their prey. They all practice on one another.

I remember that I wrote a few days ago about suicide, so I think that I shall put down what happened this morning. I find myself disturbed by it.

Last night was a hard one for T., and he said once that he wanted to know where I had hidden the bullets. I told him I would tell him this morning. Finally he went to sleep.

This morning we both woke rather early to a beautiful hot bright morning. We lay in bed for a few minutes, I stretching and he reading a magazine. Finally he said, "I suppose it's because I'm curious, but I would like to see Anne and see what the new house at Quantness is like, and I'd like to see Mother, so I think when the next check comes we'd better get an Oldsmobile and drive east and maybe show you the Grand Canyon and use all the Analgeticum I need to be really comfortable, and then come back and finish it up, after a really good time." He was very serious about it. For some reason I began to tease him. "Yes, it does sound awful," he admitted, half-laughing. " 'Dear Mother, if you want to make my last days pleasant how about sending me a nice check for a trip to see you?' " There wouldn't be enough money anyway, I told him . . . we'd be lucky to get a thousand dollars, and that wouldn't even buy the car. I was laughing at him. Suddenly he muttered, not rudely but almost laughing, too, "Oh, shut up, shut up!" And then I saw that his eyes were more than full of tears.

I felt *awful*. I hated to think that I had mocked him, and suddenly, talking so positively about killing himself in the morning, not during the night, made me sick. It almost seemed real. I still feel dreadfully upset. There is nothing to do. While I was dressing he came into the room, and I told him how very sorry I was to have laughed at him, and I could see that he, too, was upset.

It's like the surrender of France or T.'s having his leg cut off. I *know* those things have happened, but I don't *realize* it. This morning, for just a minute, I realized about T.'s possible escape from this business.

30. vi. 40

It is almost 6:00, and I am just now beginning to feel like work, so that I know that I should arrange my days differently. I should work in the morning, here in my room, I mean, and do things that take no thought, like dishes and beds and sweeping, in the afternoons. Because now, just when I begin to feel awake, T. is through for the day and will need a shot as soon as he gets out of the shower, and then, on most days about this time, there are the plants to water, and supper.

Tonight I'll get the wood together for supper in the patio. The patio is dusty, and the plants are still very small, of course, and the barbecue is makeshift, but it is already a lovely place. Several times we've had supper out there and sat quietly in the dark. It has been fine. Tonight I'll broil sandwiches of eggplant and sausages and make a salad. We'll drink some beer.

The most surprising thing about our life is our new interest in swimming. I have said very sincerely for many years that I'd be perfectly happy never to go in the ocean again, and as for public pools, I couldn't be bribed to put a toe in one. But the other day while the parents were visiting us, we decided to drive over to Soboba Hot Springs, and there in that startling cool green oasis under the bleak mountains of San Jacinto we found a lovely mountain pool that T. had seen once years ago and still talked about without remembering where it was.

It is big, irregularly shaped, with a stream pouring in at one end and out the other. There may be one person in it or nobody, and the cottonwood trees that shade it drop their leaves on the brownish water.

Father and T. and I went in. I had to rent a suit, and the only one I could get was an old-fashioned man's suit of gray wool that kept slipping off my breasts. I must have looked funny as well as immodest, but we were alone. It was fun. I wish I could swim beautifully, like a fish maybe. I am so clumsy in the water.

Then we had massages, and we all felt so nice and T. slept so much better than usual that night that it was easy to convince ourselves that we should and could afford to go often.

So I bought a cheap but pretty suit of white Lastex with red dots ($2.95 at Penney's), a white cap, some white sandals, and a pair of gabardine shorts for T., and we got out the red bath towels and the suntan oil and hurried back to Soboba the next day, and found the pool being cleaned. It was too bad. But we're going again tomorrow. I am really excited. I look very nice in my suit, which would have shocked me a few years ago, but I wish that I weighed about five or ten pounds less. The trouble with me is that I eat and drink more than I need to.

About this time every year a small idea nags at my mind about how wonderful it would be to cut off most of my hair. It creeps into my other thoughts, and I find myself speculating willy-nilly on how it would look, feel, be. I always decide, because I know it to be true, that I had better leave well enough alone, and that I would regret it, and that it would be even more bother than my long hair. And so on. But still I can't help wishing that I had nerve enough to cut it all off. I think that it might look quite nice. The trouble is that short hair would accentuate my baby face, and although that might have been very attractive ten years ago, I have no longer the flat-hipped look that goes with boyish coiffures. I don't know, though . . . I may weaken yet. My hair grows fast, and I could wear an artificial chignon on the rare occasions when I put on "city clothes."

A letter from Anne suggests that we go to the Mayo Clinic and says that her finances are in a strange state, war or no war, and that she might soon be unable to help us. We answered that we wanted to try more of Hal's treatment plus the new promise of the baths at Soboba. I can't help worrying a little about our money. It is all so indefinite. I am terribly and deeply grateful to Anne for all she has done and is doing for us, but I wish she would understand how difficult it is for both Tim and me to be living on an uncertain amount of generosity. We never know what she will send us. Sometimes she forgets, and we have to ask. She has made definite annuities for the servants, but with T. she has done nothing so that we are always in doubt and always feeling a worried gratitude that at times cannot help being almost grudging. There is nothing we can do, though. I could not get work here without leaving T. and paying a housekeeper for him, and he could not get work, unless it might be as an illustrator. Anne is a fine sensitive intelligent woman, but this is one thing I think would be impossible to explain to her—that if she is going to give us money to live on, we would infinitely prefer a small sum sent coldly at set times from a bank, to her erratic checks, which may be much bigger.

It is beautiful now, with a golden haze in the air. In the patio the two great yellow ceremonial lanterns, which Mrs. Edith Kelly once gave to Mother and which we now use for the first time since they came from Japan some twenty-five years ago, tap now and then against the thin steel wire that supports them. In a minute, I'll take out two chairs and get the wood, and while T. builds the fire I'll put the supper things on a tray. I can hear Cinnamon and Smokey mewing for their supper. Tawny has almost cut off their milk and is already flaunting her tail at Butch. I'm going to try putting some sex repellent on it. It is for bitches, but I think it would have the same effect on Butch whether it was on a dog or a cat. Tawny is as thin as a razor, and not only do I not want her getting him all hot but I don't want her having another batch of babies so soon. The little ones are seven weeks old today.

We gave one to Mrs. Purdy a week ago. It was the one that T. had picked out as his favorite. And it got crushed behind a sofa the night she took it.

She has been sick—a kind of "summer complaint," I think, although she is too discreet to go into details. (I find myself enjoying the housework and doing many jobs like cleaning the icebox with the firm if conceited feeling that nobody else is quite as thorough as M. F. K. P.). I took her some turkey soup and a little cold meat last night and found Septimus stretched out on the porch swing, with bed pillows propping him up instead of the many ordinary porch pillows. "How is your invalid?" I asked, noticing that Mrs. P. was not in bed. "Oh, we're better," he said. He tottered to his feet and called, Sweetie-pie. She came weaving in, like a somewhat pasty ghost, with her eyes off-focus. She really looked ill. "How are you, Mrs. Purdy?" But before she could answer, the old man stuck his face between us and told me all about how *he* felt. I was hot with a little flash of exasperation: poor Sweetie-pie couldn't even have a little dizzy spell to herself, without having him steal all the fun. I felt like saying, "Mr. Purdy, I am quite used to hearing all about your feelings and your symptoms and your gas pains. But *tonight,* odd as it may seem, I am asking about your wife's feelings. Move aside. I am not interested in you—*ever*—and now even less than that." But, of course, I only waited until he was through and then rather pointedly continued talking to her about taking things easily and not working too hard and so on. She was quite fluttery and grateful, and I escaped as soon as possible and left her cooking the old boy's dinner.

T. has done a whole series of beautiful pictures of vegetables and fruits, very sure and rich.

3. vii. 40

I am thirty-two today, which is a rather murky steamy day. I am dressed in my best white silk playsuit, which I bought last year at Palm Springs, and white socks, and blue and white canvas shoes. My hair is done up on top of my head, for coolness. In a little while, Tim and I will go over to Soboba to swim and have a massage and then maybe a couple of martinis and lunch. I'll wear my new bathing suit, which he gave me and Mother bought for him in Laguna. It is black silk jersey and very soft and light and becoming, although I am still surprised to find myself wearing anything ruffled in bathing. (The white and red suit from Penney's is pretty much of a flop, because it is very stiff and cold, so yesterday I wore a seersucker playsuit and was much more comfortable, although perhaps somewhat too naked for a beach censor.)

I don't know quite how I feel about being thirty-two instead of thirty or twenty, except that I much prefer being as I am now. I have a much larger capacity for everything. I see a lot more and care a lot less about things like people and whether they like me. Physically I am in much better condition than I was ten years ago, although I am now a little overweight. Mentally I think I am better off, too. Of course, I was going to school then, and now I might find it harder to follow lectures and so on. I doubt it. I should certainly find more lectures not worth following . . . which may, of course, be a form of mental deterioration. I doubt that, too. I am much less eager, in that way young people have of being eager. I find myself unable or unwilling to give anything of *myself,* that is. When I was younger, I poured some of my own élan vital into all my contacts with the rest of the world, unthinkingly. Now I am perhaps more cordial, suaver, in my relations with people, even with people I like or love, but I realize with a feeling almost of shock that I am cold and selfish about that pouring out of my élan. I hold it back, saving it perhaps for T. and myself. Now and then, after a weekend with old friends, I realize that in spite of my niceness and my ability as a hostess, I have let them come and go without giving them one spark from my own self, and I feel a kind of disappointment and wonder if they do, too, if they are asking themselves what has changed me. Sometimes I wonder if, instead of not *wanting* to give away any of my élan, I have none left to give. That is an ugly thought. Usually I do not think it, because I know that my relations with T. are warm and complete as ever. But they aren't with anyone else in the world. I have withdrawn, willy-nilly. I have been that way ever since the night in Bern, as if I were concentrating every part of my inner spirit on myself and T. It is wrong, I think. I wonder if other people are that way, too. I imagine a great many are.

We may offer to take one or two refugee children. I had been thinking rather hazily about it, and so had T. without saying anything, and today a letter from Anne about her doing the same thing made us both speak. Of course, it is a terrible gamble . . . but any children would be . . . and I can't bear not to help in some way. We could feed and clothe them better than some and send them to the public schools. It would mean more caution with our money and, of course, would change our peculiar and delightful way of living. I don't know how to go about it. Of course, every autumn I go through a kind of heat for children anyway. We can't have any ourselves. And adopting them has become complicated now that it would be impossible for two divorcés ever to get permission to do so. Which seems too bad. Certainly Tim and I, in spite of our former marriages, are a lot better qualified to raise children than many people. Well . . . I often wish we could. I think there have been several times when Sis would have let me take Shaun, but that would have been a mess because of family complications, to say nothing of Sis's bland ability to give me (or Mother, as the case is now) every responsibility and then feel quite free to criticize Shaun's manner, clothes, and everything else.

Mrs. Purdy came back today, somewhat tottery. I was hoping she would stay away longer, since I enjoy coping with the house myself. I may have to cut her down a bit, especially if we take a child or two.

I'll try to finish *Daniel* this month. That may bring us in a little money.

15. vii. 40

I finished the book three days ago and am started on the typing. It is a pleasant book, in a quiet, unimportant way, and I do hope we at least get some advance royalties on it, as we need the money.

It is steadily hot now, with delightful nights. We eat in the patio quite a lot.

The country, or our hills rather, are turning a soft coppery brown, very beautiful. In the valley the apricot pickers are living in tents under the trees.

24. vii. 40

We have decided to go back to Rochester to the Mayo Clinic. When Anne suggested it, we talked about it and decided not to (I don't remember whether I wrote all this or not). But a letter from T.'s mother makes us feel that Anne is rather hurt about our refusal, so we are going. I know that she understands our hesitation, and I am sure that she hopes, as God knows we do, too, that there may be a chance of help.

We leave Monday noon, the twenty-ninth. There will be many interesting things about it—we both like trains and, of course, the strange uncomfortable excitement of being in a new town and a new bedroom and a new toilet—but now and then I am almost sickened by a quick realization that perhaps we are in for another time of waiting rooms, of pompous puzzled doctors, of the smell of antiseptics and hospital food. I think that I cannot stand it, and then I know what T. must be feeling, remembering the poke of fingers and needles and the looking up from an operating table into the mirror of the light reflectors, and a thousand things that I cannot guess. The whole thing is wretched, and I'll be glad to get it over with. It is hard to say how I really feel about any cure except time's for Timmy's pain. I feel quiescent, I suppose you could say. Perhaps I am a defeatist. I read about fighters like Helen Hunt Jackson, and I am shamed, recognizing my own inertia.

26. vii. 40

Everything is pretty much in order for our trip . . . money came from Anne, tickets are paid for, and so on and so on. It seems strange to be packing again, after so many months here in California.

I feel sad and worried all the time, underneath my natural actions, for several people, and especially for Georges Connes. He is most probably in a concentration camp, in spite of his German decoration and so on from the last war . . . allied with Communists, Jewish name, and so on. I am afraid to write to him, for fear of causing more trouble. We would be glad to help him with the children if we could. I cannot feel that he would want them ever to leave France . . . but strange things are happening. Pierre is the most charming little boy I have ever met. I don't know Marie-Claire . . . but her parents are good.

I got hungry, so I put some cold peas in a dish and put a little soy sauce on them. The combination was terrible.

It seems queer that David never mentions anything about war and conscription and so on. I know he did feel very strongly against all that . . . but he, too, may have changed. Two summers ago, at Le Pâquis, I bet him $50 he'd be in an army, voluntarily, before he was thirty. He'll lose his bet, I think.

30. vii. 40
Raton Pass, Colorado

Dearest Rex:

Edith gave us this nice supply of airplane stamps and so forth, and I'm not even sending her the first letter. All of which shows the power of a $5 bill, I guess! We do thank you for it. It was a complete surprise, and I'm hoarding it—probably for a nice lunch and a drink of German beer at the Muehlebach tomorrow.

The train is so comfortable that we hate to think of leaving it. We had to get two "roomettes," which looked pretty cramped when we got on—but the porter rolled back the whole wall between the rooms, and now we have the most spacious room I've ever seen on a train. The toilets are super-double-deluxe—you turn a little crank, and they swing out from under the beds, complete in every detail!

It seems queer that we're within a couple of hours of Dave. I do hope we can see him on our way back.

The servants and the food are excellent on this train. There is a very nice little headwaiter, and today when we were the last people (as usual!) in the dining car, Timmy asked him if he was Swiss. He whispered that he always said so now but that he was really a German. He looked scared to death, and we left, much embarrassed.

I think we all sort of kind of jumped on you, the other night at dinner, when you confessed that when Noni said she liked journalism more than anything in the world, you couldn't see why she went into training. I can see how you would be puzzled. I imagine she is, too. But I can't help thinking she's making a good choice. You spent quite a lot of effort, when I was in my late teens and early twenties, convincing me that journalism is really no game for a woman, that it toughens and hardens her. And, of course, being a nurse won't stop Noni from writing, if that's her real talent. Look at Mary Roberts Rinehart, and Mignon Eberhart, and a lot of others. And she *will* have a sure and honorable profession behind her, in case of war or her own need of a job.

Give her and Mother my love—and tell Edie I'll write from K. C.—and much love to you from us both—

31.vii.40
Hotel Muehlebach
Kansas City, Missouri

Dearest Edie:

I got my nice airmail equipment out and then decided to treat you to a sheet of Muehlebach's best stationery.

The hotel is odd, to say practically nothing—1923 elegance plus 1903 cracked lavatories plus 1939 cocktail bars. We had a very nice martini in the Rendezvous, but decided it was too full of schoolgirls and went to the Grill, which was even fuller of women trying to be schoolgirls. There was a very loud band in powder-blue suits—somebody or other and his Sugar Blues Boys. We ate cold roast beef and drank Muehlebach *brau* (which is much better than the hotel), and although we had a lot of fun we felt as if we were escaping from the inside of a large and very sweet cream puff when we "hopped out," as Shaun says.

The trip was easy and fun, in spite of what the altitudes did to poor Tim. We stayed in our room most of the time. And when I say room, I mean *room*. If you ever go east again, try to get a double bedroom. They cost about between a compartment and a drawing room—and I've never seen such a spacious setup. We had a very nice porter—the whole train was nice, in fact. There were a few Hollywood people and a couple of loud-mouthed politicians going back to D.C. to tell the boys what to do. I took you and Sis at your words, and wore my blue silk slacks to lunch, and felt rather queer and extremely comfortable. Boiled mushrooms and bacon on toast made me feel even more so.

We came to the hotel at 7:30, and after baths and whatnot I went to sleep for three hours! I was surprised, too.

I'll write tomorrow from You Know Where. If we have too uncomfortable a night, we may do as we did today, and take baths and so on, and then take a gander at Cousin Kate's line of five hundred people in the afternoon and go back the next morning. I imagine it will be mostly schoolteachers with colitis at the moment.

Give my love to Noni, Rex, Sis, and Wee Edie—Tim's, too—

1. *viii.* 40

Dearest Edie—

We got here about 8:00 this morning—only some ten hours ago, which seems incredible.

The trip from Kansas City was one of the two bumpiest I ever took. Timmy had to sleep in the upper berth, since it was impossible for him to keep from bouncing out of the lower! You can imagine what fun it was to climb up and shoot him. I longed, and not for the first time, for a sturdy tail—or at least a couple more arms.

The hotel is very nice, in the typical chain-hotel way—a pincushion with two threaded needles on the bureau, lots of little signs under the glass tops telling us how passionately the management yearns to be our friends. The wallpaper is fresh, though, and the beds are good, and there's plenty of hot water. The coffee shop is only open when the Elizabethan Grill isn't, so we had to eat lunch (for the first and last time) in the latter. It's a ghastly place, very refined and oak-paneled. As you leave, the well-upholstered hostess gives you a smile and two little mints in a cellophane envelope.

The town is odd. I don't yet know what makes it so. The people don't look any sicker than people you see on the streets anywhere. There are a lot of very poor-looking people—farmers, I'd say—and, of course, a lot of nurses, most of them young and slender. There are a few very unattractive bars and an amazing lot of restaurants and candy stores—and drugstores, naturally. You see and hear many foreigners—Spaniards, Hindus, Chinese. There are a lot of Jews, American and not.

We went over to the clinic about 2:00. It is just like all the stories—impressive marble and bronze and wonderful direction. We were sent here and there, and after a two-hour examination by a famous young neurologist who acted very dyspeptic, Tim emerged with a sheaf of appointment cards. He is now in bed, full of castor oil, and can't eat or drink anything but tea, and has to take an enema at 6:00 tomorrow morning and be at the X-ray place at 7:00! What a life! Then, after a morning being blood-tested, he is free maybe until the next day, when he sees doctors again. These boys are thorough, at least.

I feel silly to ask it, but will you save these letters? I meant to keep a diary, but have a feeling that a letter home will be about my limit, literary or otherwise—and I'd like some notes.

Much love to you all—and thank you for the grand letter we got today. I do hope Rex didn't catch cold at the Norconian. How is the place where I gouged him? I agree with you that we are extravagant—but only now and then, and in between bursts we lead a spotlessly economical life. Much love—

2. *viii*. 40

Dearest Edie—

This note will really be one, as I am too sleepy and hot to write a letter. We got up at 5:30, after a very bad night for Tim, thanks to an ounce of castor oil which might better have been nitroglycerin, and by 7:00 were well along the path—Desk D-3, third floor—Desk N-7, seventh floor, and so on. He was X-rayed, blood-tested, etc., etc.—and now we'll see what's next when the doctors take him over at 8:00 tomorrow.

We got through at 11:00, and after some breakfast hired a taxi and drove to Winona through beautiful rolling country and fields of corn and clover. We crossed the Mississippi twice.

Tonight we had a very poor dinner in our room and then

went for a walk and decided we'd rather be hung than live anyplace but the Kahler, which is at least impersonal. It's very sticky and hot, and the worst part is that it's impossible to wash any gloves or stockings, because they take days to dry.

I'll write more tomorrow, after we've been to the clinic. Love—

3. viii. 40

Dearest family—

The first two days I spent in the waiting rooms I was interested in the people, but now suddenly I have looked at them all I want to—or perhaps more than that. The thing that impresses me most about them is a rather pessimistic feeling of their lack of dignity. Most of them are middle-aged or old and look as if they should have lived and suffered long enough to acquire that clear outline, that repose—that whatever it is that is supposed to show the Dignity of Man. Of course, many of them do look nice, or kindly, or funny, or something. But that isn't what I mean. They are *not* clear but smudged in their outlines, like a bad photograph which could show their spirits as well as their bodies. They are incoherent, bewildered, petty—and make me wonder what use there is in spending a life without really learning anything. Well—

Of course, practically every person here is completely absorbed within himself—and that is understandable, because it is hard not to be if you have a gut ache or any pain. All your thoughts and actions focus on it—and here that is true of everyone you see, except an occasional companion like me who is equally preoccupied by the pain of another person. The only way you can make any contact with others is to ask them about their experiences with suffering, either real or imagined, and since we are not interested in anyone's but T.'s and don't care to discuss it, we live in a kind of vacuum.

The waiting rooms are impressive marble rooms, very cool and spacious. There are rows of comfortable chairs, and a soft buzz of exchanged weights, temperatures, and other more clinical confidences fills the air as people wait for their names or numbers to be called from one of the two desks. Then they hobble or mince or waddle or bound or totter into one of the rows of little consultation rooms, where young and solemn doctors talk to them. Many of them are ill at ease as they go out of the big room and grin and blush and pull at their clothes and look more like self-conscious children than people going to learn about their lives and deaths.

Last night there was a mighty thunderstorm as violent as the ones in Switzerland but much longer. It made the air better.

There is a carillon on top of the clinic, which is silent at night but rings out a pretty off-key bar or two of a hymn every hour during the day. But yesterday about five o'clock it suddenly broke loose with several Schubert songs, Rachmaninoff's Prelude in-whatever-key-it-is, "Flow Gently Sweet Afton" played like a Bach fugue, part of Dvořák's *New World* Symphony, and a few other such things—and it was actually beautiful, in key and with chords of many bells at once and as many modulations as a fine organ. I looked out the window, and people down in the streets were stopped, puzzled and excited. I think it must have been some famous carilloneur, maybe from Belgium, who is here to get his gizzard fixed and simply broke loose for a while. Whatever it was, it was certainly swinging those bells around. It is the only time that I have wished you were here.

Our drive yesterday was pleasant. We went up to Winona, across the river, and back—had lunch at a fairly nice little place called Ye Hot Fish Shop, where we ate walleyed pike fixed in butter and drank a watery local beer called Bub's. The country seems like a park, with many woods and neat irregular fields of wheat, corn, barley, and pink clover, and the cows and horses are very handsome. The farmhouses are not beautiful like the ones in Pennsylvania, but the silos and the red barns with curved roofs are very handsome and look Russian.

Our driver was a pleasant young man who talked occasionally and drove very well. "From here on it's nothing but bluffs, bluffs, bluffs," he said. "All they eat in Wye-nona is fish, fish, fish." "Most of my work is emergency calls, emergency calls, emergency calls." He was not especially bright.

There are a few children here. They all yell when they get stuck for blood tests, because everybody babies them so.

The hardest thing for most people about the routine tests is having to go without breakfast until 11:00 or so. In a way it's good, because it diverts their minds so that even people who are obviously in great trouble can think of nothing but how hungry they are and for once can discuss that first cup of coffee instead of their metabolism.

Last night it was too hot to sleep, before the storm, so we got dressed and walked around the town. Looking into the sitting rooms and lobbies of all the lodging places was horrible, but we couldn't help it. Apparently the men go to bed, but the women stay up and collect in little circles and talk, talk, talk, as our driver would say.

The shopping district of Rochester looks like that of a much smaller town (it's about 28,000)—mostly candy stores, cafés, flower shops, and uniform shops. There are a couple of movies and a few very dingy-looking bars, which we seem to have no interest in, although the Kahler serves only beer, and that with compressed lips.

After four hours of consultations I brought what was left of Timmy back to the hotel (he tried to escape once to the toilet for a cigarette and got called before he had even lit it), and then we had lunch and went looking for a possible place for me to stay. (Meals have sunk to a mean average of liverwurst on rye and beer, but don't think we're starving). I looked at several hotels and will probably spend $2 more and stay right here.

Tim goes to St. Mary's (Catholic) Hospital at 10:00 tomorrow for experiments on his spine. The biggest man in the clinic (for nerves, etc.) said that he could guarantee absolutely nothing and that nobody knows why men with "good" amputations keep on suffering, one time out of a thousand, when they aren't supposed to. There are two things to do—open the whole leg and trace every nerve for nodules, etc., or block the leg nerves from the spine. They'll do the latter first, and just with novocaine. If that works, they'll cut the nerve, which will mean complete paralysis of that leg and no more chance of an artificial one. It may also do no good, because all the trouble may be coming from some trouble between the spine (or along the spine) and the brain, caused by shock, disease, what have you. In that case, they say there is absolutely nothing to do but live partially doped until you die.

Tim is in pretty good shape, mentally and otherwise, and is more than willing to gamble on getting some help.

I'll write tomorrow, probably. Love from us both—

Dearest family—

It's about 8:30, Sunday evening, and I have finished my first day at St. Mary's. I must confess it was a long one—and, of course, it's still going on for Tim. I hate to leave him, but he got quite worried about my supper, because the Kahler kitchens close at 8:00. I could have gone to a diner or something, but after ten hours at the hospital in my Sunday clothes I felt too hot and sticky. So I came back here and ate some broiled sweetbreads and a vegetable salad, both of which tasted of absolutely nothing but certainly not of sweetbreads and vegetables.

I am horrified about our expenses, in a helpless way. Of course, it's Anne* who'll pay, but still— This hotel is expensive, and the food is not only dull but prohibitive, and although I can and will hop buses, I know I'll also fall into taxis now and then. Tim and I looked at several hotels yesterday, and the only nice one is even farther from St. Mary's than this. But there's one right across from the hospital, very small and noisy but clean, where I could get a bath and room for $2.50. I think if T. has to stay long I'll go there, although he's opposed to it because the bed really did look like a soggy pancake. In the meantime, write here—and often!

I should be doing a few little jobs like getting laundry together, repainting my toenails, bathing—but all I can do is sit.

Tim goes for a trial anesthesia of his spine early tomorrow. If it works, he'll have the real one in a day or two, and it will mean the end of much trouble. If not, they may try a brain operation, or nothing.

Last night we went out about 8:00, after resting from quite a day at chez Mayo, and had two martinis at a very chromium-plated

* Anne Parrish Corliss, Timmy's sister.

little place called the Palace Garden because of three aspidistras in the window, and then went to dinner, where two very strange men who met in a circus twenty-two years ago and have cooked together ever since put on a terrific act for us, and spun full cups of coffee through the air, and cooked us the first decent food we've had here —a ham and green pepper and mushroom omelet made exactly as Tim says the famous omeletteers used to make them at Mont St. Michel, in little black slippery skillets with round bottoms. It was quite astonishing, and we left with an invitation to drive out to Lake Winnetatashahawa or some such place, to meet-the-wife and have some *real* food, and some beer, which is not served there— at the diner. I asked them why, and they said it interfered with the eating! I may go back, if I get hungry enough, but I'm rather leery of being a privileged character—if any.

We then went to a movie, since it was too hot to think of bed (only 80 degrees, but we both longed for an honest-to-God 109 degrees at Bareacres), and saw the first picture we'd ever seen but often heard about made by Republic or Monogram for the sticks. It was acted very bouncily but enthusiastically by farmish people and was about a farm boy whose uncle beat him but loved him after he rescued the uncle's $200 from a hobo, and the little city girl who realized that the country life, represented by many good shots of apple blossoms and pigs, was the best life—and I tell you, it had them in the aisles. The audience laughed and wept and muttered and nudged total strangers (us) at the hot love scenes when the hero took the girl's hand in his, and it was very interesting —especially since we already knew from Hemet that cowboys are only interested in cowboy pictures. And farmers, now, in farm pictures. So I wonder what about gangster pictures?

I hope these letters don't bore you. I'm terribly anxious to hear more about Noni—et al.—

Love from us—

5. *viii. 40*
St. Mary's Hospital
Rochester, Minnesota

It is perhaps a good thing to write about sitting here waiting for T. to come down from surgery, because if I put on paper the number of times and all that, it seems less immediately terrible—like talking of how many miles the stars are from the earth or how many pennies are in a great fortune. There were three times in Bern, the two operations and then the amputation. In Wilmington there were the two. Now here we begin again. Today is a trial anesthesia of the spine. If it works, the nerves of the leg will be killed in another few days, and as it seems to me now, we will be in paradise. But the doctors are very doubtful that it will work.

Mother asked me to write to her every day—the first time she has ever done that, and I resented it mildly. It seems—it *is*—a selfish demand. But I know why she did it. So far I have been good and have killed two birds with the one stone by making a few notes about Rochester versus Lord and Lady Bareacres at the same time. I felt foolish to ask her to keep my letters, but did so. I should guess that they have been more interesting than if I were keeping a diary, too, since I have written more about everything than I would if I were also putting it here—but I doubt if Mother has enjoyed them as much as she would more routine letters. She is always irked by what she calls "literarian" touches and likes straightforward writing about the weather, how we feel, and what we do. I think most mothers are that way. Of course, in spite of being more discursive in my letters home, because they were at the same time my diary, there are many things I've not said. Perhaps they are better, then, than a more intimate, less controlled report would be—one I did not expect to be read. Perhaps a diary should be written, not as this one, but as letters to one's family. I can see that it is probably just as well that I do not say that Dr. K. has bad breath or that I am so lonely that I have the toothache all over me, at night, missing T. I don't say things like that, feeling them better unsaid to anyone except myself and perhaps someday T. if he ever reads this. So why say them at all, then?

Across from the hospital is a short row of drugstores and little cafés. I can't eat here, so I have started at one end and will eat to the other, unless we leave earlier than I think we will. Yesterday I had lunch at Stirters, a place with a new chromium and black-glass front. It was wretched food. This morning I had coffee and a cinnamon bun in a little bakeshop, so now I feel rather sick, as always after coffee, but at least it makes me go to the toilet if I only drink a little once in a while. It's a queer reaction, I think—and can be one of the most unpleasant, like protracted airsickness.

The nurses here are nice—all graduates and much easier and less pompous than the student nurses at the Delaware. I have never been to such a big hospital—about seven hundred beds, and a new wing building. I wish I could see one of their new operating rooms. A nurse told me that they use a kind of blue light, which is dark toward the floor and then grows lighter toward the ceiling.

Yesterday T. and I decided, more or less, to try to earn our own living if he gets better. If he stays the same, we'll continue to take all the money we can get, from Anne and anyone else who will give it to us. But if he loses his plantar foot, even partially, we are going to leave Bareacres—perhaps rent it, or preferably keep it for our own vacations—and try to support ourselves for a time. We would have to go to a city, where T. would try to get some jobs doing drawings or paintings for advertising, and maybe try to have some shows, and use all the "pull" he could, and I would try to write articles or get a column job or free-lance or anything I could. It would be awful to leave Bareacres, and live in a wretched apartment, and have to pull wires and do a lot of the things we both hate. But we seem to feel that it would be a good thing. If we could we would continue to take Anne's pension and put it in a savings bank—and then maybe we would make enough money to be able to send it back in a year or give it to somebody or something.

I feel upset about Noni's going into training at the Good Samaritan in Los Angeles. It is not a particularly good hospital anymore, but the real reason I am against her being there is that she will be in Los Angeles. She doesn't like it as a city, and the climate is not at all stimulating to her, and for three years she would be expected to check in, every five weekends, at the Ranch or with us or with Sis. Her dates, her clothes, her manners—everything would be inspected, judged. Families can't help that, naturally. But I think it is wrong for a girl of Noni's age and temperament to be quite so close to her home. She'll be expected to go to Aunt Maggie's* for dinner—all her new friends will be suspect (What does his father do?)—if she wears her hair a new way it will be criticized. We can't help it. I have kept quiet to her —but perhaps I am wrong. I often interfere and never know whether it is right or wrong—but this time I'm too far away, and if she has already decided, there is no use in upsetting her. And, of course, N. is clearheaded and probably has thought about all the sides of living in Southern California anyway.

I wonder what T. will be like when he comes back—pale, sick, flushed, silent—I know he has to lie flat. He may be nauseated.

---

* Edith's relative, living in Los Angeles with her daughter Mary.

5. viii. 40

Dearest family—

I spent from 7:00 this morning until 10:30 tonight at the hospital and have to be there at 7:00 tomorrow, so this will not be a letter.

The trial operation was a failure and proves that further surgery is useless and that the trouble is located somewhere along the spine and is therefore impossible to find. They say time may help a little but probably will not, and the only thing to do is keep Tim as comfortable as possible. They say he is in wonderful condition "considering" and should continue to do as Hal says. They are working to find some substitute for Analgeticum.

The disappointment was hard for Tim but hasn't downed him. He is very shaky from the experience this morning—if I hadn't seen his bathrobe on the stretcher I would never have recognized him when they brought him back from the theater—but ought to be able to leave by the end of the week. Tomorrow, unless he has a shock collapse, he has to have some more X-rays —although it seems silly to go on when the doctors all agree there's nothing to do.

I'm upset about Noni. Why is she determined to stay in California? Why not cross the border? Surely there must be an accredited school in Arizona or some such place. I think we all could probably scrape together her fare there if she wanted to go badly enough. Probably the answer to that is that it's none of my business.

How does Rex enjoy being a political martyr? It's really a privilege to be fired from Olsen's regime, I'd say.

Much love—

Dearest family—

Tim left the hospital at 8:00 this morning, much against the nurses' and my better judgment—but in Rochester it's kill or win, and Tim says he can see how many a man comes in on roller skates and goes out on a stretcher or whatever the phrase is backwards. He could hardly walk, but we waited for an hour in the clinic and then had a two-and-a-half-hour consultation with five doctors— this with no breakfast but castor oil, to prepare for an intravenous urological examination at 1:30, after no lunch. That lasted for one and a half more hours, which he passed strapped to a steel table on his back, which is black and blue from yesterday. So you can imagine that he is somewhat shattered, as Mary Powers would say.

I don't feel very chatty, but I suppose I might as well tell you, and then we can close the subject permanently, that all the discoveries are very bad and that Tim is in great danger of losing his other leg or, if he is lucky, of dying relatively quickly. He may also get much better and live to a ripe old age, which according to the doctors would be miraculous. By living in a kind of Venetian glass box he might evade another thrombosis—no cigarettes, no excitement, no movement, no painting. Or he could live as normally as possible, as we've been doing at Bareacres, and take the quicker chance. I think I know which way he'll choose.

He has one more consultation tomorrow—the men are trying to find some substitutes for Analgeticum—and then we'll flee, if Tim is well enough. Our one idea is to escape.

Anyway, I'm getting to the end of my airmail stamps!

Love—

This is probably the last consultation, to discuss substitutes for Analgeticum and learn how to care for Tim's one leg. We are in a passively frantic state to leave and, if we were here on our own will and money, would have gone away yesterday. The ninety minutes in the anesthesia room were the second worst T. has ever spent, he says. I do not care to write about it, but think I should. He was given novocaine in the spine, locally, and then 80 cc. of ether. Then he was given an injection in the hand, probably adrenaline, and whenever he got too far away from the doctors in his mind, he had to breathe oxygen. He can't talk about it very coherently, but says that his whole body grew yellowish and numb, except his head, shoulders, and amputated leg. (The ether was given through a rubber sheet into the middle of the back.) His fingers twisted into strange shapes. He lost all sense of space and was now like a pea, now like a great echoing deserted warehouse filled with strange winds and blue brilliant lights and terrible noises. The doctors poked everywhere with a kind of cobbler's awl, asking him if he felt it and if it was dull, sharp, hot, cold, so that now his body is covered with small red spots.

When the stretcher came in, he was making strange soft noises, quite insane. He seemed to have shrunken and lay in a kind of boneless way, crying out for me. It took about three hours to quiet him and to get him warm. He was violently sick once, about an hour after he came down, but in three hours drank some vile coffee through a tube as if it were nectar. He ate a little lunch and later drank a small glass of beer—able to lift his head about noon. His back ached badly, and his little leg was terribly painful. I gave him a shot about 3:00. The big doctor came in and said the operation was a failure and that it proved further surgery was useless, and then went out abruptly.

The next morning T. was very shaky still and inclined to cry for no reason, much to his embarrassment. He had some coffee and castor oil, and then we came to the clinic, where after an hour's wait he had another two-and-a-half-hour consultation with doctors, who told him that he has Buerger's disease (a kind of chronic phlebitis), and that he must choose between cigarettes and losing his other leg, and that really there is no way to prevent another Bern episode, a quicker death, or, for that matter, a long life. At 1:30, after an enema and no lunch, he spent one and a half hours strapped to a metal table having an intravenous urological test—an injection of 100 cc. of something that caused bad neural pain for a few minutes and then a tingling all over that lasted several hours. When he finished, he was completely exhausted.

He rested, with a good shot, and then asked to go to the one pub we know, where he had beer and a sandwich, and then had a haircut. He was sick again when he got back. We went out to dinner, and he ate a little rare steak and some sliced tomatoes, which he managed to keep from losing. He slept very well and today looks better, although his hand still shakes and he feels tearful and "whuddery inside."

I don't feel like talking about this. We regret bitterly that we came back here—but, of course, the result might have been different, and we agreed to take the chance. The life the doctors yesterday said T. should lead—no cigarettes, no action, no excitement, no painting—would be less than life. If we had not come here, we'd have gone on at Bareacres as we were, living easily and compromising with the pain. And I imagine that is what we will continue to do, although T. knows that I am willing to do whatever he decides.

The man next to us has a strange, bad smell. On the other side of us, two plump women compare visits to the clinic. I am going down now to try to find out something from Information about finances, which so far have been veiled in a heavy and discreet silence.

It seems that everything is in code, which can only be read at the conclusion of the treatment. Ho-hum.

One thing we noticed in Kansas City and here when we first came, but do not anymore, was the pallor of all the faces. Of course, there are a few brown farmers, but most of the people are very pale. A great many of the women, even very well-dressed women and girls, chew gum all the time and everyplace. Many people use toothpicks.

It seems to me that if we could go back to Bareacres and see *no* one, not Mrs. Purdy, nor Arnold, nor the grocer, nor any of the family, for a few days, we could get rid of all this—get rid of having been poked and pushed and talked to and fed and smelled by all these people, the doctors and all the people in the waiting rooms and the cafés and the streets, those we have seen and those others hidden from us in their rooms everywhere.

7. viii. 40

Dearest Edie—

We leave here tomorrow evening and will spend the next day in Kansas City and arrive the next morning at 10:15 in Colorado Springs, where we will spend a day or two at the Antlers' Hotel with Dave if he is not off for the weekend and with some of T.'s old more-or-less friends if he is.

We slept until 9:00 this morning for the first time in months, and it did us both good. Tim was worn to a string. We were all afternoon at the clinic, and then after a rest we took a taxi out to a little bend in the Zumbio River and had an awful meal that tasted almost delicious.

Today I've been sorry I sent you such a bald statement of our present situation, but that is the way it is. Tim, one out of several hundred thousand in the world, has Buerger's disease, and thanks to a strong heart and Hal's treatment and the quiet life of Bareacres is in pretty good condition in spite of it. We have pages of written instructions and hours of oral ones, all of which are reduced to the facts that he must keep certain niggling care of his foot (remaining), and keep absolutely quiet, and not smoke (nicotine very dangerous). I think he is working out his own little plan for life, and God knows any man of his age and brains should have that privilege.

It will be fine to see Dave.

I'll telegraph from Colorado Springs when we'll be home. We'll get off at San Bernardino and telephone from Bareacres or drive over or something—it will be wonderful to be home again—

Much love to you all from us both—

28. viii. 40
Bareacres

At this moment my chief feeling is one of a kind of triumph that I have got T. to consider starting a journal. He writes naturally and clearly and from long since, and I think has often felt the need of it. So now he has the book half of my diary, with some sheets in it that I will add to tomorrow, and a pencil . . . and I hope for many reasons that he will begin to write.

We've been reading the journal he kept in Cornwall, and it is good because of the watercolors on almost every page, because of the minutiae of a life that can never be repeated because of war and age and other accidents, and because it shows sides of T. that he strives hard to keep covered. It also shows pompous, whimsical, wordy sides now and then, which in the reading make him squirm . . . but the main thing is good. Of course, to me as his wife it is more than that. It appeals in some ways to the Peeping Tom side of me—I feel that I am snatching peeks at a man usually well hidden, and therefore I am victorious. But there are better parts. Some of his thoughtful phrases, set down almost apologetically, move and stir me. And I am ashamed of my own sporadic and egocentric efforts at journal keeping. I realize more than ever how completely monotonous I make this fairly unrestrained chronicle . . . it is I, my thoughts, what happens to me, what I do. God, it is dull. There again the idea is probably to write as T. did, knowingly for an audience of at least one, Anne, and hopefully for perhaps me and Al and one or two others. This idea of mine is not much more than a kind of mental masturbation, which I have to admit relieves me now and then of things in my mind—still egocentric— that are bothering me and that must not be said aloud. That may be all right as a kind of medicine but as anything worth reading to another human it fails completely. Of course, I have not read any of this . . . but when I think of opening it four years from now, as T. let me do with his Cornwall journals, and reading it aloud to him and perhaps Norah, I am embarrassed not only by some of the disgusting or defamatory things that would appear but also by its inescapable dullness. How much better to write of the animals, the weeds, the changes of weather, than of my internal woes!

Perhaps I shall try to. But really I have no idea of risking such a reading as Noni and Tim and I gave his journal last week. I shall get rid of this book. And in the meantime, at least now and then, in spite of my efforts to talk of cats when my heart is full of terror, I shall occasionally if not altogether ignore the cats.

I sent off the uncorrected typed ms. of *Daniel Among the Women* today. I tried it out on Norah, who was noncommittal except for saying that she found the sisters more interesting than Daniel and that he was an annoyingly dull young man. That, of course, was what we meant him to be ... so perhaps our one guinea pig proves the novel a great success. I wish Pritchett could sell it to a slickie and make us some money ... but the chances are slim. It is not an especially exciting novel. And she is not a very good agent. And the times are bad, to put it obscenely.

T. has decided to detoxicate himself from the use of Analgeticum beginning October 1, when the weather will be better and the visits from various relatives fewer. We will do it under Hal's direction, of course. Hal and the doctors at the Mayo say it will not be too difficult, since T. is not a true narcotic. I do not look forward to it, and yet found myself last night delivering a stiff little lecture to T. about the danger of romanticizing the whole thing into another *Journal d'une Désintoxication,* complete with Cocteau's drawings and phrases like howl-like-a-dog and between-iced-blankets and so on.

To tell the truth to myself, I don't see how T. can go through with it. He has been much worse since his trip to Rochester, with an almost constant backache, probably from the spinal anesthetic, and a really frightening weakness. He paints little, although what he does is very good in a strange exaggerated way. The lines and the colors are violent and twisted. At times he is hardly rational. I have more than doubled the shots in strength, feeling that he should rest as much as possible before October and that there was no use saving something for nothing. But they don't seem to do much good. He is in almost constant pain. The last three days he has drunk more whiskey than before. He says it makes his little leg feel warmer ... and I can't see any other effect on him. But it makes me remember sitting in the Restaurant Français du Casino in Bern with David, just before T.'s amputation, and telling him that if T. lived through it, I was afraid he might become an alcoholic. That is silly, probably.

Nevertheless, I have been filled, for several weeks now, with a terrible silent inward depression. When T. goes to bed in the middle of the day and lies there quietly without even reading, I think, He'll never get up again. And when he is nauseated from a meal, which happens quite often, I think, He'll never eat again. And so on. It is ridiculous. I don't seem to brood and mope— I sleep fairly well and eat too much and drink more even than I want and talk a lot about too many things—but underneath it all is this terrible empty resignation. I hate it. It follows me like my own shadow, and I wonder for how long. Perhaps October will decide it.

We had Arnold Elliott build a fine kennel for us between the sleeping porch and the dry brook where someday we hope to have a little swimming pool. It is about twenty-by-thirty feet, with a three-section roomy house at one end, with a top that lifts up for cleaning and airing, and at the upper end a hydrant so that I can keep fresh water there without too much bother. Saturday Arnold will cut out some steps down to the gate so that it won't be so hard for Tim, and me, too, to get down there. Now all we need is a dog for it. We are afraid to put Butch in it alone because of wildcats. T. wants a dachshund. Myself, I would like a large mixed-breed dog with a heavy yet easy frame and loving brown eyes. Perhaps we can get both, which really would not be much more trouble than one. Of course, two, especially if one were large, would be more expensive to feed. . . .

While Noni was here, last week, Arnold came up with a box of very pretty little pins and buttons and so on that he had made from tiny pinecones. T. gave Noni a pair of becoming waxy brown-green earrings, and I got some sweater buttons for Sis. Arnold is ingenious, but like so many such people, he will soon lose enthusiasm for this new pastime and drop it just when he had promised to fill many orders for his buttons and such. I have a lovely cluster of pepper berries that I picked Sunday at Soboba, and I think perhaps he could take such clusters while they are still juicy, and dip them in a kind of shellac he uses on everything so that they would not shed and crumble, and make very pretty boutonnieres and hair ornaments of them. I must remember to speak to him on Saturday. But by then he probably will be heart and soul in some scheme to change the drinking fountains at Ramona Bowl or to become governor of a western state, which last he confessed to Tim was his great ambition.

Norah's week here was a pleasant one. I think she and Georges Connes are the two best people to have around . . . best in that they are both easy and stimulating. I noticed that although T. and I led an almost uninterrupted life while she was here—not so easy for two people and a guest in five rooms—we at the same time made an enjoyable effort to be more entertaining, more interesting, more amusing. That is a good sign now and then, I think. Some guests make existence itself seem a bloody chore, no matter how fond you are of them as people, people unassociated with the private life you must lead no matter how many extra meals there are, and clean towels, and beds, and tender feelings. Rex and Edith, for instance, exhaust me almost painfully after only a few hours, and it is not only the many extra things I must do for them —things that they take for granted that are quite foreign to T.'s and my usual life, like breakfast with eggs-toast-marmalade-coffee-morning-paper—but it is their constant *presence*. They are always on my mind. No matter how well I know them nor how accustomed to their manners and their lives, I am spiritually unable to accept them easily. I must constantly *think* of them . . . of the chairs they are sitting in, and the look on their faces, and the way they slept last night, and the cigarettes near their hands to be smoked or not, and what I shall next say to them and they to me. That all makes for fatigue. I think it is stupid and try very hard to combat it. But the fact remains that I cannot live easily with them, as I can with a few people like T., Norah, Connes, sometimes David, in the past Larry Powell, and now and then Eda.

The last weekend was miserable. At first, until a few hours ago in fact, I was much upset by it, but now I see that the best thing is to think of it as something long since past, instead of writing letters in my head about it to Sis, Noni, myself.

When Sis arrived with Dave she looked exhausted. Her hair was untidy, and her face was gaunt and sallow, with swollen eyes. We sat for a time and had a drink, and then at my suggestion she went in and took a shower and changed into some of my play clothes and came out, looking fresh and happier. Supper was pleasant, and afterward we went in and built a fire with the windows open, which is always especially nice.

We played some records . . . I began to play certain ones for certain people, I must admit with some amount of flattery and cajoling in my mind, for I have known for a long time that the best way to have a pleasant time when Sis is around is to flatter and soothe her in every possible way with her favorite foods, colors, sounds, and all.

Then, for some reason, we began to talk, and before we knew it we were having a pretty emotional argument about modern cemeteries and how despicable the whole system of graveyard hypocrisy has become. Sis likes her job, as we all know, and we all said we were glad she did and that she had it and was making a decent salary, but in our own ways we all told her that she should not let the crap she has to hand out from 8:00 to 5:00 each day ever creep into her relations to her family. I talked, inevitably, of the strange experience Al and I had getting his father buried in Forest Lawn,

where she works, and Sis said quite plainly that I was so prejudiced
by one experience, which she intimated broadly was pure imagination, that I had influenced the whole family against the place. At
that Dave, who was fairly silent, said that it was wrong to think
that I had given Mother and Rex ideas that they had held strongly
ever since he could remember. Tim kept saying things very calmly.
We all talked without any shouting. I remember that Sis looked
very pretty, sitting on the couch, and that Noni was upset. None
of us had had much to drink, but once I found myself almost
crying at the thought of Sis's being swept away by the vulgarity of
the things she was saying—all about how people needed F. L. and
how happy it made them to be cared for in their sad moments by
trained grave psychologists, and so on—and I left the room for a
minute. Then I came back, and it was still going on. There were
some more sharp criticisms of the system as *we* hated it, not as the
public, and then Sis said something like, "Why, those fine people
out there are *glad* to do anything in their power to assure the
poorest man in the country perpetual care for his loved ones," or
some such phrase that was obviously part of a sales talk, and I said,
"Yes, at 25 percent." Sis looked at me, not pretty anymore, and
said very calmly, "Dote, that's the dirtiest, most low-down, sneak-
ingest thing you have ever said to me."

I was simply floored. I truly had no idea what she was talking
about. I kept thinking, Well, here it is. Here it is. She had always
hated me, and now it's out. Now here it is. We can never be easy
and nice together again. At last she's come out with it.

Then I began to think of Mother, and of the awfulness of
family quarrels, and of how Sis and I have always hated sisters who
fuss in public, like Constance Lewis and Mrs. Hall. I knew it could
not go on from there and that if I did not do something that very
moment, it would be impossible ever to stop the tide of malice and
suspicion that had opened there between us. So I said that I was

very sorry that I had said anything to make her feel that way and that I hoped she would forgive me. It was one of the most difficult things I have ever done, especially there in front of the children.

She did not accept my apology, nor did she offer to apologize to me for saying such a hateful thing. Soon after that we all went to bed.

The next morning she was fairly nice but never once looked at me. I felt wretched, as I had all night, even in my dreams— wretched that such a bad thing had happened at all and that it had happened for the first time in either of our lives and in front of T. and the children. I had talked about it to T. when I went to bed, and he said very quietly what I should have known all along, that, of course, Sis was planning to sell lots or some kind of funeral business at Forest Lawn and that my remark about percentages caught her unaware on a spot of uneasy conscience. I think he is right. It is a bad business.

We were all to go to Soboba to swim that morning, but David asked to stay home to draw. He was polite but obviously upset. We went swimming and had a nice quiet time. Sis and I walked to the Lonesome Pepper and talked casually of Shaun and the weather and such. T. and Noni talked a little, waiting for us, and Noni said that Anne was almost speechless with rage, not only at me but at all of us—that she felt we had deliberately ganged against her.

Driving home she made some of her unpleasantly sneering remarks about Mother's friendship for and dependence on what Sis calls her "inferiors"—Mrs. Svensen, Lera, and so on. Of course, I don't like either woman, but I made a few platitudinous remarks about nobody's ever liking anyone else's friends and so on, because Noni is currently pleased by Svensen, and I thought that any chance the poor child has to have a little fun and go to concerts and so on should not be hindered, stuck as she is there at the Ranch. But Sis said that it was very queer how I had changed, since I always used to agree with her about Lera and Svensen and Mother's other stooges. To her it was another proof that I was siding with the children against her. But how could I go into it in front of Noni? I just had to say something about not being too harsh on other people's friends. We finished the drive in uncomfortable silence.

Then at lunch David descended from his tower of silence, and we all began to talk about influences in art, and I made some very silly and really rather funny remarks about Rouault, and we were all laughing, and then Sis began to talk about me—about how much less dictatorial I used to be, and so on. I found myself trying to hide her ill temper from the children, wondering at myself as I did so. It was a kind of vanity, I suppose . . . not wanting them to see how she, and therefore I, as her contemporary, could be small. But it did not work. Their faces grew stony, and we all tried to talk of other things.

She did not look at me as she left but spoke politely, as did I. I had ashes in my heart, truly, and longed to say, No, no, don't let this bad weekend stay so, don't let all this go on. But there seemed nothing more to do. I planned to write to her at once. I talked to T., very troubled. Then I waited for the Monday mail, thinking perhaps she would write and accept my apology and tell me that she had not meant those cold mean words. But no. Tuesday a postcard came, asking me to send up her bathing suit and coat, which she had left, and thanking us for a grand weekend. There is nothing to do, I suppose, but I am upset and sad even now. I wish that I could write to Sis, because I have a long and deep horror of family trouble. But there is nothing to say, I suppose. I think if I did write, she would laugh and pretend at least to have forgotten it. Perhaps she has. Perhaps it was all in my head. But sometimes since Sunday I have thought that she is basically a bad-tempered

woman and that as she grows older she is making less and less
effort to act any way but exactly as she feels at the moment. It is
one thing in novels about tempestuous and beautiful nitwits but
another when one must adapt not only one's own life but the lives
of one's guests to an undisciplined person such as Sis is becoming.
As I said, the only way to have a good time with her . . . and she
can be a lot of fun if she wants to . . . is to direct all attention of
every kind—food, light, drink, conversation, color—to please her.
As it was, for that hateful weekend, I debated a long time over the
menus, knowing that Sis would not eat melons, that onion made
her ill, that she hated beer and white wine and red wine, that she
would not eat in the patio because of insects, that she liked her
bed made with the blanket around her face . . . and so on. It is
ridiculous, I kept telling myself . . . because she does little to please
other people, unless it is to her advantage in either a physical or a
material way.

Well, it was hateful. I shall not mention it again. This weekend
will please her, since she is to drive to Laguna with David and a
friend from Princeton and spend the weekend down there with
them and Noni. She will feel beautiful and attractive and domi-
nating, and she is all of those, especially when she is far from me.
And that, of course, is what the whole thing is about.

But I shall never feel the same for hearing her say those calm
hateful words to me.

30. viii. 40

This morning, after a wretched night during which I prickled
here and there constantly as if little fleas were nibbling me, and
once felt very put out with T., and then went into a little nap and
dreamed that I was really making to him the icy speech that I had

only thought about . . . this morning about 6:30 I got up to give T. the sixth shot he had asked for and got since 10:00 last night. I gave it to him—they were all double strength, too—and then said very calmly and noncommittally that the last two days had proved how impossible it would be ever to live with narcotics available without strict discipline, since he had been asking for more shots every day and had had as little help from them as if he only took one or two. In fact, yesterday was an almost impossible day . . . in spite of the fact that he had five and a half ampules instead of the usual one and a half. He said that the days had been unusually bad, and I said that perhaps that was because he knew that he could have as much help as he asked for. Then I pretended to go to sleep again. I had not been at all cranky and had said what I had to say very simply.

He dozed a little, and then I began to read and the new kitten Blackberry climbed up the screen and began to cry, and T. woke up and we listened to the 7:45 news . . . which seems a little better lately, especially since French Central Africa had pledged to support de Gaulle and the Allies. Tim looked at me with his face quite flushed and a strange embarrassed look and said, "Now for a good breakfast of cereal." I said, "Fine," and then realized that he wanted me to say, "Why?" So I did. "Well, I've gone on the dope wagon . . . bang . . . like that." I said, "Oh, that's good," or something like that, and we decided to let Dave come down Tuesday as planned, and live every other day on watermelon as Hal said, and keep ourselves mildly occupied. It was all quiet and easy. But inside I was in a tremble and still am. It means more to both our lives than almost anything that could happen, and now that it's finally here I am not at all scared, as I have been increasingly as I waited for October 1 to come. I think T. is brave and good and that he has been infinitely wise to decide abruptly this way, both for himself and for me. I have been miserable and frightened and have noticed it in my sleep and all the time . . . a kind of nervy bravado about thinking and talking and even eating. Now we can do what there is to do and then perhaps start all over again, in a few days or few weeks.

After breakfast I put away the Analgeticum and the alcohol and the distilled water and the syringe, and as I did it I found myself cold and a little sick with a really live disgust, especially for the syringe. I hated it and could hardly bear to treat it with care and gentleness. Of course, I must . . . there may be times when I will need it, to give T. a shot of Pantopon if he ever has any more of those mysterious cramps of the rectum. Perhaps he never will . . . or not for months, anyway. In the meantime, I feel as if I had been freed from a noisome enslavement to that horrible little metal box. All the horror it used to give me, to see even a needle or a photograph of an injection, all the struggle I had over my own nerves and stomach before I could even watch the doctors shoot Tim in Bern, all the times I practiced in Adelboden and then hurried into my room to drink water with ammonia in it . . . all that came over me this morning as I put the things delicately away, and I was nearly sick.

Now I feel strange and light and a little silly. I hope it lasts. I am keenly interested in the various stages of poor T.'s next days and will write what I remember of them . . . perhaps.

We are both of us disturbed and worried by what we hear and infer about Anne and Jo and Quantness. Of course, Mrs. Parrish, who has been writing often lately in a passing rush of loneliness and ill health, is still bitter about Anne's marriage. In fact, I think she is more so than ever, since she sees that after two years Anne still prefers Jo's company to hers. She pretends that she is only happy at Anne's happiness and says all her reiterated things about Jo's deceitfulness, snobbishness, weakness, on and on, as quotations from Uncle Boney and Doctor Springer and the McCartneys and so on.

Anne, who has only seen her mother twice since she married almost two years ago, although she has lived within from two to four hours of her, writes voluble letters about how terribly busy she is, and how "frighteningly ill" Jo is, and how desperately tired she is, so that it is impossible to go to Claymont. In the meantime, she entertains a constant stream of Jo's friends and, in an effort to amuse her mother, paints lively pictures of their various oddities. She also invites Mrs. P. to come to Quantness, at the same time telling of her rushed fatigue, and has twice committed the unpardonable sin of entertaining the McCartneys. It is all miserable . . . mainly because Mrs. P. is very old, is ill, and through years of adoring and generous treatment from A. has been turned into a spoiled child, so that now at Anne's apparent heartlessness she is bewildered and hurt.

T. and I have always felt that Anne was foolish to let Jo's friends build Quantness and to run it for him and them in an almost hysterically generous way, and now we are almost disgusted with her for the way she is talking about Anthony Hope, the refugee they have taken in. It was all a mistake, as well as a silly mix-up, due, according to Anne's first written admission that some of Jo's friends are not only foolish but definitely crooked, to Auriol Lee's promising to get them eight-year-old girl twins and then telling them casually that a fifteen-year-old boy was on the way. So Anne, frightened and dismayed, has made no bones about being disappointed and writes with her usual entertaining garrulity about its unfortunate heredity and worse environment and what in God's name shall she do with it. And T. and I think that is a wretched preparation for any child, no matter how bad he may be. It fills the air with prejudice and discomfort. Worse, it seems to indicate to us the whole unhealthy atmosphere of Anne's home, which more than most should be clear and good.

It is wrong for us to criticize her, I suppose. But we both know her pretty well and like and love her . . . and it is impossible not to wonder about her. The fact that she sent us a present of $500 after Rochester does not make it any easier to dismiss things she does that worry us.

We decided to spend some of the money on a kennel, which we would then fill with Butch and one or two other dogs, preferably a dainty little dachshund and a nice big sheepdog. But yesterday morning I telephoned Walkerdine and the Humane Society and talked to a lot of other people . . . and no dogs. It was something of a letdown. Today we may go to Juniper Flats or some such place, where we have heard of a man who raises coon dogs, the only kind that are known to kill wildcats. In the meantime, Arnold is making some unusually nice steps down the embankment to the kennel, which he insists on dyeing with a bright brown cement paint he invented himself and is proud of. I hated it . . . but perhaps it will fade, and the outline of the steps is good.

I am somewhat at loose ends, but only temporarily. I do puttery jobs about the house and yesterday read a book about some Anglo-Catholic nuns in India that made me wish that I had written it, because I would have done it better, I think. But I didn't write it . . . and what is more, I probably could not.

31. viii. 40

It seems strange to eat the half of a melon with precision, pushing the spoon meticulously into its side for each bite, and listening to the radio play some goddamned silly *Variations on a Theme* by Elgar, and feeling jubilant that T. has gone into the bathroom to wash his teeth but anxious, when he coughs, that he may have gone in there to be sick again.

He started at noon yesterday, some six hours after his last shot, to be violently sick at about two-hour intervals and to cry ceaselessly into Kleenex tissues without wanting to. He cried until about 3:00 this morning, but from then on he cries only occasionally and, to his surprise and distaste, when I touch him—because the time before he liked it—or when Butch brings a little rubber chewing doll into the room. He is somewhat sickish still but without vomiting. I rubbed his back and buttocks about every one and a half hours during the night and today, and it seems to relieve him for the time and to divert him. He is not so much jittery, although he is that, as in great pain. As he says, he has no special craving for Analgeticum as such but simply a great suffering. I can see that he is better even than he was yesterday or four hours ago, but, of course, I would not tell him so. He perspires freely and naturally, and in spite of absolutely no sleep, his eyes are quite clear.

I called Hal at 8:00, feeling that he might be away for the Labor Day weekend, and almost in spite of myself my heart was warmed to hear his enthusiasm, his thankfulness almost, that Tim had decided to do this. He said it wouldn't last more than two or three days, and that the vomiting was a good sign, and that T. would never right it. He said no food or yeast for two days, but frequent glasses of hot water with a small pinch of baking soda.

I think T.'s washing his teeth is a very good sign. Last night I slept on the porch, while he was in the bedroom. He drew a few horrible pictures of monstrous tortured faces, and had at several magazines, and kept the radio on at some scratchy all-night station. I was in a state of subacute horror, I think. I made my ears stop hearing his cries and the sounds of the worn-out records—almost —and my mind stop thinking—almost—and slept in many patches to dream unusually agreeable dreams, mainly about the duke and duchess of Windsor, who came to see us and precipitated a terrible war in Hemet between us and all the social matrons led by Oliver P. Dusley's worthy if uncomfortably pompous woman.

Those were the *Enigma Variations*. I think Elgar often tried to add a little depth and interest to his musical piddlings by such titles or by saying they were portraits of his friends—guess who— Quite possibly I malign him, but fortunately or not, it doesn't matter.

A nice letter from Noni, thoroughly swept on by the familiar family-tide of Take-Shaunie-to-the-dentist, doctor-it's-time-to-go-uptown-let's-go-to-a-movie, so that she has not even one word done on the two stories she thought to send us this week. I know all that too well. Tim, too.

Thunder behind Tahquite makes me look up at the mountains in spite of myself and see in their dark heavings the strange flat slopes to the Grammont and a storm rolling from the Savoie, oily and portentous. San Jacinto is farther and bigger and finer, as mountains go, and I have a better feeling about it, but sometimes I try hard not to look at it because of something there that brings the Grammont into my mind's view with a sad feeling of right and pain and homesickness. I never felt "put" there, as I do here. But it is true, in spite of my fairly skittish feeling that such a phrase is hackneyed and literary, that I left much of my spirit at Le Pâquis. When we drove past it, a year ago, I could not bear to look. Someday I shall go back. Of course, I looked at the house. I saw that it was sweet and well cared for—not now, all sandbagged and alone—but I did not really see it, for fear of seeing us there, in the garden and under the federal wall and pollarding the willows and sitting at some silly picnic with Mary Powers and David and Noni and Anne in the forest of Arlburg.

Louise Elliott, Arnold's oldest, a fourteen-year-old with a wise pointed face and a tiny body, is singing a song that reminds me of one I used to hear from an unseen Majorcan woman in the place on the Rue Monge in Dijon. She is stringing wire into the fence of the new kennel. Lena, Arnold's wife, is talking as always in her harsh flat voice, and Arnold answers her abstractly. The thunder grows nearer. "Gee, don't it seem, don't it seem, honey, as if it ain't no time from Christmas to pageant, once Christmas is here?" Her voice rasps amicably into the crisp air. "Arnold, this morning I was walking down to the spring and *Honey* and this crazy old man says—and I says—and—" she laughs. Arnold laughs and slops a little cement onto the rock steps. Lena bores him to distraction with her gabble, but there is a nice feeling between the two of them, and I can see how she is a good wife, generous, severe, with a trim waist and full firm breasts, attractive in spite of her cockatoo voice and her strange stringy Egyptian hair.

It has begun to rain, large drops but sparsely, so that the hot air has that dusty but cooking smell that I have almost always liked. Little Louise, wrinkling her thin face, laughs and prances between the drops delightedly, looking at me without shyness as I stand on the front terrace watching Arnold get an old tarpaulin from the Bantam to protect the steps.

A few minutes ago I heard Louise call to her mother to come watch Arnold take off the leaf. I watched, too, from the porch, as he peeled the big castor-bean leaf from the puddled cement on the bottom step. It was thundering nearer, and Lena was shrieking amicably with her hair in curlers for Saturday night, and Louise was talking excitedly about some black granite that her father had once shown her near Pala, I think. I could hear T., at the other end of the house, retching violently in the bathroom, for the first time since 6:00 this morning.

The shower is over, but the air is still heavy and gray. I have paid Arnold ($19.50 for labor for kennel and steps, with a bill for about $30 yet to come from the lumberyard), and we are alone here on the hill. I made T. a little drink of cold water and whiskey, but doubt if it does him any good. He feels very sick, but it is the pain in his phantom foot that is torturing him. Still—he is much quieter than yesterday at this time, partly from fatigue and partly because he is accustoming himself, I think.

I am sticky and shiny. It is no use bathing yet, though. I remember a day like this in Laurel Canyon, when John and Gigi and Al went swimming and I was afraid to write to T., so I started a long letter to Al about our six or seven anniversaries. I typed it and bound it together, months later, with his beloved stapler, and gave it to him. As far as I know, he never read it. Finally, in La Tour when I was going through the books last year, I tore it up. It was interesting because it showed how very much I wanted him to love me instead of some misty picture he worshiped called My Wife and because it spoke of the first time I ever saw this valley, on our fourth anniversary [1933]. I loved it and wanted to live here, and we talked to Bev Grow in San Jacinto about renting an old mill or garage, but we knew that we had no money to live anywhere but in the family's home in Laguna and that Al would really loathe it anyway. I remember writing about San Jacinto village, and the hot sweet night as we walked back to the Vosburg from the movie, and a big rich car full of haughty careless young people with dark eyes and hair, who swept down from the hills and through the village as if they had owned it since God. They were beautiful, in a wild ugly way.

N.B. Soeur Irma—I have always had a certain precision about my actions, but it was from her that I came to crystallize my need to formalize, to "tidy." Now, when T. goes into the bathroom, I straighten the bottles of alcohol and Dorothy Gray Hot-Weather Cologne, the Mennen's Antiseptic Oil, and the Squibb's Baby Powder into one line. I wipe off the top of the little radio case and the table with a piece of Kleenex. I empty and wipe out the ashtray. I put all the magazines in a neat graduated pile and tighten the bottom sheet of the bed and plump the pillows. I do all this and more as I would wash my teeth to avoid feeling fuzz on them, because I know the hopeless fuzzy feeling, especially in a "sickroom," of a place without order. And I remember that big room at the corner of the third floor of the Viktoria Hospital, with the round parlor table and its completely unused complement of two armchairs and two straight chairs. The table was covered with a cut-velvet "throw" of green or red or mustard—God knows—and over it a clean white cloth edged with wide crochet. On it was the formidable array of bottles, ranged thoughtfully according to their usage and all toeing an invisible line some inches back from the blotting pad and the inkwell for the clinic sheet. A chair waited for Dr. Nigst's handsome, outwardly confident behind, and the pen was wet for him, and the bottles were in their recommended order for his daily ballet of injections—and behind all this Soeur Irma moved quietly, automatically, just as I move now to put the four-inch powder can carefully in front of the five-inch oil bottle and the two-inch cologne bottle. Nobody cares but me—and Soeur Irma—but to us it makes, perhaps, the difference between reason and delirium, the inch of order that justifies a mile or so of agony and sweat and chaos.

This may sound foolish. Truth to tell, I do not care.

Adelaide Arnold just called to ask us to a tea tomorrow when the illustrator of her next book would be able to chat with us of mutual acquaintances—probably Dorothy Lathrop and the children's librarian of the N. Y. Public Library. I asked about her book. She spoke wearily, deprecatingly. She asked about mine. I spoke nonchalantly. Then she said that "old friends from the Smithsonian" were going north with her. I spoke of the lovely weather in San Francisco now, and while she said knowingly that it would be cold later and I murmured, "Yes, yes," inconsequentially, I thought, They would be old—from the Smithsonian—like my little dressmaker, always little.

1. ix. 40

Today, at about five o'clock, it is dark and almost cool, the first straight gray day we have had since we came here. The rusty bloody slopes of wild buckwheat glow in the impersonal light, and all around the valley there are occasional shots from the heights, as there were this morning, for the opening of dove season.

Last night we went into a complicated soothe-Timmy routine, as he said, and gave enemas, warm drinks, massages, this and that. Then I went to bed and immediately to sleep, about 11:00. After about two hours of concentrated fidgeting, including several trips to the toilet to get rid of the aftermaths of the enema and a violent bout of sickness, not to mention a severe coughing spell and so on, Tim, who according to himself was twitching like an old mule with hives, set himself foggedly to sit out the night, complete with rugs, water, cigarettes, and radio. He dimly remembers throwing himself on the bed for a minute, and he woke up some four hours later. I gave him a rub then, and he slept for another hour.

Today, although he is obviously in great discomfort, is nothing like yesterday. He looks worse, probably, with pouchy eyes and a swollen lower lip, and his wrists are swollen, too. But he is able to sit still for half an hour at a time, and has laughed several times, and told me that although he felt god-awful in his poor little leg, it was wonderful not to feel the dreadful time sense that he felt when he knew that six o'clock or two o'clock meant a shot to help him. He feels freer now, and that is good.

Contrary to Hal's council, he has eaten a little today . . . some

vegetable broth and for lunch a broiled peach and a slice of bacon
. . . probably foolish, but I can't help believing that the psychical
effect of a somewhat exotic dish offsets the harm it might do,
whereas a plate of unsalted zucchini might send T. into a little tizzy
of depression. I would not feel the same way about a child, probably . . . but a man forty-six years old cannot be built or rebuilt in
one day or year.

I feel tired and will write no more.

I have been invited to a lunch at Freda van Benschoten's on
Tuesday and am going. I like her a little more than I dislike her,
probably. She is harmless, I think, until I see her in my mind's eye
the frightening heroine of a strange story full of well-bred murder,
arson, rape, and mayhem, always discreet and always speaking like
a lady.

Later

Gastronomically I have in me the makings of one of those fat old
women who before this war lived in expensive hotels in Europe,
mainly because of the cuisine, which was heavy for the rich old
German women, solid for the English "ladies," complex and rich
for the old French women, and thoroughly delightful for the Ital-
ians and everyone else.

Or, on the other hand, I have in me the makings of the old
Czech peasant woman, Otto Truttmann's mother-in-law, who
came once a year from her little farm to rich, beautiful, wonderful
Switzerland and tried so hard to eat enough goodness for the next
eleven months that she had several *crises de bile* and made poor
stingy Otto call out the doctor more than once at night, which cost
double a day call.

In other words, I see in myself signs of a strange piggishness, which might be called with more nicety but no more precision *gourmandise.* It usually crops up during times of undoubted strain, such as now, when I am almost shocked to find myself sneaking a bite of potato chips (stale at that, in the kitchen when I am really not hungry, and after a weekend of unusual boredom, when I usually crave pâté and champagne for breakfasts and, that being impossible, eat leftover chops or bacon and a glass of beer).

This is a strange sign of unrest . . . or rather one of its aftersigns.

2. ix. 40

Now and then I think my heart will break, listening to T.'s low weeping under the sound of the radio or watching him try two or three times to get up from a chair. He slept about an hour last night and is quite weak now and depressed. There is nothing I can do, nothing—except rub him, which I do every two hours or so.

We talked last night of my writing a fair, lively (if possible) journal of my own experiences in American restaurants. It might be a good idea. Many people thought I was biased and unfair to our native gastronomy in *Serve It Forth,* which annoyed me, because it was a hasty criticism. I can never say that all apple pie is delicious simply because apple pie is a great American dish. Nor would I ever damn all apple pies for the same reason. I have never made the usual gastronomical pilgrimages, of course, to places like the restaurant in New Orleans's old quarter for Huîtres Rockefeller, etc., etc. But I have traveled an average amount here at home and had to go to average places—with perhaps a more-than-average amount of interest. So—I am milling it over in my mind. The book would be controversial, naturally—and in order to write naturally I would have to do it straight, which would necessitate a lot of name-changing if it ever saw light.

Today is a fresh gusty day, with moving clouds and an occasional slamming door. The air is good.

About 6:30 P.M. I just had an unusual experience, brought on partly by fatigue and anguish, partly by a diet of watermelon to keep T. company, and partly by a generous lot of wine I drank at noon. I felt, after a half-hour massage for T. at 5:30, so tired that although I knew the air was beautiful and the plants were thirsty, I could only look out the windows as I walked languidly past. I lay on my bed, watching the golden shimmering of the cottonwood leaves, and my mind seethed with words—the lush reptilian blue-green of the tobacco leaves, and so on and so on—while I broke into a weak steamy sweat. I went to the kitchen to get more watermelon and tried not to stagger, wondering if I were unconsciously dramatizing my own position as the timeless loving wracked automaton. I got the watermelon and ate it calmly, and I began to feel better. But I cannot describe, ever, the feeling of almost-complete foolish trembling that came over me. I still feel queer and have about decided that if I want to get through what might be a difficult night, I had perhaps better eat some eggs and toast than try to live on melon.

For the moment T. looks quieter, but I have put in a call for Hal to say that he is weak and has only slept five hours in four nights and can I not do something to relieve the constant pain in his poor leg? I have little hope of help, except Hal's warm voice and another assurance that it will soon be over. But will it?

I don't yet know whether we'll have David down tomorrow or not.

Saturday, 8. ix. 40

The air in the Ramada at the Soboba Hot Springs is cool and gray and full of the soft sounds of falling water from sprays tended at twilight by the gnomish gardener. Below me on a rustic seat a young man talks with apparent charm to a girl whose hair is pulled into a soft dark knot on her nape. She is more at ease than he, but both of them laugh too soon and twist their hands unknowingly.

David left Bareacres a while ago, with Shaun down the hill from camp. I thought it would be best not to have him come out and indeed decided strongly not to, but then I said all right, and it turned out to be a very good thing. Having him in the house made it necessitous for quiet, so that sometimes when if we had been alone T. would have cried out, he was quiet—and that was probably better. Dave took us on drives, and talked when spoken to, and was easy and friendly.

This is the ninth day since T. started to stop, and I can see that this far at least there is great improvement. He feels discouraged, because the pain in his leg is there constantly, but I know from his physical shape, his reactions to things, that the pain is less now—or else that he is more able to combat it. He seldom cries and is able to sit for sometimes an hour at a time without twitching about. Occasionally his conversation is rather flighty.

The night of the last day I wrote in this—when was that? three days? four?—was the worst. I rubbed him and gave him milk and so on—did I say that Hal said to give him milk or raw meat every two hours?—but toward morning he broke down more completely than I have ever seen him do. He had slept only six or five hours in as many days and was wracked, literally, with the pain and with nausea. He quite lost control. I had been expecting it, but to my intense surprise and chagrin it was a terrible shock to me, and I was immediately and almost overwhelmingly sickened, so that I swayed with nausea. I did what I could for T., with arguments and scoldings and massages and so on, and then drank some ammonia in hot water and sagged into my bed, where I lay for perhaps an hour in a kind of passive physical revolt against things I could not even name. My guts heaved and my heart flapped in my chest, and I was an uneasy soul from stem to stern. Finally I went to sleep, and poor Tim slept.

The next morning I decided that Hal or no Hal, a few sleeping tablets would be a good moral companion, if nothing else, so I telephoned Edith and explained to her that I did *not* want an opiate of any kind. She sent some out that night from her doctor (I tried unsuccessfully first to get them from Ginager, the local druggist—it would have meant prescriptions and on and on)— Dave brought them—and the first night T. took two, and the last three nights he has taken one and has slept about six hours every night. So I think the harm of the soporific is offset by the benefit, and perhaps I am criminally wrong.

It is queer, or perhaps not, that when I hear of what must have been a very nice easy weekend with Sis and the children and a college friend of Dave's, I am in a minor way jealous. But I am, because I want the children to see Sis and me together in a nice way. But when they see us, Sis is very conscious of sides: are they on Her side or on My side? And the only way to avoid that is to have a man for her when I am around (with them, at least): she is very conscious, I think, of being thirty and unattached, and there I am with T., and she hates every move of courtesy David or Rex or even T. makes toward me. And unfortunately for our sisterly harmony, T. and David have been the only men when she was around, so there has been not only the siding of me versus her for the children's favor but her unwanted while I was wanted. Oh, dear. Anyway, I wish sometime I could invite the children and Sis and some completely pushover man for her, so that she would have a really nice weekend and would be happy and fun and the children would see that she and I could be together and still agreeable. As it is (I may imagine the whole thing), I feel jealous to hear of how gay and easy weekends are away from us, and wish desperately to be able to show David and Noni that Sis and I are not always queer and ill-tempered with each other. God knows I don't feel so—and God knows that several times this winter Sis has had a really good time at Bareacres. But when Noni came it was changed—and when Dave came it grew impossible. Dave's being male precipitated the whole business.

Two days ago T. and I paid $200 for the beginning of a gray, green-leather-lined, convertible, six-cylinder, hydromatic-drive, cabriolet Oldsmobile, 1941 model, which is to be delivered, we hope, on October 1. I feel rather awful about buying anything like that and wonder if we'll ever pay for it—but T.'s intense pleasure at being able to drive the demonstration car (there is no clutch) is worth even bankruptcy, I think. Now we are trying to figure how to build a garage for $25.

10. ix. 40

I am continually irked, as if by a dormant eczema, by the knowledge that I not only should but want to start work on a book about American gastronomy. But I find myself unable to, partly from procrastination and partly because of things like the constant attention I must pay to T.'s food and how much he sleeps and whether he goes to the toilet. I do not need to tell myself, even in print, how much more important such things are to me than the partial accomplishments of a chapter finished or a story brought to its end. Such pip-squeak reassurances of my own intelligence are unnecessary. But when these sad tasks are over, when my poor

Timmy no longer counts sleep as a perfumer would his drops of attar . . . that seems a queer thing to write, but it is what I thought . . . then I will get to work and write what I think about American gastronomy. And in the meantime, as I said, the knowledge that I should be doing it and that I could earn money by it irks me. Does that negate my whole paragraph?

It is still a gray day. There is a storm somewhere. David is here, presumably to help us build the garage we have found would cost too much, and sits on the wall of the front terrace, sketching the black clouds or perhaps the blacker mountains. T. is painting in the studio. I, after putting the kitchen to rights, am in my little honey-colored workroom, all open to the occasional air, thinking that my mouth tastes too much of the cold cauliflower we ate in the salad for lunch. Perhaps in a minute I'll make myself a drink of vermouth à l'eau or even whisky.

I have never remembered how to spell whiskey. Perhaps it is because I am basically afraid of it. But on the other hand, I have never remembered how to spell parsley, and certainly I have no fear of that fine strong upstanding herb.

T. and I have been reading aloud rather a lot lately, and twice I have been haunted by such strong memories of things that I cannot even now remember completely that I have been almost unable to go on. Once we were reading . . . well, the last one we read was so good that I cannot possibly remember the one before it . . . but a book. And suddenly, in a passage that had nothing to do with hotels, I thought so deeply and thoroughly and intensely about hotels, and walking along the impersonal corridors, smelling of wax in Switzerland, whether it was the Trois Couronnes or the Bärem in Interlaken, and of cigar smoke in America, and of opening the door in the long row of doors and suddenly finding myself in a room that even in five minutes had mysteriously assumed the character positive or negative of the person stopping there, and then of what that character might be and whether or not I liked it, and even of other people walking down hotel corridors not even in my memory and what the rooms meant, warmly, passionately, horribly well, when they opened the impersonal doors—I thought of all this and much more while we read aloud some passage that had nothing to do with hotel corridors, and could hardly go on reading.

In the same way, while Tim and I were reading an unusually well-written book called *Verdict of Twelve,* by an Englishman, which is much too good a novel to be billed merely as a "murder mystery," I was almost silenced, somewhere with complete irrelevance, by a memory so intense that it was tactual, sensual, of the mosquitoes that beat slowly up and down the cold white tile paneling of the bathroom at Le Pâquis. I remembered that small room, stuffy as soon as it was warm, and intolerably cold if it was not stuffy, which the architect put in grouchily as a concession to our foolish exaggerations of sanitation. It was irregular in shape, not from whimsy but because it had to be sandwiched in over the pipes and between the clothes closets. It was a room that was conceived and built grudgingly, and from the beginning that was plain. It was too high for its size, and the walls, which we tried despairingly to soften with a tile more on the creamy side than the blank white or the poisonous turquoise that were suggested, rose hardly and stiffly to about eye level and then whuddered into plaster of a deeper, more indeterminate yellow. There was one window, a miserable affair that canton law made us fill with opaque glass, the kind of window that was so hopeless that I never even bothered to hide it with a curtain of chintz or voile. The toilet, offset in a half alcove, flushed directly into the ceiling of the living room below, with a loud sucking Swiss enthusiasm, and continued to do so in spite of consultations and wavings of contracts to the contrary. There was no washbowl, since Timmy in a moment of Continental enthusiasm

. . . also Swiss, largely . . . had decided that the idea of having a lavatory in each bedroom was really the best in every way except perhaps the aesthetic. The tub was ample, although, of course, not up to the 1890 standards of the Three Crowns. There was a fine soap dish . . . built into the tile wall.

I remember several things about that bathroom, besides how stuffy it got. Several times boys, and even girls, would swing down the road from Chexbres, which ran outside in a fine curve at almost roof level, and they would yodel, inexpertly but with that same Swiss enthusiasm as they pelted along. I would be lying in the tub, which was filled with Le Pâquis luxury to its brim with the hottest water this side of hell, and I would hear the clear youthful voices, tremulous but exuberant, come toward the horrid opaque window and then shoot by it full and fine, as unworried as apples.

But the thing I remembered about the bathroom . . . I remembered other things as I suddenly thought on it, the other night while I went on reading about the terrible murder trial in *Verdict of Twelve* . . . I remembered how hot and perfumed it smelled after Anne Parrish would bathe in it and how she never washed out the tub, and I remembered finding little splashes of blood when Mary Powers was there and thinking that she had left them there on the toilet seat deliberately to frighten Anne and us into thinking she was desperately ill, and I remembered feeling ill one night and how T. fixed a tub for me and undressed me and brought me a little glass of brandy warmed in his hands . . . but most of all I remembered how the several large mosquitoes put their noses against the tiles, always cool, and buzzed up and down, up and down.

They made a strange noise and seemed quite absorbed in what they did. They seldom bit, and then only absentmindedly, as if it were their unfortunate duty. Their bites were strangely virulent and raised big white welts edged with angry red, but I never hated the mosquitoes, as I would have had they not been so driven. Up and down they went, their sensitive proboscises pressed painfully against the hard white tiles. Up and down. Through steam and stink and the fine Swiss odor of Pine Bath Essence, they filed away at the white tiles, never making anything but perhaps a tiny track on the mist, which soon vanished. They buzzed like little serpents and bit with violence at the smooth blankness of the solid, sturdy, ugly, practical white Swiss bathroom tiles.

And that was what I remembered, only much more, as I read aloud something that had nothing to do with it.

I should very much like to get myself a little drink. The day is dull, I feel dull, I feel depressed. There is something to drink and make me feel less mindful of everything. But I know that I am inclined, at least at this period in my life, to drink too much. Not much too much, but a little. So I shall try to combat it. Because I think any person, or even any beast, who is not quite in focus is not only pitiable but despicable.

My typing is bad. I could make it better. Or even worse, if I tried. But the thing is that I do not try to make it better. This is the place for a well-pointed moral.

I think instead I shall go and take an enema and a shower and perhaps manicure my toenails and my fingernails.

T. and David are painting now in the studio, and Butch tick-tocks.

. . . T. just came in and said, among other things, "I can't remember what it feels like to have two legs. Sometimes I look at people in amazement and think, 'How can they go along on only two sticks, when I have three?' It must be very queer to be that way. It's funny." I said, "Not very funny." I wasn't grim . . . but it simply didn't seem funny to me. He said, "No . . . perhaps not funny. But it seems very queer. Only two legs."

There is rain, now and then, on the roof. It sounds beautiful, dripdripdrip, and strange in this dry land.

The new dog Wheeler whimpers and scratches at the door, trying to get Butch out into the brush. He leads the little dog miles away, and we call and call, and finally they come back, Butch too tired even to greet us. So we have Butch locked in, and Wheeler the foxhound whimpers, foxed for fair.

15. ix. 40

The air is changing fast so that it is cooler and filled with a fresh golden color and a different smell. I am quietly excited to think of winter here.

Timmy is better, I think, although the nights are bad. Sometimes he takes only one of the yellow capsules I got Mother to order through her doctor, but more often it is two. I hate to have him take them, and I hate to trick Hal this way, but I couldn't endure the nights any longer . . . not for my own sleeplessness but for what they were doing to T. Today he seems to feel better than yesterday, and I find myself able to look forward to things like winter.

Winter means some work, too. It is only about 5:30, but already I can hardly see to write. I'll have to get some kind of good working lamp in here. And the same thing must be done in the bar, where we will perhaps eat suppers more than we do now that we can stay on the porch, and for the studio. Then some shelves and so on must be put in the front bedroom if we are to sleep there. And worst of all, as far as expenses go, we must soon see about buying an oil heater for the house. It means about a hundred dollars. The check from Mr. Sheppard has not yet come—I dread having to go through the humiliating business of telling Anne again that it is late and that we need it. I wish to God she would do what she planned to and settle some sort of annuity on Tim, even if it were half what she sends him now. We are in an almost constant state of worry and embarrassment.

Arnold may come for supper tonight. He was here about 6:00 last night and talked with many sighs about how dull it was to eat in cafés while Lena was staying with her mother, but I did not ask him to stay for supper, partly because that kind of obvious hinting always annoys me and mainly because we already had Merle Armitage here.

He came down within two days after I had thanked him for a note and told him that T. had been very ill but that we hoped to see him sometime later. I was really cross when his letter came Friday saying that he would be down Saturday for the afternoon and dinner. It seemed callous and pushing, but, of course, he is an unusually callous and pushing man. It is partly his boundless vitality and partly his thirty years of being an impresario, which probably left him feeling that all people are to be treated with the same naive protective boldness that he used on Chaliapin and Mary Garden and Stokowski. He is something of a glandular phenomenon, I think—looking nearer forty than fifty and with an enthusiasm and vigor and curiosity that are not only tiring but frightening.

He is tall and fattish and wears affected clothes: last night, a well-cut loose suit of blue cotton with a navy-blue shirt and a red cotton bandanna wound under the collar and knotted in front. His heavy suede shoes had exaggerated square toes. He has small hands and feet and a very small short nose, which looks almost boneless. His left eye is larger and higher in his skull and has a mad mean look in it, like Peter the Great, while his right eye at the same moment may be twinkling and genial. He talks continually and loudly, with many gestures, and occasionally laughs with an unconvincing joviality, always at something he himself has said.

He gave us a copy of his latest book, *The Navy*, which Ward Ritchie printed beautifully for Longmans Green. We talked about that for a long time, while he drank three highballs. Then we had supper, which I really made just about as we would have had it (grilled steak, a salad of lettuce and shoestring potatoes, iced grapes, coffee), and listened to him tell about his trip this summer. He has unpleasant table manners, by the way, even though we did not sit at a table. He talked for about four hours and ate all the grapes and drank all the coffee. Now and then he would say, "Do you really want me to go on?" and before we could say yes, he would go on. Or he would say, "Shall I tell you about a most amazing and wonderful thing that happened on the road to Milwaukee? It will take perhaps ten minutes, and then if I tell you about that weekend it will take about thirty minutes more?" And on he would sweep. He was interesting, in a way he did not realize . . . so completely the pusillanimous snob, bragging about the riches of his friends and whimsically referring to his various hostesses as ghastly old bitches.

16. ix. 40

I started to work this morning . . . got all my notes in order for the book on eating. I don't want to write it particularly, but I want to write. It is like having the itch. Now that I have started to work again, I am easier, as if I put ointment on my mind.

17. ix. 40

Yesterday afternoon I wrote quite a lot about patriotism and gastronomy, none of it good enough. This morning, though, I have finished collecting everything for what should be a good section about oysters and eating them. I'll try to do at least part of it this afternoon.

It rained now and then all night, and at times the air was so heavy with the smell of sage and wild buckwheat and wet stones that it was like breathing a rich sweet Greek wine, so that it was almost better not to breathe consciously.

T. was in such pain that he did not even go to bed but sat up all night or wandered quietly about, fixing himself warm milk and looking at the wild moon-edged clouds of the storm. This morning, after a massage, he is working again. I don't know what to do for him. I wrote again to Hal, asking really for some further reassurance that the pain would diminish as he and the men at Rochester said. But he probably will write a note asking us to come up to Pasadena and hear some new records, in reply. It is not that he is callous . . . but I think he has nothing to say to help us.

This morning T. and I were sitting in the bar, eating some grilled steak for breakfast, and he looked out the window and said, "Butch must be terribly constipated. He has been trying to drop a turd for about five minutes." I looked, too, because I was surprised, and almost at once we realized that it was not a turd but that the poor little creature was in the grip of a really terrible erection. We went down at once to the kennel and found him immobile, unable to walk, with his back curved high and his penis as big as a large man's and dark purple. He did not seem to suffer but had a bewildered look on his face. It was terrible to see, because it looked so hopeless—his little body curved and stiff and that monstrous organ hanging from it. I ran to the phone and got Walkerdine, who said to put ice water on it. By the time I got the ice and a towel, Butch was much better and lay quietly while we put compresses on him. As the inflammation went down he began to jerk, so I thought to distract him by taking him for a little walk. But the poor little wretch could hardly make his hind end follow his front, so I put him alone into the kennel, and now he is all right, although quite exhausted.

Tawny is pregnant again, with an unknown mate this time, and is so crazy and disagreeable that we think we may take her into the Riverside animal shelter and have her killed. She has never been an agreeable or even friendly animal, and since her first heat, which was unsatisfied because of the astonishing lack of any Toms in that part of Moreno valley, she has been definitely disagreeable ... snarling and dour, and really mean with the new little kitten Blackberry, who is one of the merriest animals in the world.

4.x.40

It is so long since I have written that I almost dislike the thought of starting here again. Too much has happened.

Last night sometime Tawny had five more kittens in Tim's paint-rag bin and is cheerful now for the first time in weeks. I moved her into a box in the toilet, but she is still rather mussy, although this time was much cleaner than last. I can't help liking her again, so proud and purring, but I dread having to go through the business of disposing of the little things and feeding the rest and on and on. We now have ten animals!

Two weeks ago tomorrow, Rex and Dave were here for lunch on their way to Colorado. Rex was happy as a child at the thought of a week with Dave. But that night Mother collapsed with angina pectoris, and by Wednesday Rex was home again by plane, and the whole family had gone through one of those lightning changes so that all our positions are different and strange and even difficult, and we are bewildered for the time. Mother is still in the hospital, perhaps a little better as far as blood pressure goes but having attacks of pain irregularly, which must be helped by shots. At first she protested at being there, but now she is content to stay, frightened of having an attack at home when the nurse might be away.

We went up as soon as we could get the things in order here and stayed for about a week, with one night down here in the middle of it. At first the doctors thought Rex need not cut short his vacation, and they told me that Edith might come home in two or three days if we could get Shaun away and muzzle the cook. Edith, too, told me that she longed to come home but could not bear the thought of Grace's talking, and asked me to speak to her. Sis and Tim and Noni agreed that I should, so I had a fairly sensible talk with the woman, who parted from me at the end with tears of love. For three or four days she was much less chattery and worked quietly and well.

Rex came home . . . and the second morning he was there she pounced on him at seven o'clock and apparently told him that I had told her we did not want her anymore and that we had another woman to take her place. (This was probably the result of her constant listening via the kitchen door to everything we discussed in the front of the house, and once Tim and I had said to Noni that perhaps we could get Sweetie-pie to help if Grace had to leave, since she was having her change of life and had been too "poorly" even to do the washing when we arrived.) Father was much upset, naturally, at the thought of changing cooks along with everything else, and although he said nothing to me, I knew from his manner and from what Noni said that he was disgusted with me for precipitating all this with my meddlesome ways.

I was disappointed that Noni, who knew why I had spoken at all to Grace and knew that I had not told her either that we wanted her to go or that we had another woman engaged, should not tell Rex that I was less interfering than he thought me. But Noni was, for the first time, showing a side that I had never suspected before and that has been a shock to me. She almost openly resented my being at the Ranch, and grew cold if I even suggested helping her with the marketing, and said things like "Well, I'd *thought* that I had things pretty well in hand . . . but, of course, I'm delighted to have you step in and manage everything, Dote." It was difficult for me, because I am the oldest and the most used to assuming responsibility in a thousand crises at the Ranch, and I was really straining to give it all to her and at the same time help her without seeming to, because I knew that she was the nominal head of the house and that it would be unpleasant but good for her to have some responsibility. But things got less pleasant all the time, and we came down here as soon as we could. Now I telephone every night, and all Noni will say is that Mother is all right. Occasionally when I pump her with questions, she will admit that Mother has had another attack. But I know nothing, really, about how she is. It is very hard. Last night I tried for two hours to get the Ranch (Sis and I both asked Noni never to let the Ranch be left alone, even if it meant hiring someone to sit by the telephone at night now and then, because Mother might need some of us), and finally called the hospital, where someone told me with customary hospital vagueness that Mother was fairly well and had had two attacks that morning. I was terribly upset and angry with Noni, since I had told her that I was going to call last night and felt that if she had gone out with Rex or to see some people she could at least have called me first and told me how Edith was. It is wrong to be so ready to be upset and exasperated, I know . . . but I am down here simply because it was impossible to stay at the Ranch, where I want to be, near Mother, and I feel really depressed that the result of twenty-three years of my being Noni's older sister is finally, at this unfortunate moment, turning against me with her sudden cold resentment. I know, and none better, that too often I have felt obliged to step in, to boss, to direct, where perhaps it would have been better, and certainly easier, to let things go every which way rather than antagonize the younger ones of the family. I have always been given too much responsibility, because I usually took it well, and sometimes I have taken it unnecessarily. It is easy to see things like that as I grow older, and I regret the fact that I was so willing to lead and that so many people who should have known better were so more-than-eager to give me jobs that were really much too heavy and old for me to assume. Now, at a time when I could and would like to help at the Ranch, these sins of omission and commission, not alone mine, are putting out a fine crop of antagonism and misunderstanding between Noni and me.

Of course, the whole thing is difficult for her. She is too young to be stuck there and knows it. She is alarmingly anemic and listless and probably morbid. We urged her not to stay at the Ranch when she first got back from Honolulu, but with her characteristic torpor she said she thought she'd stay a few months and then maybe move on. But now that her freedom is threatened she is inwardly frightened and furious at the trick and told T. that she *would not* be caught, that she *must* escape. She must, of course, and we'll do all we can to help her . . . but at the moment she can no more escape from the dreary routine of running the Ranch than I can escape from my helplessness at being here instead of there where I feel I should be. Noni is egoistic with that bland egoism of a young person, and quite possibly feels that she is the only one who is caught. She is unwell and given to defeatist thoughts, I know.

Grace, after talking "confidentially" to every member of the family and apparently trying to turn each of us against the other for some strange unhealthy reason of her own, is now on a two weeks' vacation, and as far as I know, Noni is running the house and doing the cooking, with the cleaning and the laundry done by Goldie. I asked her please to get extra help now and then, and to take care of herself, and so on, when I telephoned the other night.

But she barely responded, and I felt like an unpleasantly boring old woman who was quite obviously poking my nose into what was none of my business.

Shaun is in a school that was picked out by Rex over Sis's head, so that, too, was unpleasant at home. Of course, Rex has all the financial responsibility of Shaun and feels fairly correctly that he should have the say in where the poor child goes, but Sis was upset and angry at his lordly disregard of her. And no one can be more lordly than Rex. He is difficult to live with unless he is constantly flattered and appeased.

So it is plain that for the moment, at least, the family is at odds—and at a time when by all the rules of sentiment we should be knit closely by our concern for Mother. It is a strange and disturbing thing to happen, and quite unexpected, by me at least.

6. x. 40

Night before last I called Noni, who said that Mother was much worse. I told her I would call again the next night.

In the morning a letter came from Hal, and I read it aloud without thinking that at last he would speak the truth in it, so that before I could stop myself I had read that there is nothing more to do for T., no way to help him. I was so sick that I turned very hot and tried not to realize what I had read. T. cried, but not much, and said that he wanted to wait a little longer, and then perhaps start taking what Analgeticum is left. I thought that probably I had never been so sad and went about work filled with a leaden bitter hopelessness.

At the same time, I had a pleasant day. I worked violently about the place, raking and cleaning the kennels, cleaning the patio, straightening the paint and nail shelves, on and on. The day was mildly hot, and part of me felt almost happy to be working that way.

Arnold Elliott came up, much discouraged that he was laid off work for two weeks with a bad back, so to cheer him, Tim and he went over to Soboba . . . or rather to the Soboban, where they drank rather a lot, and did not get back until about 3:30. I waited quite a while, mildly annoyed that Tim would not telephone me, and then had a nice reckless lunch of beer and celery and raw beef, with a nip of whiskey first, in the patio. I knew why Tim was staying away, and I wanted him to, much more than I could ever be cross. When they finally came back, they looked quite cheerful and rather mellow.

After Arnold left, Tim said he'd like to go over to swim and have a massage. The water was cold and fine. We were alone in the pool. The sunset in the air was the goldest I have ever seen, so that as we floated on the water the air seemed to shimmer and vibrate between us and the tall cottonwoods with their yellowing leaves. I had a drink in the bar and then sat in the Ramada while Tim was rubbed.

About 8:00 I called the Ranch, and Father answered. He is hard to talk to because of his deafness, but after the first noncommittal answer or two, he told me quite a lot . . . for him. The doctor wanted to see him in a few minutes. Mother was worse, especially in her mind. Father seemed for the first time to have admitted to himself that she was terribly ill. I asked him how Noni was getting along, and he said that she had got a fine dinner and was a good cook. He sounded affectionate and courageous.

In a few minutes Sis called, also from the Ranch. She was rather incoherent and upset—had been getting some furniture out of storage and then had spent almost an hour with Mother, who wept and talked hysterically of being useless and wanting to die. Then Sis came home, much disturbed to find Rex and Noni at a football game, while the phone was ringing with people like Aunt Mary frantic for news, and found the house full of dead flowers and dirty ashtrays and so on. Sis made drinks, thinking they were going out to supper, and when Rex and N. came home, was disgusted to see Noni open some canned corned beef and some canned beans. She told me this on her second call, from Los Angeles two hours later, since Noni was listening at the Ranch. Sis said that when Rex went up to Barmore, Noni announced that she was willing to stay and take care of the Ranch for one year exactly, and then she was leaving. Sis was furious at what she thought was Noni's cold-blooded selfishness and said that she was so busy dramatizing herself as the martyred spinster daughter that she could think of nothing else. This is partly true, but Sis did not like it when I said that it was hard for any twenty-three-year-old person not to dramatize herself. Sis was almost crying with annoyance and depression, and our two conversations were incoherent. She said that Barmore had told Rex that Mother was growing worse and that if she ever had another good day, she should be moved to the Ranch where she would be happier, but that it was doubtful that she ever could be moved. Apparently there is a progressive thickening of the walls of the heart.

Last night was wretched, and poor T., in spite of taking two of Hal's blue capsules instead of the one prescribed, was not able even to lie down until about 7:00 this morning, on the couch in the living room where he slept heavily until about 10:30.

I called Noni, who seemed genuinely glad to hear my voice. She said Rex was at the hospital and then was meeting Mrs. Kelly, who had arrived last night in Whittier and wanted "a good long talk" with Rex about Anne's impossible and vindictive actions with Ted about Shaun. Poor Father. He is very good with Mrs. K., and I think will be able to smooth things out.

I am going to call Noni now and if possible go over there this

afternoon. Tim should not make that 175-mile drive in the shape
he's in, but he wants to come, too. I feel that if I can, I must see
Mother. She has confidence in me, and it may help her to know
that I am there, even for a minute or two.

. . . Mother is much better, and neither Rex nor N. wanted
us to come, because of the long drive, but we want to, so we are
leaving soon. I'll see M. for a minute, and we'll have supper at the
Ranch and then drive home.

7. x. 40

We drove up to the Ranch and had a drink with Father and
Noni, who had just got home from seeing Shaun at his school.
They found him well and happy. Rex was worried because Shaun's
service uniforms, which cost $10 apiece, did not fit at all well, and
had told the captain to send them to the local tailor for taking in a
bit here and there.

Rex looked thinner and tired but was kind and gentle and
thoughtful. He came out into the kitchen later and stood leaning
against the sink, talking with a highball in his hand while Noni and
I got supper and Tim sat in the "nook." He is being patient and
good and is so sweet with Noni and so bewildered by the changes
that I could weep at him.

Noni looked very badly, thin and white, with no life in her at
all. I think I will try to take her to Hal or any other doctor she will
go to, sometime this week. She admits that she is anemic, and at
this time when she should be taking especially good care of herself,
she is sinking deeper and deeper into ill health and lassitude.

The house looked bleak, with no fire ready and one small vase
of dead zinnias that I took up from Bareacres two weeks ago. The
ashtrays were dirty, and we ran out of coffee and had to go up to

the corner market for some. I got supper, of ham in cream, baked noodles with mushrooms, a salad by Noni, and very bad coffee by Noni. But it was a pleasant meal, and we talked with rather too much liveliness about a great many completely dull things. Rex is wound up to a flow of conversation, doggedly trying to avoid any mention of present things. When they inevitably appear, he answers or remarks briefly and then swings again into an interminable monologue about the Indian weavers he saw in New Mexico or what Mike Robinson told him about trying to heat a big house in London many years ago.

We went up to see Mother about 5:30. The room was dark, and when we went in she was startled, mildly, and had a hard time coordinating her voice, which was high and small, like a sleepy child's, to her words, which were mumbled and drunken. She concentrated once or twice, and her eyes seemed to focus, but for the three or four minutes we were there, she was for the most part very muddled. I thought she had been doped again, but apparently she had not had a shot for many hours, and it was weakness and yesterday's pain that had addled her usually precise speech. We stood up to go once, and she cried out, Oh, don't go . . . the days are so long! So we sat down again, although we knew we should not . . . and then she almost went to sleep, as quick as a mouse. When we left, she said, Take some flowers . . . they are so lovely, and then she held out her arms to T. She had always loved to kiss him, over and over again, so that her subsequent kisses to me have seemed perfunctory and dutiful, and yesterday she held him close and kissed and kissed him with that weak ferocity of sick people. Then he stumbled away, and she put her arms softly about me and began to sob, in little quick sobs. I whispered to her of her soft sweet cheeks and left, ready for tears but filled instead with a dry pity that made me dizzy and aching as if I were ill with influenza. Take some flowers, she whispered, lying with her eyes shut and tears on her cheeks, almost asleep again with exhaustion. I pulled a bad red rose from a vase and went into the hall. T. stood leaning against the walls, weeping. We drove home and I rubbed him, and he cried more at the foulness of our own natures that we must make people live when they are through. So that now when Edith has an attack, we will give her restoratives to make her live for another one.

We drove back before midnight, against Rex's wishes. It was better, though, and T. slept well with only one capsule, for the first time in several nights. Today he is painting again, and I am fussing here and there, rearranging furniture to make places for the two ugly heaters that Mr. Ankum and his airy-fairy son are installing in their own lackadaisical way, and putting off getting to work.

We had a letter from Pat, written in his cellar during a raid. A great many English people are doing that, until I am almost sick of hearing about what gallantry it represents. God knows it does, but I get sick of being told so, every time I meet anyone who has had a letter from the Old Country. I must write to him, but I will put it off a little longer. He will be sad indeed to hear of Mother. She has always had something more than a maternal affection for him, and he has reciprocated with the kind of flattering love that lets him tell her every time he confides something in her that he would not in his own mother. Poor Alice Maud . . . I wonder if she is still doggedly living in her service apartment in London with her shell-shocked butler. The big American-style buildings in Madrid held out better under bombing than the old stone ones . . . perhaps she is wise to be as stubborn as she was when I last heard.

The air is full of smoke, not for the first time this autumn, and we are watching the horizon. It makes a good smell, and we know what to do if we see clouds pouring with the wind in our direction, but still it would be terrifying to watch the flames and the brown fumes racing toward our house in this capricious air.

Sis called the Ranch last night from a party. She sounded drunker than I have ever heard her, and breathless. She is to call me tonight, after a visit to the Ranch. I kept thinking, Thank God I am not at a party, all the way home. She was almost hysterical, in a restrained, dramatic way. She has read too many cheap novels about gallant young beautiful career women who drown their sorrows with complete sophistication. I can say that with sincerity, but I know, too, that she is unhappy. Different people have different ways of showing their sorrow and pain, and she is suffering, even if she does it at the top of her voice at a rowdy cocktail party, just as much as Z. or Y.

Material came from the government today about the oyster. I am working in my head and have sent off one chapter, which is a short story. T. suggested a good title today: *The Wild Life of the Oyster.* I think it is amusing and will use it for the chapter on vital statistics, probably.

Our car will not be here until Saturday, in spite of being promised for Thursday or before. It is annoying.

9. x. 40

We went up to the Ranch yesterday, and I saw Mother for a few minutes in the hospital. She was more coherent—they had cut down on the doses of phenobarbital—and can come home whenever she wants to. But she doesn't want to much. A nurse is engaged and a hospital bed is in place, but everyone hopes she'll stay longer at the Murphy Hospital, including Edith.

Noni looked better—thanks largely, I think, to Lera's self-assured and efficient presence. Lera will be there a few hours every day. She had baked a large chocolate cake—and I, thinking how bare was the larder, took up a large box of cookies and a cake by

Mrs. Purdy! Rex, too, looked better. He had won $3.35 at Pang-ingee—winning always cheers him. We had a drink with him and then a mediocre enchilada up along the road with Noni, and got back here by 11:00.

In the moonlight the house looked like some strange land crab, with two antennae feeling the sky. The two new heaters were in but with ridiculously long chimneys. The Ankums are cutting some ten feet off each one—poor dolts.

I have an uncomfortable thumb—am afraid it may be something disagreeable like a felon. I'll see a doctor this evening because it makes me awkward.

We drowned three kittens this morning. Much less messy than other ways—but it is true about the nine lives. After almost half an hour they were still kicking.

1. xi. 40

It is the first of the month, and perhaps I should make some promise to myself to write every day or to stop drinking or to do something. Instead I shall only admit that I have no idea where I last wrote nor when, and do not much care.

We went up to Pasadena, after a discussion that enough was enough, and stayed in a sterile, tidy "home" run by one of Hal's old women. We felt penned, even though we would go out during the day, and for one night I was as unhappy as I have ever been . . . more than that . . . thinking of what I had heard about T. and so on. But in the daytime we could go out, and during our stay there we had a decent time, driving in the new car about the towns and stopping once for beer and fried shrimps at a drive-in place, and so on. When Hal said we could leave, sooner than we thought, we fled like bats out of hell. I insisted on shaking hands with the shriveled old woman who ran the "home," and she was embarrassed and held out a hand covered with soapsuds that felt like a rubber glove filled with lukewarm consommé and old fish bones. Her name was Mary Elderkin.

Two days ago we went to see Mother. She was in bed, with the door closed. Timmy, who had had a bad fall helping me put down the kennel top the night before, planned to lie down with a massage and a pill, but we learned through Noni what surprise Mother planned, so I stopped T. from disrobing in the guest house and we came in to find Mother's door open and her in her Chinese robe in the Irish chair. She looked very pretty—her skin was younger and fresher than it had been for years, and I felt that she smelled better, probably, in her intimate cracks—and she was playing "The Pretty Tyrant" as she has not played it since she was a bride, I wager. It has its boring side . . . mainly because her twenty-five-year habit of talking anywhere in the house and expecting everyone anyplace else in the house to listen has become exaggerated by her power, as an invalid, so that she talks in her rather weak voice almost constantly and expects us to listen no matter where we are. That may be one reason why Rex is such an accomplished deaf person. Anyway, we are so relieved to have Mother still alive that we submit with fatuous and unbreathed gladness to her coquetry, and only occasionally do we admit to boredom.

Noni is long overdue for leaving and has had a quarrel with Anne. I heard about it from N. and then from Rex who drove out unexpectedly for the weekend, and then from Sis who wrote a furious letter just after the quarrel. It was about Noni's refusal to come in and fetch Sis out to Whittier for the weekend. Sis blames it entirely on Noni's smugness as Present-Savior-of-the-Situation, but Rex and Edith both refused to let Noni drive through the Saturday traffic in her present inexpert state, and Noni, to cap things, got rid of a lot of rancor by telling Sis she didn't care if she *never* came out. Sis, on the other hand, feels ousted and hurt. She hung up. Mother had a bad day. They all stew mildly. It is to me but one more sign of the disintegration of my family as such.

Tomorrow we take Arnold Elliott into Riverside to see Dr. C., who fixed my slipped sacroiliac and can perhaps do something for the sprained back that has kept Arnold out of work for some seven weeks. It is all bootleg and may make trouble with the insurance doctors, but Arnold is willing to take the risk.

17. xi. 40

Just now T. and I went out from the warm lighted study and the whuddering firelight of the living room to the porch and watched a half rainbow grow and die against the hills. Sunlight, long and yellow, flung itself against the middle distance of San Jacinto in an intense blot—San Jacinto hills, not the mountain, which was blue and far from us. The hills showed their folds and meadows like old elephant hide, and in front of them the valley and the little lizard of land blazed with arsenic, Paris gray, as violent as dying California leaves can be, yellow and hideously beautiful. The rainbow curved up, more and more intensely, never higher than the quarter-arm but plainly from Soboba, and then it faded. We felt cold and came into the reassurance of the house. The harsh yet measured beauty of the scene before us was disturbing.

The Powells were here and departed in a warm friendly mood, I think. Fay was older physically but more attractive—her beautiful feet and her slim beaky skull have always drawn me to her in spite of some less handsome features—and Larry was mellower. They were genuinely stirred by some of T.'s pictures, which pleased me.

It's long since I wrote here. There are days when I want to, but I am too content—and other days my spirit is too black. Today, after a weekend of company and, just now, a highball, I am verbose but uninspired—and today I choose to write. My mind is full of my own despair, muted fortunately. It is best to write of things like weather and furniture.

The weather toys with rain: to rain—not to rain. I long for rain, to help the plants and more especially the springs—which are still strong, thank God. There is an occasional spate of warm gray drops against the patio windows, and the fire feels good. I brought in several logs, just as the weather changed, and the incredibly fine brown powder from the wormholes made me sneeze.

I look at the cat who sits on the couch beyond my chair and see by the tawny patch beneath her chin that it is Suesky Jo, Tawny's first daughter, a cold neurotic virgin still, rather hateful usually and for no reason since we treat her well. Tawny has grown lovable since her second litter, and her one child from it is a pretty creature, striped white and gray, either male or female.

As to Bareacres: apparently we owe one-half of 1939's taxes but are tax free because of T.'s veteran exemption. The land is as we found it, except for a cleared firebreak around the house, and the road up to the flats has been smoothed out a bit by Old Man Gibbel. The springs are flowing sweetly. The tank springs leaks, and we go up now and then and whittle a plug or two of soft pine and fill the holes. In a year or so we'll have to build a reservoir, preferably of stone. The land around the house is much as we found it. I've cleared it off near the buildings, because of fire, and behind the house have cleared and nourished a little rocky knoll planted with tamaracks, which may someday be beautiful. It must have been planted there among the rocks by old Captain Hoffman. The little dwarfed trees respond almost pathetically to encouragement. As soon as this possibly rainy spell is past, I'll scratch the ground here and there and scatter the wildflower seeds that Arnold gave me.

The house is fairly well tightened against winds and rain now, and as I lie on the couch before this gentle fire and know that in another room is a good oil furnace, I feel coddled as an orchid and, in spite of myself, apologetic.

We have a handsome harrier, who leads Butch the little Pekingese far into the hills so that they both come home exhausted. We keep Butch to please ourselves, and we keep Wheeler to please him—but if Wheeler steals him from us, what is the use of keeping either? Butch just came in, completely fatigued. I hear Wheeler bugling in the hills, and so does he. But he's not built for chasing hares. He pleases and amuses and charms us more than Wheeler. Therefore, we should get rid of Wheeler. Perhaps. But Wheeler is so handsome—

Later

I have fed the cats and dogs, and now, with a Charles McCarthy program on the little portable radio and the fire chattering and a cigarette fuming in my holder, I look out past the blue Swiss chair, through the little hallway, into the kitchen. There, past the top of the smooth white icebox I see the rafters of the high wooden kitchen, satiny and brown and reassuring.

My heart is heavy, thinking of my friends in France and of England so hard pressed. I can hardly bear to think of anything at all these days, and dwell resolutely on the growth of a kitten or an acacia tree and the progression of clouds in a winter sky.

4.xii.40
Globe, Arizona

The second day of our trip to Delaware has been one of the strangest of my life, because of the road we took. We went only about 115 miles, but it took us most of the day and left us tired in a good hollow way, and exalted. It was no more like ordinary motoring than childbirth is like ordinary pain, or *épinards en branches* at Foyots was ordinary spinach.

We started at 11:00 from the fake-posh Westward Ho in Phoenix, where we had a comfortable room and excellent service and good hotel food and yet hated everything for its standardized comfort and excellence and goodness. The doorman said, "Well, you folks going over the mountains? It's like riding on the pantry shelf all night!" We said no, but after a stop at the AAA for guidebooks we decided to try it—the Apache Trail, which is longer and more mountainous than the ordinary road through Superior to Globe. We drove a little through the Papago Saguaro Park near Phoenix—and laughed later to think we'd been awed by those first giant cactuses. (I know that's cacti but I don't like the word.) The red rocks there were handsome.

At Apache we did not stop at the zoo, which advertised animals of the country like Gilas and wild hogs but also had spider monkeys. We headed northeast into the Tonto country, on a fine dirt road, past a mountain that is the most beautiful mountain of my life. We knew there were Superstition Mountains near there, and I didn't want to know where they were because it seemed as if that one beautiful mountain should be the Superstition, even if it wasn't. But that was it, sure enough—on the map. It made me feel good. The mountain was red and like a Gothic dream, more or less.

Things got stranger and stranger. There were badly defaced

signs pointing to various landmarks, but they were unimportant. The colors of the rocks and mountains were red and pink and black, with a greenish moss now and then turning the surfaces sulfurous. The *palos verdes* and *ocatillas* were green, and different kinds of small cactuses grew everywhere, almost too prettily in the crannies, like a professional garden. Everywhere, even up to the tops of the fantastic mountains, were the saguaros, stately as a forest, without visible leaves. Some of them were taller than houses, fifty or sixty feet, with a dozen strong fingers or new sets of little light green balls beginning on their sides.

The road was excellent. There was no traffic, although near Canyon Lake we passed a car and an old woman and a girl eating lunch, and we all waved as people do in wild places. Twice we passed roadworkers, friendly thin men with brown faces. The road once made my knees weak, near the Walls of Bronze—it was the steepest mountain road I'd ever been on, and everywhere I looked was so beautiful that when we got to the bottom of the gorge I drank some whiskey. I felt quite exhausted.

We kept going up and down, and everywhere it was beautiful and terrible. I never had the feeling, though, that the country was sinister the way San Jacinto is, or the Bodwin moors in Cornwall. I wanted to lie flat on the red earth and close my eyes. Then we passed Roosevelt and the dam, which Timmy said was an ugly dam with the wrong curve to it (I think he disliked it partly because it had sucked the great fjords of the Salt River down into little scarred creeks), and I drove the easy half of the way over the smooth curving dirt road to Globe. I can never say, even to myself, what happened today between me and that country, driving as I was with T., beside him in the car in all that red wilderness.

We are stopping at an auto court, my first. It is clean and pleasant and decorated with so many red-yellow-blue-green Mexicans sitting under cactuses or riding burros, painted, embroidered, drawn, that I feel almost as if I were undressing in the middle of Tijuana or some such place. The beds are good. The man next door snores. There are many advantages to these courts, certainly, and one of them is price: $3.06 here with no tips, for a nicer room than we had last night for $7 and many tips. But, of course, we do all the bag toting, and it upsets T. not to be able to help me with that—and we must drive downtown for food—

We went, somewhat unwillingly, to one of the first restaurants we passed in this typical little mining town, down by the copper mine in the "rough" section. It was small, neat, blue—the Sobeston's Pic-a-Rib Café—and when we saw it was recommended by Duncan Hines's loathsome and unfortunately popular guidebook, *Adventures in Eating,* we said *no.* But the landlady said it was very good. We went, and so it was, and yet we came away feeling irritated at what we didn't know. The martinis in the hideous black-and-metal-painted bar were unusually good. The waitress had pretty legs and a tired pasty face and served deftly and intelligently. There were tea-roomy dripping candles on the tables in the small dining room, but the seats under the foolish curved awnings were soft and comfortable. The people were uninteresting—well-fed and smug. The proprietor actually made the salads himself and the drinks, and brought a big chalked blackboard for us to order from. We had good vegetable soup, at his command, and delicious grilled spareribs cooked with sherry, and a fine salad made with wine vinegar, and goodish French bread, especially in a town this size. And still we left feeling vaguely irritated. I don't know why. I'd certainly send other people there, and I'd like another plate of the spareribs, and yet I don't want to go back myself.

We drove westward after supper—busman's holiday—through Miami. It was all saloons, with the mines and smelters upon the hills all lit. We stopped at the one little grocery we saw in the whole town and bought some bananas and two little tins of sardines for tomorrow's lunch.

I told Edith when we left that I'd write to her instead of in my diary, but I'm not doing it. In some ways, it is a good idea— my letters home are thus more interesting, to me at least, and I kill two birds because I ask for them back later. But on the other hand, there are many things I can never say in my letters. I can never say, for instance, how wonderful, how nearly miraculous and fine it seems to me to be going *away* from them all, to be gone willy-nilly from any part of their involved lives. They would never understand, nor would I probably, if my child tried to say the same. But it is true. And I am happy now in a completer way than I have ever known, to be alone and unrecognized with my love. Now, to me, is always—more surely than I ever thought possible.

11. xii. 40
New Monteleone
New Orleans

Dearest Edie—

We were disappointed not to have any letters from you when we got in this afternoon, but maybe some will come tomorrow. I do hope all goes well at the Ranch.

I'll write a real letter tomorrow. This is merely to tell you a few vital statistics. The trip goes like cream, with perfect roads and weather so far. We're a little slower than we'd planned, since we find that Tim needs to "lay over" every two or three days. He's only had two really bad nights, though, and his morale is better than for some time. As for me, I'm in the pink of health—my only trouble is that I doubt very much that I'll drop that superfluous two pounds I'd planned to, since (believe it or not) we have struck such odd drinking water that I've been easily talked into taking beer instead— However—

The New Monteleone is a typical convention hotel, complete with hordes of supercilious clerks, fat drunks with cigars and buttons saying "Call me Joe—or Butch—or Gus," dirty bathtubs, and running ice water. I think Aunt Petie romanced a bit about looking out over the river, since it is several blocks away and well hidden by factories and warehouses. However, the room is fairly quiet—and I doubt if we could do better in "Nawlins," which after some six hours reminds me of a mixture of salesmen's convention, the American Quarter in Paris in 1929 (full of shoddy bars and whiskey-voiced blonde divorcées), and the brothel district of Colón.

We caused a minor revolution by refusing to go to Antoine's our first night here, and went instead to a fine place recommended by the cabby, which was so much like Lipp's in Paris that we felt like ghosts. We'll remedy our heresy by going to Antoine's tomorrow night. We may even order oysters Rockefeller—but I'll be damned if I'll have crêpes suzette, guidebooks or no guidebooks.

Much love to you all.

It's swell to hear the river steamers. They moo like divine cows, musically and with a kind of maternal lonesomeness.

12. xii. 40
New Orleans

Dearest Edie—

It was good to get your letter this morning—and don't ever say it was dull. I was glad to read every word of it. As you know by now, I'm only writing from big towns. It's silly to send postcards from little ones, since they'd reach you long after you'd got letters from big ones—and at night sometimes our one idea is to take a bath and fold.

I've meant to tell you for the last week how wonderful the heater is. We've used it almost every day (not down here in the gray mugginess, though) and have blessed your bones a thousand times. It works beautifully and warms the car up in about a minute flat. I don't see how we could have got along without it.

New Orleans has got us down temporarily, and we're leaving in the morning, with the definite idea of coming back on our way home. The combination of low altitude and very gray wet weather has played hob with poor Tim, and we're going to leave as soon as we can. We plan to be in Claymont December 23 or perhaps earlier, if all goes well. It has been slower than we'd thought. We've had a lot of fun, though.

How nice of Aunt Gwen to send us a present!

And speaking of presents, we've been sending a few packages to the Ranch. Please don't think we're crazy to have sent such silly things to you and Rex—but we decided the house had enough brass candlesticks and snuffboxes and that you'd like something you could use—at least once!

I'm so glad you nabbed off my coffee cups from the bazaar! I've bought some New Orleans coffee for them—the best I've had in America—but don't know whether I can make it right in an electrical drip thing. It has a lot of chicory in it—I think you'll like it and will split my box with you.

We plan to do some sightseeing next time we're in town. In the meantime I can smell fine smells, even up here in the room.

We stopped in Lake Charles night before last. It's a pretty little town on a sort of bayou, and the hotel was adequate and agreeable, with nice Negroes and bad food. You'd love the little towns in southern Louisiana. There are big old wooden houses, painted white, and the most enormous oaks I've ever seen, all green-gray and mysterious with Spanish moss. There are lots of sugar refineries, and the Negroes still live around them in the old slave cabins, which are gray now and quite beautiful.

There seem to be two main types of people here, the Cajun-Creole type, long and dark, with small black eyes under thick brows, narrow-lipped mouths, big noses, small heads on stiff thin necks—very proud looking, rather of Rex's and Dave's type—and the carp-faced, soft, sly, shrewd type rather like Huey Long. The latter have bad manners, generally. The Negroes are slow and thin and the most primitive I've seen. They hardly speak so I can understand—it's rather like Stepin Fetchit in the movies, only worse.

We'll probably go to Mobile tomorrow, if Tim feels like it. I may write from there. In the meantime, don't expect too many letters from me, but for goodness' sake don't worry if you don't hear every day.

Our love to you all, and very much—

24. xii. 40
Claymont, Delaware

Dearest family—

This will probably be a note, because Tim and I are driving down to Wilmington in a few minutes to collect a bundle from his uncle's office, and I want to get off a word or two to you while I can. You know what being company means—you think you'll have long quiet hours to yourself, but somehow they all went into talk and delivering Christmas baskets and so on and so on.

We got out here for lunch yesterday and found Mrs. P. much better and livelier than she was two years ago. She is even tinier and is slightly deafer—but since she talks constantly herself, it isn't necessary for her to hear what others say. She's an extremely attractive and interesting conversationalist most of the time, fortunately, with a good sense of satire and drama.

Uncle Boney, home on the dot of 5:00 or something, at the table at 6:00 sharp, to bed at 9:55, looks less well and to everyone's amusement was almost garrulous. T. says tonight he'll be taciturn and by tomorrow will have lapsed into his usual monosyllabism—ordinary treatment of honored guests.

As far as I can figure, we decorate the tree tomorrow morning and have presents tomorrow night. There is no early communion at All Saints'—only midnight mass and a 10:30 A.M. service—so I'll probably go to the latter. Uncle Boney disapproves of the former because it's "high church" and because it's decadent.

It seems queer to be in coal-soot country again. The weather is cold and sunny—very beautiful, but I had wished childishly for a white Christmas.

Sunday's ride through Washington and Baltimore was tiring —typical Eastern traffic. We were glad to get to Wilmington and fall into tubs and broiled lobster in the Darling Hotel.

More later—

26. xii. 40
Flower Hill Farm
Claymont, Delaware

My darling Edie—

This is to tell you we're still alive and that I plan to write a decent letter, so help me, before the sun sets on me. Last night we had Christmas, which was one of the most exhausting of my varied experience, largely because of sheer dullness. We fell into bed at 9:30, and from exhaustion and the fact that we hadn't slept much for two nights, woke up at 9:00 this morning! (I got up twice for Tim, but hardly remember.)

Much much love—and thanks for telegram—

14. ii. 41
Bareacres

I have two queer ugly pains, one on the inside of my left knee and one between my second and third fingers near the second joints on my left hand. It—they—feel like bruises, throbbing and not constant and never together and not in my body really but about half an inch in the air. They are ugly, as I said, and might bear out the neurophysics of some such addlepated astrologist as Larry Powell's mother—or equally well support the invert philosophy of any typical hypochondriac.

Tonight small showers beat on the roof. Tim prepares himself for bed. Butch taps about busily—his nails should be cut. Tiny, back from a disastrous spaying at the vets, sniffles and stinks and twitches on a pillow, and I should be caring for her now, putting Vaseline and cotton on the ugly hole in her back that came from too many glucose injections and tucking her into her little red coat for the night while I do my best not to smell her incredibly foul breath. Poor little rat—I should have said kill her—and now a kind of vanity tells me that in the two days she is home there is a great change for the better. I don't know. I see she is chipper, and that her ugly wound—infection from a careless injection? I want to believe the new vet is good—is closing, and that she coughs less. Vanity. And yet I think of the hopelessness of seeing any creature weak and ill and ugly, and of my mother and of Tim and of my own self occasionally helpless with acid-ridden guts, and I know that if we had the power of yes and no for suffering, most of us would be dead. If I could say—for others—what they may have wished poignantly to say for me—I'd be dead long since and they, too, and probably, possibly, things would be better. Yes or no, I must go now and make myself swab sensibly at a hideous white-rimmed hole, bolstered by the proud certainty that Tiny, poor do-less bitch ex-bitched, may soon be better for my care.

12.iii.41

I've been unable to write in this notebook lately (I am almost unable to now but because of Tawny, who, about to drop the third litter in sixty months, is unusually fond of me and even more than usually snarlish with the other animals). It has seemed foolish to write, partly because although I have never reread any of this journal, I remember it was shamefully personal and thoughtless. Of course, I can say to myself, Is it necessary to prove a capacity for profundity in every paragraph? Is it best to comment, when I watch a spayed bitch humping like an old bull as she plays on Butch's back, that Mussolini still plays with Latin bombast on the unconscious, scornful backside of die Führer? Or that life, etc., etc., etc.? I could probably dish out a certain amount of this philo-sophical (quasi) guff, and even sell it in condensed form to the *Reader's Digest* but I am a defeatist or a realist or a procrastinator (God help us all if that still lies before me!) and cannot as yet steel myself to such wholesale crap mongering. Instead I shall go on, my lap full of cat-cum-kittens, my ears filled with Tim's flattering sweet melodies as he plays our new piano, my thoughts resolutely non-thoughtful.

Tonight I wanted several times to write here. I knew that it was because my heart and my mind were too full and that I would relieve myself, like a purged man, of a lot of self-pity and self-praise. So I withheld this doubtful pleasure from myself—and later indulged it in becoming captious with poor Tim about how silly it would be to keep the dogs out of the kennels when doubtless the whole house was infested with Butch's attack of lice. I grew grim and almost peevish, and made things no easier for Tim, and suddenly realized that it was simply because I had too much within. Perhaps it would have been better to write here in the first place. But I should have said much more than now. And why say it? The fact that I am dismal is enough, or even too much. My hands smell of liniment. If I read this years from now, which I do not plan to do, I would remember why: that Tim's other leg had increased in pain, like a scalded thigh, like skin held under steam, so that at nights sometimes he howled like a dog. Well—why go into all this? I hate myself—I'm like some women who have to tell someone, anyone, even their hairdressers, how they had three lovers in one night—

I've had no great drive to write here, or in letters, or stories or books, for some time now. I finally made myself answer a few letters, one of them eight months old. Now I don't feel like writing at all—I brought out this book simply because it's a wet lazy day and I felt I should be "doing something." This is not it.

18.iv.41

Tonight I have not much more inclination than usual to write anything in this spasmodically attentive journal, but I think it might be a good idea. The night is cold . . . we have a fire and even one of the oil stoves lit for the first time in days . . . and T. sits wheeling through the Haydn sonatas at our lovely little new piano, which perhaps I've not yet mentioned here. (It is small, with a good tone, and although we were fools to buy it at $10 monthly for some three years, we have not yet regretted it.) T. says this [typing] doesn't bother him, and perhaps he is right. I am in my room. I could fill my empty pen and write silently on my knee by the fire, where I'd rather be . . . but I am too do-less tonight, and such small jobs irk me even to think of.

Tomorrow probably I shall buckle myself up a bit and concentrate on several things that need such attention. For one, I shall stop drinking whiskey, partly because it is expensive and partly because I am definitely overweight: I weigh about 150, which is at least ten pounds too much for me at my age. Then I shall try to finish staining and waxing three wooden chairs already built for the porch and build, stain, and wax three more . . . this week, if possible. Then I shall gradually oil all the floors, while Mrs. Purdy is on a two-week vacation in El Paso. She has some definite skunner against using oil or even an oiled mop on the floors, and in this climate oil is the only possible way to treat them . . . so, while she's gone, I plan to do all the wood in the house and then issue one of my timid ultimatums when she returns. Mrs. Purdy, I hear myself say, I want you to use this mop only for oiling, and please have it freshly filled each time you use it. This broom, also, is to be used solely on rugs . . . and the toilet floors must be washed with oily water once a week. Instead, I'll probably wave my hand vaguely at

the O-Cedar mop* and then look at the soapsuds all over the
floors. She exasperates me, but she's a good soul in her way and
better than we could hope for here, I suppose. At times her blurred
outlines, her vapid sentimentality get dangerously on my nerves,
but . . . in the meantime, I am truly enjoying her vacation!

We have done a lot to Bareacres this past six weeks, and today
Arnold came and built a fine stone staircase from the patio around
the big rock and up in a good curve toward the hills. We arranged
with him to help him buy a truck, for which he will come on
weekends and pave our patio . . . good enough, since everything is
in shape except the ground, by now worn powdery and soft and
untidy on all our feet through the house. Arnold is the man to do
it, with a real feeling for stone and how it should be laid, and with
his new truck he can haul it, too.

Timmy made us some nice shelves on brackets for pots of
petunias along the patio walls, and with them and the four strips
of red and green and blue awning, all we need now is Arnold's
floor and my chairs to have a lovely shadowy place for the summer.
And in the winter we'll be there a lot, too, if we ever get the floor
. . . any day with sun is warm and lovely there.

I almost hurt Arnold's feelings by saying in a joking way that
amongst us we'd turn Bareacres into a damned park, but it's true
—we fix one thing and then see another. This last week Leonardo
has cleaned off all the weeds and with his extraordinary neatness
has made the ground so smooth that I hate to walk on it, with neat,
tidy, almost perfect circles around each tree.

We've built an arbor along the west side of the house and
spent more money than we meant to on four grapevines. We've

---

* The O'Cedar mop was one that could be filled from the top with oil for the
floors. Elsa preferred soap.

tended them as we were instructed for two weeks now, and they are all growing. The most amazing is the Rose of Peru, at the south end . . . we snipped off forty-three fine bunches today and left four on. The other three vines were almost empty of bunches, but we left one or two on each to see what would happen. They will be beautiful if all goes well and will make the end of the house cool and green-shaded in the summers.

I finished a book, *Consider the Oyster,* a little while ago and sent it off to New York, with a slight fanfare thanks to Idwal Jones. The three chapters sent to Mme. Metzelthin of *Gourmet* did not please her, but she wanted me to cut down a thing I wrote about Swiss restaurants, which I did with partial success. She wants me to write a series of articles about gourmets of history, which I should be glad to do . . . but I'd want at least to make enough money to pay for a week's research in Los Angeles, and she is on a limited budget. Oh, well . . . it would be good for me to do something with a deadline, probably.

Yesterday T. started again to take injections of cobra venom, at Bob Freeman's suggestion and under James Long's care. It will take ten days or so before there is any reaction, except the slight numbness and dropping of temperature that follows each shot. I have a feeling they may help. Something has to . . . the supply of Analgeticum seems pretty well stopped at San Pedro, thanks to the war.

Almost every word I write makes me think of another, and almost every word makes me think of something that has happened or is happening about war. I think of the hysteria, controlled so far, of people like the E.'s, who practice shooting at the whites of "their" eyes each morning and discuss hoarding food and tear bombs with passably self-contained passion. And then I think of David so lax and bitter about having to go into the army, probably this fall, and then I remember that I should write to J.B., a hospital orderly and apparently happy at Camp Moffett. That makes me think of the letters I ground out to Pat Nuttall and the Beutlers, word by word about the weather and such when I was wondering what the air was filled with around them and whether they were alive or dead or sane or screaming mad. I must write some more, to Mlle. Vodo-do-og-do and so on. I wonder about Georges Connes, very much, and Matruchot, and even about Paul Musset —or was his name Moussey?—and the Simonots and Michel de Vautibault. My mind is full of pain and speculation, underneath all the ordinary chaos of our lives here in this temporary quiet zone. I am puzzled about all these people and about my mother and about Noni and even about myself. I am puzzled and disturbed about the slow growth within myself of a need for religious faith, which has no reed to lean upon. I am not puzzled by the life between T. and me, though, and in that I am indubitably blessed above most humans.

Last night Blackberry, our strange lovely cat, developed a hunched gait and a painful glassy way of sitting down and squeaked with his usual good manners when we touched him ever so lightly at the base of his tail. He is still infinitely cautious about moving. I think maybe he's been stung—Arnold found one salamander, one angry scorpion, and several spiders and centipedes in his rocks today, and I've seen many blue lizards about. I'll take Blackie to the vet tomorrow if he hasn't loosened up a bit.

Today I deliberately watched the mother-cat, Smokey Josephine, vomit. Always before I've shut my eyes and my ears, if possible. I knew she was going to do it, out on the front slope, and thought to myself, Well . . . I'm almost thirty-three and supposedly have experienced many things, so I'll make myself watch this. It was queer the way her very red tongue stuck out in a kind of slide and then out shot an almost-perfect pale-blue lizard. Smokey seemed quite pleased by it all, but in spite of my reasonableness I felt a little nauseated.

We are taking care of Mrs. Purdy's little bitch Tiny, and I don't like her at all. We owned her for a time and decided she was too much like Mrs. P. to have around. Which indeed she is. I don't see, occasionally, how I can stand her for another ten days. She is so damned fawning. There is nothing bad about her, except bad temper now and then with the cats . . . but she brings out all my latent exasperation at other things so that I have to be careful to be nice to her, instead of whacking at her because I have broken a dish or stubbed my toe or some such thing.

9.vi.41

One reason I write this is that I am putting off getting to work on my notes for a series of articles for *Gourmet*(?), which one moment is ordered and the next not, and the other is that I have just finished a stupid dutiful note to Aunt Maggie and am thinking about her and myself in relation to her.

I say the note was dutiful, and that makes me think of many reactions I have in spite of myself.

I remember with pleasure the times she used to come out to Whittier when I was little, and I know now that even then Edith loved her, rather as we did but much more so, as freedom and romance and what would almost be called glamour now. Aunt Maggie always brought us presents . . . always until Grandmother learned that we looked forward to her coming for that reason and forgot that there were many others, and told Aunt Maggie never again to bring us anything. Aunt M., even at some seventy years, obeyed her. She used to bring us each a little Japanese parasol, or in the winter once a fuzzy bathrobe covered with little rabbits and bears, or a box of crayons for each. Grandmother, when she heard us wonder what Aunt M. would bring next, decided we wanted her to come only for her presents and forbade them. Perhaps she was fighting against her own shame at never giving us anything gay like that. She did not know that, presents or not, we loved to have Aunt Maggie come.

Aunt M. had a tic that made the whole front of her face lift in one movement toward the top of her head. It lifted up her whole scalp every few minutes. It had begun when she was married, and when we knew her was gradually lessening, so that now in her ninetieth year it almost never shows. It fascinated us then, as such things will when you're a child, and later I remembered the irascible snarling man she married and could well see that something bad had caused it, which she forgot gradually as the years passed and Uncle Doctor died and she forgot the tantrums and neuroses of her nine high-tempered children.

She was a little girl with flat hair, according to the stories, and when my grandmother, several years older, decided that she should have curly hair, twirled Aunt Maggie's hair untiringly around a stick, nobody was surprised either that it turned actively kinky or that several of Aunt M.'s children had hair almost like a Negro's.

She was a happy creature, with a long thin jaw and one eye—my wee eye, she has always called it—that was higher and smaller than the other. I forget which one it is.

She married an adventurous man who practiced medicine but was at heart and sometimes actually the kind who went to Chile for silver (and always smoked Chilean cheroots afterward), who had a terrible cruel choleric sense of humor so that he tormented his patients by telling them they had scabies when it was really only a scratch, who begot nine or so frightened, spirited, truculent children.

Aunt Maggie also took care of her strong willful mother for many years, so that now she says without much bitterness but with her own kind of strength that she never knew what it was to have a home of her own until she was too old to have one.

For the last several years she has lived with her strange, painful, attractive daughter Mary, whose own unfortunate life is a plain result of her parents' and who has been good and kind with that unmistakably martyred kindness of neurotic women. The two women have lived together in what many would call luxury, usually with two ill-trained and mismanaged servants, in a mournful and extremely banal California suburban villa. And Mary, really in spite of herself, has managed to tell everyone what agonies she suppresses every time Aunt Maggie twitches her brow or, more lately, sniffs. It seems she sniffs nervously and constantly. To add to it, Aunt Maggie was raised to turn all her social energies into the church and consequently has made it almost imperative for Mary to do the same. Mary has been both intelligent and generous about this and goes every Sunday to a class she leads, apparently forgetting forever the days when she was one of the toasts (in champagne) of such rich-bitch country clubs and sets as flitted about Sewickly and such Eastern hangouts.

Aunt Maggie now is very old. She is a small woman who is unruffled at receiving callers in bed, mainly because she is still truly and delightfully vain and knows how attractive she appears in a fine ruffled linen nightgown to people used to department-store pink chiffon. She has great calm, partly because she probably does not care much what we think of her and partly because she is old and partly because she is a real lady. She does not hesitate to scold, knowing that her manner is too winning to annoy for long.

She is vain and spends hours choosing a silk, always expensive, for her summer or winter or fall dress, which is always made about the same way and yet never looks out of date except that it is long always. She wears nice low pumps and usually a piece of rich but very conventional jewelry given her by her children for some fete . . . the children being both rich and conventional themselves.

I am fond of Aunt Maggie for many reasons. One is that she was generous and gay when I knew no other age than the stiff and disapproving one of my grandmother, her older sister. Another is that she is a nice old lady now, after a rather twisting and hard life, and in spite of her enslavement to her sister, her mother, her husband, is a quiet, strong personality by herself. I like her because she is clean and dainty, too. And I like her because she has always been good and generous and merry and sweet with my own mother.

That is probably one reason why I am sometimes rather stupid about her. Mother, as she grows older, sometimes becomes actively fatuous about Aunt Maggie, and I feel not jealous, as it would seem on the surface, but embarrassed and wishing Mother would be more intelligent . . . a case of hurt vanity, of course, as always when someone you love does not behave as you think she ought. I think, Oh, for God's sake, when Mother says or does some silly thing about Aunt Maggie, and then Mother feels sad and hurt, and I feel badly and know that I can never explain how warm and grateful I feel to Aunt Maggie, not only for myself but for Mother. But when I try to say so, it all turns into hurt and ridicule and misunderstanding.

That probably explains why I write this now. One of Aunt Maggie's sons, a man I consider without much provocation to be a cruel, willful autocrat, has suddenly developed an almost diseased sense of mother worship—he has portraits painted, etc., etc.—and has sent special sheets to each cousin and so on to be filled out for a great birthday book on Aunt Maggie's ninetieth or something year. Everyone, even Edith, agrees that she will be bored . . . probably. But we must all do it.

For a long time we all laughed, Mother among the loudest . . . but now that the time approaches we are practically forced to write "tributes" to this grand old lady of the family, the matriarch, etc., etc. There was a great deal of family discussion about it, mostly my fault because I would quibble and balk. Finally I wrote in the book. Now I regret it, because in an adolescent way I insisted on being truthful and said that A. M. was the nicest old lady I know, and now I feel that I should simply have handed out the usual family guff and skipped everything I really meant.

The whole thing has been, I suppose, a kind of protest against sentimentalizing a family character. It is inevitable—I should know it from Mother's predilection for such novels as *The Matriarch* and some of Galsworthy's and so on—but I hate it. So instead of keeping my mouth shut and letting Mother have her little literary orgasms of family pride and Aunt Maggie her hard-won tidbits of whipped-up family loyalty, I must be truculent and worry Mother and not write what I should in the Birthday Book.

The thing is that I like A. M. probably as much as most of the people who will write to her . . . more I think, complacently, knowing my own strong secret gratitude to her for many things that I cannot even write about . . . but something stupid and antagonistic to seeing such people as Edith make fatuous fools of themselves forces me to be difficult.

I love Edith and would like her to know that I love Aunt Maggie . . . but I don't think I could show her how, behind my partly jealous, partly hurt reactions to her sappiness, I see her own respect and feel my own . . . or know my shame at being stupid and truculent and all that myself.

18. vi. 41

I am in one of those spells of putting off getting to work, which I suppose hits every worker who can choose his own speed. They are destructive, in some ways, because they make working patchy and difficult, and they are purely a mental state, so that I feel ashamed of my own dilatory frame of mind and spend almost meaningless moments trying to talk myself out of it. Logically I succeed, but physically I do not, so that, as now, I wander about the house and lie down and get up and drink Coca-Cola and occasionally write a letter or read a recipe.

I finished a short book about oysters a few weeks ago, typed it quickly and for me fairly well, and sent if off. It was sold easily, to Duell, Sloan, and Pearce, thanks partly to the kindly interest of Idwal Jones, who still likes *Serve It Forth*. Then I got into a little spate of correspondence with Madame (self-titled) Pearl V. Metzel-thin, who edits *Gourmet* in N. Y., and partly through her vagueness (Mrs. Pritchett says she sometimes suspects Mme. M.'s head is filled with maline) and partly through Pritchett's enthusiasm, I thought I was supposed to do a series of articles about famous hosts and hostesses and dashed to Los Angeles for five days, where I grubbed in the library through unpleasant memoirs of Boni de Castellane, and Harry Lehr, and such creatures. In a few days I found Mme. M. had been mistaken—that was an old idea abandoned over a year ago, etc. I wrote a testy letter to Pritchett, and at present she wants me to do one article about a gourmet as a kind of try-cake and sit tight. The result is that my secondary mind is filled with data about what I somewhat glibly term the "Gilt-edged Gluttons" that I gleaned in Los Angeles, and yet I am halted in my fine frenzy to write about them by the knowledge that nobody wants to read about them and further halted by knowing that I should be turning out an article about some damn silly old boy "as a gourmet"—Richelieu or somebody—already safe and well known. Meanwhile I stew mildly about the house.

My secondary mind is well occupied, but my primary mind is a pained and aching blank, filled with the hollowness of realizing that T. is not well. He took fourteen shots of cobra venom over some four weeks, and no good came of it. When we were in Los Angeles, I saw for the first time what I should have known weeks before, except that we don't move about much here in the house, that stairs and even straight walking are almost impossible for him anymore. He must stop and rest every few steps, and it humiliates him who even with one leg has hopped about like a cricket. He suffers mildly and constantly on his good leg . . . a kind of tired yawning, rather like the preamble to what took off the other but slower, and his little leg is terribly sensitive to touch. Then there are two or three places—where an injection made a little swelling, where Blackberry licked his skin—that seem dry and red and painful. Christ, I think with that impotent half-blasphemous calling out of helpless people, what can I do? I don't admit that T. has any tenuous thing like Buerger's disease. Then I see strange signs like his increasing weakness and these occasional tiny dry painful places on his beautiful firm clear skin, and my mind grinds out a slow word *Christ,* in several syllables, willy-nilly, a kind of impotent protest, a kind of acknowledgeable acknowledgment of something I do not know but must recognize. What goes on in T.'s mind I cannot think. He is for the most part quiet and, in a controlled way, happy. Now and then he cracks open, like a hard-boiled egg that is accidentally dropped, and what I see then in his eyes and hear in his voice frightens and horrifies me so that I want to lie on my bed and go into a faint, or become a believing nun, or anything to hide from it. But I know that I cannot hide, any more than he can, and I know, too, most of the time that what he is doing may not be worth it but is the only decent thing to do.

The reason perhaps for writing diaries, among people who seem to have to write, is that they learn a certain clearness and focus. This I do not seem to acquire as I grow older. In fact, this journal, although I have not read it, impresses me with its agglomeration of careless typing, weighty incoherent sentences, and undisciplined moods. I hope that I have sense enough and *soon* to destroy it unread. T. knows I write it and sometimes speaks of it, hoping I think to read it. I have said nothing in it I would not have him see, but I am sure I have said many things that it would be well if he did not. Why bother, why worry, why exasperate people?

We are godparents. Jane and Bill Evans's daughter Barrie is the cause, and in two weeks, if all goes well, we will christen her. I am bored but tolerant, and when I hold the little smelly peeing bodkin in my hands, if I do, I shall quite possibly cry, wishing it were my own. The sentimentality, the pomp of procreation, and the ceaseless mystery cannot but affect me, and my sincere thankfulness that I am sterile is often swept away by stirrings that are as raw and gnawing as any sexual orgasm. I shall wear a white linen dress and gulp a bit and help the Evanses dry the dishes after the usual noisy lusty supper in the old wooden house in Santa Monica.

Anne's book I have finished at last and told her, without saying I liked it, that it is beautiful, strange, painful, sincere. It is indeed. I did not like it, because I thought it was undisciplined, and I feel more and more that a writer must know and self-impose discipline, of the tongue, the mind, the spirit, more than anything else in the world. I think I know many of the fallacies and pitfalls of that argument. But I still believe it. And Anne's book, in spite of its sincerity, was muddled spiritually and was a terrible hodgepodge of words and images and research and prettiness and realism and mysticism (what T. calls misty-schism, viciously), so that in the end my feeling was one of fatigue at having read it and a kind of intellectual nausea. It needs discipline. Anne thinks she knows it. Perhaps she does. God knows the book was sincere and full of prayer and work and thought. But still it was clouded, and I do not know what is the answer for Anne herself. She is a fine creature, but I think she has been deluded into thinking of herself as an intellect when she is really a strongly natural body with too large a vocabulary for her own strength, so that what she and some of her friends think is brain is really a sensitive and highly articulate nervous system. She is a wonderful sensual writer, and I wish, probably vainly, that she could realize it and not try to be a sort of Hearstian Saint Thomas Aquinas.

20. vi. 41

It is a hot day, and outside . . . It is another hot day now, the next one, and yesterday I was probably going to say something obvious and startlingly dull about the noise of the cicadas or the sound of cottonwood leaves on the brick patio.

David and Norah left about two o'clock for Mexico. They forgot their only map and came back for it, but otherwise got off with unusual finesse, acting much calmer than I could have under the circumstances. All their plans seem dreamy, and our only touch with them for the next few weeks is Wells Fargo, Mexico City. It is a sign of the difference in our ages that I cannot help wondering what we'd do if Edith should die or some such thing, while they seem never to have thought of such emergencies. They plan to reach the city in about a week and stay in a pension for a while and then go to a less expensive place. Noni is taking her typewriter and will probably write about Hawaii, and David thinks he will do a lot of sketching. They looked well, in brownish cotton clothes, but physically they seem too finely drawn to me for their ages: thin, pallid, with slender controlled hands, David's with curved nails, and both of them with tense lines at the corners of their mouths and smudges under their eyes. Of course, David is almost completely bald. And Norah, often, looks older and more worn than I do. I pity them both, for they seem finished too soon. They need new blood in them.

Last night I told Tim what he was waiting for me to say, that I can too easily get into an easy routine of doing research and writing articles and books about gastronomy and that I'd do this one small series about Gilt-edged Gluttons, which *Gourmet* does not want but which I can probably sell elsewhere, and then sit myself down to writing a novel. I've always thought that novels should only be written if there is something in them that *must* be said, and now here I plan to write one simply because it will be good for me. But maybe I'll have something to say that I don't know now. It will be hard, and I feel lazy and yet gnawed, so I'd better get to work.

There was a little bird in the house today, not very nervous. We took the screen from the closet window, and I think it is gone now.

Twice lately I have dreamed about oversized lizardlike animals. Last night I looked down from a window and saw Blackberry holding against the bloody ground a long gray lizard, about three feet long, and I saw that the cat was exhausted and that as soon as the lizard rested a little it would whip away. I knew that I must go down and pick it up with a towel over my hands and I was wondering what to do next when I awoke. And the other night Tim and I were on a small ship as beautiful as the *Normandie,* and an enormous crocodile was caught and tied firmly alongside the ship like another smaller ship before we all realized that it was our undoing. One whip of its great tail almost capsized us, and we knew too late that if it were freed it would destroy us at once and if it were held captive it would destroy us more slowly but just as surely by gradually weakening all the seams of the little ship with its occasional terrible lashings. There was despair among us all, but I didn't feel any fear . . . just a resignation and a curiosity that made me look down at the half-submerged malicious eyes of the creature and speculate about its food and its life and its possible thoughts.

3.vii.41

Today I can't remember any other birthday than this. I got up early and fussed quietly around the house, in a vague spate of getting ready for Father's and Mother's coming this afternoon. Finally I dressed in work clothes, ready to clean the patio later, and now I sit on the porch on my little tuffet eating potato chips and drinking beer. My mind runs with absolute distraction on food for this weekend, on the pets, on the hack articles I've been writing grimly in the last few weeks. But inside all of me, like the bone in the flesh, the stone in the fruit, is the hard core of thought about T.

For some time now—perhaps six weeks—his leg has grown more tired, with a gnawing sickening tiredness. Yesterday the doctor tested it and found it strong and apparently normal. But when he went to bed, Timmy and his leg collapsed. It was a dreadful time. It was full of fright and agony. Now I don't know whether he can get up this morning. In a little while we'll see. Will he ever get up? I know he is abysmally discouraged. His eyes look strangely at me, and even when he is asleep I feel them rolling under their lids, looking for help or me or anything but despair.

15. vii. 41

I pause on my way to a bath and bed to record, here on this hot and in some ways hopeless night, that today I slew a literary god —or demigod. I perceived at last that E. M. Forster, the first and almost the last writer I nearly wrote a letter to, is but an intellectual E. F. Benson. That is praise—but for what Forster once meant to me, it means damnation indeed.

18. vii. 41

I try to imagine in my mind, in the part that sees colors, and smells, and tastes, what it is like to be Noni and Dave in Oaxaca, sitting in the *zócalo* drinking beer and watching the stately sexual parade each night while the band plays. Or working in the hot thin air, hearing the life in the patio and writing or drawing of quite another one.

Sis is here. Now and then we go into the patio and play water from the hose on each other. It is fun, childlike, and yet in a peculiar way more enjoyable, since I think we share a pleasure in looking at each other, sparkling and glistening in the leafy shadows of the cottonwoods, with the water spraying out from us into the sunlight. Her body, in spite of the scars on her belly, is fine and slender, less full than mine, with sloping hips and small breasts with brown soft nipples.

3. ix. 41

The old adolescent days (or nights) of lying alone looking at moonlight on the eucalyptus leaves are gone. Now when I turn off the switch, I twitch. Now I am afraid of quiet and the dark, and my mind, riddled like an old oak chest with four thousand loathsome wormholes, creaks and crunches at itself and makes insufferable such earlier pleasures. I drink a too-hot, too-strong toddy in bed, and if my luck holds I go to sleep after some dutiful trash reading (*Mystery of the Police, Death Holds the Cup,* et al.), and then in a while (I have no watch) I wake cold and sober and my unwilling mind leaps like a starved dog at the poisonous meaty thoughts. Finally, stiff with resolve, I achieve another bout of sleep, terrible with dreams that at last, in a few minutes or hours or seconds, wake me sweaty with nightmare. I get up, as soon as I'm able to unhinge my joints from horror, and weave to the bathroom and bathe my face and sit on the toilet and drink some cold water. In a while, diligently, I sleep again, and either dream another nightmare or sleep lightly, fitfully, almost peevishly, until after dawn. Then, about one morning out of three or four, I sleep heavily until 8:00 or so, without hearing the shot. I try to live (even asleep?) with what dignity I can muster, but I wonder if there is much in this abject procedure. I write it down here partly because this is the first night I am really alone and partly to shame myself, like a whiplash. I can hear a night dove in the arroyo, and Freda van Benschoten's spaniel, whose voice has just changed, barks heavily across the flats. I shall live, I know in spite of myself, and where and how?

9. ix. 41

I discovered several years ago that in order to stay at the Ranch without becoming almost frantic with boredom I must, early in the visit, establish some kind of excuse for leaving Mother and going to my own room. That is why I am typing now. I hope she can hear me. I want her to think that I am working. I *must* be able to come up here to Rex's room, where I am sleeping while he's in Chapala, and pretend to be doing something so that I can't be interrupted. It is a stupid trick, and I'm ashamed of it, but it's necessary. Otherwise I would spend all day, every day, sitting in the living room or on the porch trying to read, and all the time listening to Mother and having to answer, and eating too much, and listening to the radio news, and going uptown to do the marketing. Of course, I'll do those things anyway, but not *all* day . . . just most of the day, because I am trying to be nice and make Mother feel that I am grateful to be here. She is being nice to me and coming out to Bareacres when she really would rather stay here, so I must be nice, too, about these few unavoidable days at the Ranch. It is four weeks and three days now, though, and I know even if the rest of the family does not that I must stop this ghastly life of compromise and get to work. It is bad for me, this drifting about and postponing the truth: I must live alone. That seems to horrify everyone. But to me it is plain: I *am* alone, completely and unalterably, and living with other people or having them live with me can never make me any less so, as long as I live. So I might as well get down to it. I can't stand much more of the hopeless stupid life I've been leading since T. died. I must get to work. I must practice being dignified all by myself, instead of always having an audience to make it easier.

Pretty soon now I'll write about T.'s death, because I think I should. Of course, I wrote at once to Anne and later to his mother in answer to her first hurt, bitter letter. But I haven't written to myself yet. I keep putting it off. There are too many things that I can't write yet. They're in words in my head, but I am afraid of writing them. It is as if they might make a little crack in me and let out some of all the howling, hideous, frightful grief. It is difficult to know, certainly, how to live at all.

I won't keep up this typing any longer without getting too near subjects that scare me. Perhaps it would be better to write about other less inward things. I like this typewriter, for one, and wish more than ever that I knew how to use one properly. My half-taught system is not bad for composition, but when I have to copy anything, it tires my eyes not to be able to type without looking at my fingers all the time. I could go to school again and learn. When I consider that, though, I always decide to get along as I have for so many years. T. made Anne learn to type properly when she turned into a writer, and her typing is perfect . . . easy, even, correct.

Butch is lying beside me on a cushion, just under the end of Rex's bed. His coat is about half grown out now, and if the autumn turns hot, I'll have him shaved again. I hope I do: I love to see him all naked because he has such a funny trim little body. He has been all right for the last three days, but until then I worried that he might die of grief, as I have read that sensitive dogs sometimes do. He ate without enthusiasm, and his coat grew dull, and he almost never played but instead walked heavily about the house all his waking hours, looking for T. Occasionally he would fall into a kind of frenzy and run frantically through the studio and the porch and my workroom, sniffing and whimpering at all the fading odors of T.'s crutches or hands or body on the chairs and the floor and the books and curtains. It was sad to see, and there seemed nothing that I could do. Butch was polite with me but quite unresponsive. Now and then he would seem to be interested in Sis or in Mrs. Purdy, but in a few minutes he would begin his search again. A few days ago he began to notice me again, and now he will not leave me if he can help it and seems almost to be trying to entertain me and accompany my spirit.

I left the little puppy at the vet's for the first time. He was very quiet in the car to Riverside, but the ride loosened his bowels and he made several messes, poor thing. He is a jolly little mongrel, and I love him. T. did, too, and asked that he be called Colonel Timothy instead of plain Colonel, and then I added Arrow Ass because of the little buff arrow under his stub of a tail, so he has quite an impressive name. I usually call him Colonel and refer to him as "the" Colonel. He is glossy black, with curly spaniel ears and what looks rather like a Doberman body, with buff feet . . . a thoroughly comical mixture. His eyes are black, and he rolls them so that the whites show, like a blackface actor. He is very quick and imitates everything Butch does, so I'm hoping he won't be too hard to train. He is stubborn, though. I am proud of how healthy he is. He is now three months and one week old.

Blackberry is in good shape. He seems to hunt all night, and I have to keep the cat doors closed or he brings his catch inside to eat. He sleeps most of the day on the red chair in the guest room. The strange pearl-gray tufts behind his ears are clearer than ever and more obviously made of fur unlike the rest of him. It is almost like cobweb. He is less impish now that he is older, but is very attractive. He still hasn't learned how to purr but has a large vocabulary of sounds, most of them tiny and theatrical.

Susie, now about three months old, I think, who was given to us the Sunday before T. died, is still very small. She is very funny and appealing and impudent, with a big-eyed pale face like a marmoset. She has a painful habit of walking up people's legs as if they were trees.

The other night when I took Butch and the Colonel down to their kennel, Butch ran into the thick weeds in the arroyo where Sis and I heard the two rattlesnakes a couple of weeks ago, and he refused to come when I called. That is unusual for him. He was silent, but I could hear him moving. I knew it was not a human he saw or he'd have growled, and I could not hear the snakes. I got a cane and the flashlight and rather unwillingly went after him, because there seemed no tone of voice or threat that would bring him up. He was leaning his front feet against the trunk of one of the big trees. Blackie was down there, too, watching. Their four eyes gleamed like lamps, and they were quite silent. I flashed my light all over the branches, and there in a high crotch I finally saw a tiny black and white creature, with a round innocent face like a teddy bear's. It peered down at me, blinking cautiously, and I peered up wonderingly at it. Maybe it was a chipmunk. I know it was not a baby skunk, in spite of its definite black and white markings. Finally I dragged Butch away and left it. I am sure Blackie could not reach it. It was a sweet little animal. I wonder how Butch knew that it was up there . . . it must have been two hundred feet from the house, but he went to that tree as unhesitatingly as if it were rehearsed beforehand and made not a single sound.

Mother is having her massage this morning. She seems fairly well, I think.

We are anxious to have a letter from Mexico.

14. x. 41

When you look at a man, it is easy to imagine what may have been his pleasures, given a certain destiny—that is, given a way you might place his present or future action. If he is a murderer, you can become completely involved in the things he saw and thought and dreamed and ate when a child, that he should thus evolve.

But if you look at a man who is nothing, a man like S., who at fifty-two looks eighty-two, who snarls and hawks and spits and inches thinly through his miserable days, what can you give his past as pleasure? Did he ever see straight? Did he ever smell right and clear the smell of a rose or a woman or a toasted bacon sandwich? Perhaps he went to a few pasty brothels, and probably he was seasick coming from England to Chicago as a lad, and certainly he got irascibly drunk quite often, in the inimitable way of tall thin men who are to die of stomach ulcers. But where was his pleasure?

My spirits heave at the thought of this human waste.

The other day his wife flushed and tittered at a sudden flurry of excitement among the animals, when Butch, upset by the smell on himself and the Colonel of a new flea soap we'd used in their bath, began to hump and move himself over the puppy. S.'s wife, wet as I was from the scrubbing we had given the two dogs, watched them sideways until I broke up the business, and then giggled, "I hope S. doesn't take a bath today!"

"Why?" I asked absentmindedly, and then laughed dutifully to realize that she was trying to be intimate, "just girls together." I was shocked at the connection of these innocent dog movements with human copulation, and then sickened to think any woman could feel thus about her chosen man's desires, and then I averted my mind from the hideous pictures of S.'s thin white bones thumping flaccidly up and down between her soft-fleshed thighs. And then my mind filled with those intolerable lines, "Christ, that my love were in my arms, and I my bed again." And I shut off words.

10
War Story

Almost all the books and stories now have touched war, vicariously or with true sweat and noise and fear. Of course, people, too, everywhere have touched it, even in the quiet dead-end valley where I live. I know that the iceman's daughter, soon to have a child, has lost her husband on some dry far island. I see the women in the unused store building bent over their piles of bandages, rolling and rolling, with their heads wrapped prettily in white and their hearts perhaps heavy with the pain they prepare for. And now and then a boy who graduated from high school a few months ago has his picture on the front page of the weekly paper. He is dead, or he wears a new medal maybe, or both.

Things like that go on, but when I read printed books, the war seems far from here. We have no stink of it, no frantic tortured eardrums, none of the strained gallantry of men and women who have touched it. I sit passively on my hill, reading about the stench, the roar, the high courage.

In letters from England, people I love say defensively each time they get a box of food from here, "We are really *quite* well off, you know . . . but the powdered lemon *did* avert a wretched chest cold."

And Emily Hahn in Hong Kong decides not to walk up to tea that day, because there is really too much going on, what with all the bloody bombs and then the ack-ack and the rioting. She has tea at home instead, with refugees and her baby and the cook saying Charles is wounded badly and she cannot get to him. . . . The tea is hot, what there is of it.

Or I get word from a man I've never heard of at an unknown Midwest college, saying that a friend of his has heard through the underground that Georges, dear gaunt fine-browed Georges, was safe a year ago somewhere outside of Dijon and sent word for none of us for God's sake to try to get in touch with him because of his kids who were still in Caen with their grandparents.

So I read all this—and even books by correspondents—and it seems sometimes as if I had already died, here on my quiet hill.

The other day, though, I knew I was still alive. J.B came to see me.

J.B. is the son of Spittin. They all lived at the turn of the road where it went into the main part of the valley, and I had to shift gears there after the curves and the tricky ruts, and I got so I stopped to wave and then to talk. I would have had to stop anyway, because of all the children under my wheels.

One time I asked Spittin, who was called that because he spat so much, how many he had. He was slow in answering but finally figured out, "Abaht nine livin', and fahve dade."

But his wife told me that more than that had died, and she seemed sad about it. She was pregnant then, and soon after our talk I heard long cries, like a lost calf, and finally I drove down the mile of road and found her writhing on the bed, with only three or four of the smallest to watch. There was almost nothing I could do by then, and I was very ignorant, but by late afternoon when the children started coming home and Spittin rolled in from whatever pub he'd been at, things were fairly much all right again, and he could think a while and say, "*Six* dade."

J.B. was the oldest of this clutch of hostages to fortune. He was about seventeen when I first knew him, and probably the dullest of the lot, a tall thick boy with pasty skin and eyes emptier than a dead man's. He was still in school, but his grades were so bad that they weren't even marked on his card, and he and his teachers longed for his next birthday when he could legally stop going to classes. He used to shamble up the hill to see my husband, and I'd hear him talking, slowly, painfully, in the studio. Gradually he began to pose, and some good pictures came out of it, although he did not seem to see them but only the Coke bottle he held permanently in his hand. After perhaps ten Cokes, he would talk more, and we began to think that the reason he was so slow was that he was never spoken to as a grown boy but always as if he were the same age as the current baby in the brood. This was partly because Spittin and his wife were not much older either—about seven or eight, at most. They didn't realize what they were doing to J.B., of course. But he was *lonely*. We'd say something about how cool weather was easier to work in, something simple like that, and J.B. would think for a minute, and then his clay face would lighten and he'd answer, with a kind of piteous delight, "That's right." What he needed, we thought, was to get away from all the babies.

Finally he was eighteen, and right away he left school and drifted to the nearest beer parlor. He was too clumsy to play pool and too poor to drink much, but a couple of times I picked him up on my way home from the village and he was mumbling drunk, for the other men would give him liquor so they could tease him better, with his baby speech.

Spittin was worried, and whenever he saw J.B. come into a bar, he'd leave by the back way. He talked to my husband. We suggested that J.B. enlist—this was just before the first draft. J.B. did, but the night before he was to report he ran away. That was bad; we felt to blame. Then he came home, and as soon as he could, he enlisted again. He was in.

It seemed queer at first not to see him when I stopped by Spittin's house, sitting on the doorstep with his heavy puffed face between his hands and two or three little siblings climbing over his thick legs. His mother stopped doing the daily washing in an old tub over a fire of chopped-up auto tires, too, and when I went in one day to see why, thinking I might find her bedded again, she beamed and showed me the rattletrap washing machine J.B. had made her buy with his first pay.

A few days later she walked up the hill to see us. She had on some kind of corset, and her hair was curled, and she looked almost my age, although I knew she was really younger. We sat formally in the living room. She thanked us for getting J.B. to go away. It seemed strange, because she never had mentioned anything personal, like the time I helped her when she made the long ugly noises. We drank Cokes in little polite sips, and then as she went away, she smiled shyly at me for the first time and said, "You see? I ain't got my bar' feet!" And I saw that she did indeed have shoes on, cheap high-heeled fancy shoes. She was really happy, and I never saw her again, although I have heard that she is working in the laundry of a training camp and has finally heeded the country nurse enough not to have any more babies. She left me a Christmas cactus, which still thrives.

I thought that was the last of them all, because they moved

away, and new people came to the little house and picked up all
the empty hominy cans and raked the yard clean of empty Coke
bottles and dung.

Then last week J.B. came back to see me. When I went to the
door, I didn't know him, of course; he seemed taller, thinner,
with a fairly clear and almost intelligent face. His uniform was
immaculate, with the shirt buttons, the buckle, the fly all in line,
and the creases just so down his arms and thighs and over his deep
chest. He looked fine, for Spittin's son or anyone's.

I was busy, but I was glad to see him, too. We sat in the
garden in the gentle sunlight. He fidgeted, but not as he'd used to.
His hands were still clammy to the touch, I noticed when we met,
and there was nervous sweat on his face, but as we talked, he
looked straight at me instead of sideways and almost didn't stam-
mer. He was in the medical corps. He wanted to learn about
surgery, he said. He shook his head about the fliers at his base.

"They're crazy," he said firmly, kneading his hands together.
"They crash, and they see their friends spread all over, and they
go right up again. They're crazy. They don't have to pick up the
pieces the way we do."

He shook his head, and his hands looked moist and frantic,
but he had improved. He spoke coherently, if very simply. He
knew my husband had died, and when he said it was too bad and
asked if he could have something, I went into the house and got a
necktie. He folded it carefully and put it in his breast pocket and
then went on talking about the hospital and an operation he'd
watched there on his own stomach. I was glad to see how he'd
grown up, but I was busy, too, and wished he'd go.

Then he seemed almost to pull his hands from their arms and
told me, with his eyes on the ground, about how he had a three-
week furlough because of the operation and had only been home
two days and couldn't stand it.

"Nothin' to say," he said miserably. "My folks don't talk much. My dad was in France last time, but he don't know nothin' about this one. There's too many kids. And I can't eat the food. It rises on me. We eat swell at the base. But I can't eat at home no more."

He was trembling. He was lost and terribly lonely for his prolonged childhood.

"I just can't stand it there no more," he said, so low I could hardly hear him.

"Let's have a Coke, J.B.," I said, and without waiting for an answer, I went into the kitchen from the garden, leaving him with his head low, as if he were wounded.

I felt awful. I felt that something was my fault: I had helped to pull up his roots, and now he was alone, nevermore to be a child with other children near him. Suddenly the hill seemed emptier than I could bear. I felt like running away. Alone, alone, my heart cried. *Seule, seule,* wept the dove imprisoned in the tapestry. I, and he, and all of us . . .

I left the Coke in the bottles, the way he used to like it, and when I got to the door into the garden, I stopped with a horror that seemed almost a natural part of my inchoate misery.

J.B. stood weaving and winding in the middle of the stone-flagged court, turning slowly round and round, with his hands hanging at his sides like an ape's. He has lost his mind, I thought at once. He has gone mad with all the blood and the pieces of fliers in baskets and not being able to talk to Spittin. I am here with him on the hill, and he is mad.

I stood for a minute with the two Coke bottles steady in my hands. Then I went out without banging the door and touched him on the shoulder.

He swung around until he faced me, and his dull little eyes were full of tears, and his face was lighter than I ever thought it could be, almost as if something had turned itself on inside his thick pasty head. He smiled at me, and a tear ran down into his wide mouth.

"Ain't nothin' changed," he said softly. He swung around once more, as if something had spun him from above, and his eyes touched the rocks, the hills, the far bending silvery eucalyptus trees, before he looked square at me again.

"Ain't nothin' changed, really."

He drained the bottle and handed it absently back and then very simply wiped his cheeks with the back of one clean pudgy hand. "I got to be gittin'. Gonna send myself a telegram to report for duty."

He looked seriously at me, with more intelligence in his face than I'd ever seen there. "We got ourselves to think of, you know."

We shook hands, and his was dry and firm, and then he swung off down the hill. He had escaped, and I, alone but no more lonely, felt that for a few minutes I had touched pain and death and strength very near me, instead of on the written page or even on the bed of childbirth or at the grave.

—*Bareacres, Hemet, California, 1940*

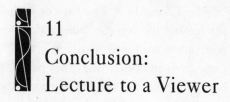

11
Conclusion:
Lecture to a Viewer

Yes, this painting is a very strange one. You will notice the shell and the involuted use of both live and dying flower, and it seems to go far beyond the shell and the flowers, the dahlias or whatever they were—yes, dahlias. There is the limitless horizon, which was there in the near-desert when the picture was painted.

The air and the brush were dry. The flowers were vivid but dying. The painter was dying, too.

We went often to the graveyard of the Pala Indians, farther south from our place. We knew a young man named Leonardo who was of the Palas and who for a time had moved up instead of down on their scale by marrying a Navaho. This did not last, and he moved away from his agrarian culture, northward toward a lower tribe, the Sobobas. (This word *lower* sounds very snobbish, and such it was: the Sobobas were not as skilled and perhaps as subtle as the Palas. They were far below the Navahos in that complex pecking order.)

So Leonardo was perhaps or probably ousted from his tribe for leaving his Navaho wife, and he moved up to the Soboba reservation and lived with one of their best women because he came from an upper tribe. They had a fine little son named Cowboy, about two feet tall and two wide when I knew him.

Leonardo and I understood each other, I think. We pruned tobacco bushes and walked past a couple of rattlesnakes without resentment.

One day he said that my husband and I should go down to Pala to stay in the cemetery for a few hours. It seemed to be a message, and we obeyed it.

It was not the first time we had been there. The quiet old mission was a haven. There was the chapel, of course, with its basically pagan symbols on the plastered walls covered thickly with whitewash. And there were the softly reverential garden and its burying ground, all one. At the western end, as I remember, was the bell tower in a separate clumsy adobe structure, which an old man climbed up and into to ring the bell.

On the dry mounded graves, out past the few small Anglo-style tombstones, there were shells that had come up from the Sea of Cortez. They were laid out in puny crosses or in opulent outlines of where the bodies lay below. They were broken, rarely whole, and they glowed like pearly gems on the dry rich soil. The people had carried them this far. We knew that nothing should be touched, but I would have liked to take one faraway shell to help me remember these days of return, of farewell.

Then, the last day, an aged man climbed down from the stubby crude bell tower. He walked toward us, with a shell in his hand, and he was smiling confidently. He came right toward us and put the shell from his hand into my husband's. They looked deeply at and into each other. Then he went back toward the mission.

My husband held the shell for a few minutes or seconds or years and then handed it to me, and we went on toward the car and home.

Once there, he painted the message, the shell. And I have the canvas, very reassuring and beautiful, and I have the shell, not as a fetish but perhaps as a kind of guarantee of peace or fulfillment.

—*Bareacres, Hemet, California, 1941*

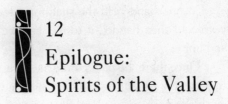

12
Epilogue:
Spirits of the Valley

Some people believe that it is a fortunate thing if a person can live in a real valley instead of on flat open land, and they may well be right. For some sixteen years, from 1940 on, I lived most of the time on ninety acres of worthless land southeast of the little town of Hemet in Southern California, and they were fine magical ones, important in the shaping of many people besides me, perhaps because Hemet Valley was a true one in every sense. At its far eastern end rose the high mountains that separated coastal land from desert, and our little town lay almost as near their base as Palm Springs did on their other side. Mount San Jacinto loomed on the north; to the south, high rocky hills rolled toward the Mexican border, and westward the valley opened gently, as any proper valley should, toward broad coastal flats and the far Pacific Ocean.

My husband, Dillwyn Parrish, and I bought our land for almost nothing: it was haunted, for one thing, and completely untillable. And we lived there intensely until he died three years later, according to medical schedule, of Buerger's disease. Then I stayed on, through another marriage and two little daughters, who spent their first years there with me after I divorced their father. When the oldest was going on six, we moved to my family ranch near Whittier to live with Father after Mother died. I worked half-time on his newspaper and ran the household, and as often as possible (weekends, vacations) we went back to Hemet to the little ranch house in the wild rocky hills.

It became clear that I could not raise two growing females there alone, where I had decided to remain. Now and then I found someone to repair storm damage and so on, but finally it seemed wise to sell the place. I felt thankful for everything I had learned there, and when I said it was no longer mine, I withdrew forever from it, even though ashes of my love and my mother may still blow from under some of its great rocks. I know the wind still sings over the Rim of the World and always will.

Tim (my husband was always called that by people who loved him, which meant everyone) named our ranch Bareacres, after a character in *Vanity Fair* who had several marriageable daughters and countless acres of barren land. He managed to sell the land, bought a string of pearls and a husband for each girl, and he and Lady Bareacres lived penniless but happy ever after, as I remember.

Certainly our land was bare! It rose in rough steep hills, with one deep canyon that split it down from the Rim of the World, its horizon, to the wide dead riverbed that was its northern boundary. A thin little road track went up from the valley floor, past our house and on up past the trickle of our only spring, to a deserted old ranch on the Rim of the World. There was a big sturdy red-wood tank at the spring and a handful of stubby cottonwoods, and down nearer our house in the canyon, dry except for an occasional

mud puddle from the underground trickle, stood a few tall eucalyptus trees. The rest of the place was covered with great harsh
boulders, some of them bigger than a house. On the flat top of an
enormous rock above the spring, two oblong tubs had been
chipped out centuries ago, and we were told that sick Indians were
brought there to lie in the hot sun while soothing water was poured
over them, water that we found was heavy with lithium.

In front of the house, which stood about a thousand feet up
off the wide dry riverbed that separated us from Hemet Valley, the
land was steep but with fewer big rocks, almost like a meadow,
covered with sage and mesquite and low cactus. Across the riverbed, northward, between us and Mount San Jacinto, lay the flat
valley land, rich with apricot orchards. It was neatly laid out with
roads and little houses here and there, but we could see only a
general kind of lush carpet, flowery in spring, then green, and then
winter-silver. Hemet was westward, invisible.

Our narrow dirt road went straight across the riverbed and
up to the valley floor to meet Crest Drive, which curved the whole
length of the valley. Directly opposite us, a small grove of eucalyptus trees grew down the slope where Fredrika van Benschoten had
a little orange orchard along Crest, and in that grove the Squawman, who had left his land for us to find, had a correct Navaho
house built for his bride. It was of adobe, one room and a wide
closet and a corner hearth, and it was so heavily plastered that
there were no hard corners or lines but a softness to everything
under the thick whitewash, as if it were a robe to be worn, firm
and protecting but with no part of it to cut or hurt or rub against.
The floor was of dark crude tile. The beams across the low ceiling
were slender eucalyptus trunks. There was a kind of kitchen in the
closet whose wall came up only eye height, and Freda had piped
cold water to a small sink. There was no toilet, and since the

Squawman had not made an outhouse, I decided the grove was answer enough.

I spent much time in the squaw house, mostly after Tim died. I wrote a couple of books there. I never slept there, strange to say, but would go down from Bareacres in the mornings. I always took a thermos of broth or a cool drink, and about 11:00 I'd go out and look up across the riverbed and see my home there, sometimes with my two little girls waving from the west terrace, with a neighbor to watch them until I got back. The trees Tim and I had planted back of the house and down into the canyon were thriving: sycamores, eucalyptus, tough cottonwoods.

When Tim and I bought the place, with a veteran's bonus of $2,000 plus $225 we borrowed (we were dead broke after his illness made us leave Switzerland in 1938 when World War II got under way), it was flatly undesirable, even according to the realtor who showed it to us. It had been owned by a shady fellow said to be a degraded government Indian trader, an army officer, whose Navaho woman followed him to Hemet Valley. He bought what we called Bareacres twenty years later, but she, of course, did not live there, so her relatives unwillingly came from New Mexico and built her a decent house across the riverbed in Freda's grove.

Because of strict caste laws, the Navaho was not only called a lost member of her own tribe but could not have anything to do with the local Indians, the Sobobans, who were beneath her social level. It must have been very lonely for her. The Squawman, as he was always scornfully called, had a lot or some or a few valuable Indian artifacts, depending on who was talking about him to us, and most of them were gone when his body was found in the house and a clean bullet hole showed in the south window. Perhaps it was robbery? Navaho are good shots, we were told. The little house in Freda's grove was empty, with not even a blanket or cup left. Nobody knew "anything." Up on the hill across the dead riverbed the air blew through the unlocked door of the Squawman's house. Everything in it was stolen, gradually and without real harm . . . no vandalism, no ugly dirt, no mischievous fires. It was haunted, for sure.

It looked empty and welcoming when Tim and I first saw it in the kind January sunlight, and we stepped into it past the bullet hole as if it had been waiting. We rented an airy little house near Moreno, toward Riverside, and came every day over the Jack Rabbit Trail around the base of the mountain with two old carpenters Tim found. We shifted a few walls around and screened the long front porch that was held up by six trunks of cedar trees that Indians had brought from Mexico, it was said, for the Squawman.

His rock foundations were good. The porch floors across the north and east sides of the little U-shaped house were of well-poured smooth cement, and there was a big fireplace of rough brownish stone in the living room. We made one room and its porch into a fine studio, and put in another little toilet and lavatory there, and slept on the porch outside, looking east. The kitchen spread out to the east, too, over the old cement porch. Down in the canyon we built a big doghouse, with a fenced yard to fool the coyotes and the occasional lynx. On the west side of the U was an entry and office for me and a bedroom and bath for anybody we liked enough. (Hemet had no motels then, but there was a small adobe hotel behind a half circle of fine palm trees in town.) And in the hollow of the U was the patio, the most delightful one I have ever known—indeed, the heart of the place. French doors opened onto it on all three sides. We paved it with flat stones from the canyon. Tim devised a series of strips of bright canvas on slanted wires that pulled across it at will, so the air and light would stay filtered. We pulled them back and forth according to wind, weather, the time of day.

There were low tables and chairs, all-weather stuff, and two chaise longues that could be beds. A wide Dutch door opened into the kitchen. The south side of the patio was a stone wall perhaps four feet high, and on the terrace above it were cottonwood trees and some sycamores, so that always there was the sound of leaves growing, blowing, falling. The Squawman had started the wall, and we carried it on past the house to make a fine terrace of sandy earth. Tim and I kept native succulents and cacti growing in the wall crevices, and when my girls were small, they played out there in the warm dry winter days, and now and then we put out a croquet set for the long hot summer twilights. And often we pulled the chairbeds out to the terrace in the brilliant August nights and lay naked in the silky air, watching the meteors shoot and tumble in the pure black sky.

Bareacres bordered the Ramona Bowl on the west, where the pageant based on Helen Hunt Jackson's book about Indians was given every year in a lovely little open-air theater. Tim helped rewrite some of the new script, and we maintained an aloof cordiality with the cast every year. The Indian hero was played by a skilled actor from Hollywood, much as summer theater on Long Island is now held together by stage stars who need fresh air and a nice piece of pocket money, and we knew a few visitors like Victor Jory who came to Hemet. Ramona the Beautiful Indian Maiden was always played by a local girl. And the finale of the long afternoon performance was when a posse of thirty or forty of the valley's best horsemen thundered through the amphitheater and up over the eastern horizon and down onto our land! We always had bottles of cold ale, open and ready, for the excited riders on their panting prancing horses. It was fun. . . . We waited to hear the guns sound to the west and then opened bottles as fast as we could. And they would come pouring over, a thunder of hooves, wild yahoo yells. We forgot that they were hunting the Indian Alessandro, poor devil, every afternoon at precisely 4:54 for three weekends. (He, or some reasonable facsimile, was safely panting in a hidden bunker up the theater hill.)

We stayed aloof from active life in Hemet while Tim was there, because we knew his time was short and he had a lot of painting to do. We made fine firm friends, though, and some of them still live. And later I made many more, when my little girls were starting there. Of course, they don't remember much about people, but they still know how to walk away smoothly and quickly when they meet a rattlesnake and how to listen to what the wild quail mothers say.

Freda stayed my dear friend until she died, a very old woman, the last of all her group of strange witty people who seemed to take Tim and me for granted as a part of their own very private lives. And there was Spittin Stringer, who lived in the cottage at our turn off Crest Drive down into the riverbed and on up homeward. Spittin was called that, of course, because he spat a lot. He was the only man we ever met who had gone to France in World War I and then back to Oklahoma without setting foot off dry land. He knew this was a fact because he had just gone with his buddies into a big dark room that had bumped along the road a long time and then they had gotten off and started fighting. There was no arguing about a fact like that. What's more, nobody in his whole family could rightly remember how many kids there were. He said around thirteen. His wife couldn't rightly recall either, and if she had ever counted she would not admit it in front of Spittin. But the oldest boy, J.B., said flatly it was fourteen.

J.B. used to pose for Tim, once he and his mother had walked up the hot hill together so that she could see if we were decent. When I met her at the door, she had on a store-bought dress and shoes, but she took off the killers when she saw I was barefoot and went back with them in her hand, satisfied that J.B. would be all right. Though I never saw her smile, the next time I passed she called out, "Hi ya! Still got mah bar' feet!" and stuck one big muddy toe out from behind the washtub by the door.

When J.B. enlisted, Spittin could not think of what the initials might be for. J.B. was simply his oldest boy's name. And on second thought, maybe his, too. So Tim suggested putting Joseph Benjamin on his papers to satisfy the army, and perhaps he is still alive to remember that J.B. might as well stand for that as anything else. Tim painted one unforgettable picture of him, a thick young boy sitting dully, vacantly, with one hand on his knee holding a green Coke bottle. Tim called it *Kola High*.

On the other side of our turnoff, up on a knoll in a grove of trees, was the Lee house. It was something of a palace, at least compared with Spittin's place or Bareacres or even Freda's prim little white house behind the orange trees on Crest Drive. The younger son of its owners lived there with his wife and a burgeoning family, and they raised turkeys and a few noisy beautiful peacocks and stayed pretty much to themselves, the way we did. Later, though, my girls and theirs were peers, and their mother Isabel became a quietly true-forever person in my life.

And over all of us rose proud San Jacinto Mountain, sacred to many Indians of its own and other tribes. The Jack Rabbit Trail snaked around its west side, between Hemet and Moreno, and it seemed to hold the raw steep slopes up almost like an invisible wall. The Indians called it a hot mountain, and steaming water burst out of it, more or less controlled for human bathing, in places like Gilman Springs and Soboba Springs and even downtown in the little town of San Jacinto just outside the Indian reservation. Once when I was about ten, relatives came from the Midwest to spend the winter at the Vosburg Inn so that an uncle could "take the baths," and I was embarrassed to have my aunt tell us how Mrs. Vosburg cut up her very fat husband's worn trousers to make clothes for all her small children. Years later one of the Vosburgs was a very beautiful Ramona in the pageant, and I helped with her makeup and never told her what I knew about her father's pants.

A man named Leonardo came often to help us. He was a Pala Indian from the agrarian tribe farther south, but had lost caste by taking up with a Soboban girl. He was cut off from his tribe, and gradually I watched him turn heavy and morose. He was always courteous to me but did not really see me, the way one does not see every leaf on a tree. He loved Tim but would not pose for him. Now and then he drove his girl and their little son Cowboy over to see us in his shabby truck. Cowboy was a dimpled brown nugget, but we only smiled at each other. The girl was silent, unsmiling but not hostile. Leonardo and Tim talked in his studio. Then they would go away, without any words to me but a quick wave and a smile between the two men.

After Tim died, Leonardo returned a few times and cut back some branches in the cottonwoods and made the little tool shed outside the kitchen very tidy. But he grew heavier, and I knew that he was drinking much of the time instead of only for the few religious retreats that the Sobobans were allowed to mix in with their Catholic celebrations at Saint Hyacinth's Chapel on the reservation. And, of course, every year it was almost as ritualistic to round up him and a few other gifted braves for fire fighting. They were sold or perhaps given spiked gallons of sweet muscatel wine, fixed with a half pint of straight alcohol to fill the drained tops. A friend who ran the local bar showed us how this was done.

The men got drunk very fast, and the one cop and the judge who was also the bartender knew when to move in. I felt as shocked as I ever have in my life, and as disgusted. But it was considered fair play there in those days, when good fire fighters were as much a need as water itself and the best ones could be had for a gallon of spiked wine and a couple of nights in jail to make their indenture legal. The awful thing was that every time it happened, it got easier for the men to *stay* drunk, of course, so that after several seasons Leonardo was half lit most of the time, with a fat body and a bitter dull face, no more the lithe man who ran up our road with a flashing smile when he saw Tim wave from the big studio window.

Another fine friend was Arnold. He was always thin, although I am sure he had drunk his fair share of rotgut all over the world. He had been a desert rat for many years, the kind of shadowy drifting loner who becomes almost dust colored—protective coloration, it is called in toads and mice and serpents, and the few real desert rats I have met were the same. By the time he came to be our friend and protector, he had married a little round brown girl named Lena and they had two little round brown daughters, but he still wore dust-colored cotton clothes, and his eyes were as hard and colorless as stone, except when they smiled at Tim and now and then toward me.

Arnold knew more about native desert plants than anyone I ever heard of, and while he was the caretaker up at the Ramona Bowl, it was a kind of secret paradise for botanists and crackpot gardeners who came to watch him plant the unplantables and whom he in turn watched like a hawk, because they almost always tried to steal some of his cuttings. It was a game they all played, and Arnold reported every sneaky trick, every artful dodge, of this unending tournament of trickery among the famous people who came to watch him. He turned weeds into jewels, for sure.

After Tim died, Arnold buried the little tin box of clinkers [Tim's ashes] under an enormous hanging rock. I said, "Let's go up to the Rim of the World and let the winds catch them," but he said, "Nope," and simply walked off. I knew it was all right, and went back to Bareacres and waited, and when he came back, we had a good nip of whiskey.

Arnold did a hitch with the Seabees, and I felt responsible for Lena and the little dumplings, for a time anyway. Then they met him someplace up north, and I never heard from him again, except that he is still clear and strong in my heart.

That is the way Bareacres is, of course. I am told that the fine pure air that first drew us there, half mountain and half desert, is now foul with smog and that the rich carpet of fruit trees we looked down on is solid with RVs and trailer parks. One block on Main Street is now in the *Guinness Book of World Records,* or maybe it is *Ripley's Believe It or Not:* something like 182 banks and savings-and-loan offices on that sleepy little stretch of sidewalk! And there are almost a hundred doctors, most of them connected with "convalescent homes" of varying status and opulence. And Crest Drive is lined with million-dollar villas, with the subdivision where Bareacres was (a "ninety-acre hell of red-hot rocks and rattlesnakes," as one New Yorker described it to us after a lost weekend there) the most snobbish and stylish area between Palm Springs and Los Angeles.

That is the way it is, I say, and I do not grieve or even care, any more than I did when Arnold went up the hill with the little box. I have taken and been given more than can ever be known that is heartwarming and fulfilling forever from that piece of wild haunted untillable land we named Bareacres for a time. No doubt roads have been cut into it and rocks have been blasted away, but I know that the contours cannot change much in a few hundred years in that country. And meanwhile the ghosts are there, even of the sick sad Indians who went to lie in the magic lithium waters of the spring, and even of the poor Squawman with a bullet in his heart, and of my own mother who loved the place . . . they are all there to cleanse and watch over it. They, and many more of us, keep an eye on things so that time itself can stay largely unheeded, as anyone will know who spends more than a few minutes in country like Bareacres.

There are many pockets of comfort and healing on this planet, and I have touched a few of them, but only once have I been able to stay as long and learn and be told as much as there on the southeast edge of Hemet Valley.

When I decided I could not stay there alone with my young girls and then had to decide further that I could not pretend to be an absentee owner, it did not hurt me at all to sell it. I felt serene about it then, and I do now. I had found what I needed there, and now other people will. I do not care how many millions of dollars Bareacres is now worth, nor how many days of smog alert there are each month in the little valley. I do not have any of that money, but I still breathe sweet fine air. My mind and my heart are bursting with unsuspected scents and notions and strange whiffs from other places, and I would like to write ten thousand times more than any human could about that one spot in my own tiny cosmos! All I dare hope, with perhaps some embarrassment for this unabashed gluttony, is that other people can open long-locked doors in their memories and enjoy some such rediscoveries of bliss and pain and beauty and foolishness and general enjoyment of our human condition.

—*Glen Ellen, California, 1984*

About the Author

M. F. K. Fisher was born in Albion, Michigan, in 1908 and spent most of her childhood in Whittier, California. During ensuing years she lived in Dijon, Vevey, Aix-en-Provence, and southern California before moving to the northern California wine country in 1954. She authored over sixteen volumes of essays and reminiscences, including *The Art of Eating, Two Towns in Provence, Among Friends,* and a widely admired translation of Brillat-Savarin's *The Physiology of Taste. To Begin Again: Stories and Memoirs, 1908–1929,* was published by Pantheon Books in 1992. For the last twenty years of her life she lived in a house built for her in Glen Ellen, California. She died at Last House on June 22, 1992.